Contents

CHAPTER 3

All Children and Adolescents Have the Right to Culturally Relevant Literacy Instruction   25

CHAPTER 4

All Children and Adolescents Have the Right to Literacy Instruction That Is Individually Appropriate   43

All Children and Adolescents Have the Right to Access to a Quality Literate Environment   58

All Children and Adolescents Have the Right to Choose Their Reading Materials   69

All Children and Adolescents Have the Right to Schools That Create a Climate for All to Learn   108

All Children and Adolescents Have the Right to an Education That Involves Their Families and Communities in Meaningful Ways   119

Preface

We wrote this book because we believe that teachers make a difference in the lives and learning of their students. Over the years, we have become saddened and worried that educational policies, prescribed curricula, calls for increased accountability, and high-stakes testing are making it difficult for teachers and students to engage in meaningful literacy experiences in school. We are worried about the large numbers of students who drop out of high school because they don't feel connected to their teachers or engaged with the ideas discussed within school contexts. We are alarmed by the differences in achievement that continue to widen between diverse students and mainstream students. And we have tearfully bid farewell to gifted teachers who have left the profession because of the lack of support and intense frustrations they experienced in their schools. In short, we wrote this book because we are deeply concerned that students, especially middle and high schools students, are not receiving the education that is promised to them.

A high school English teacher recently told one of us that the field of education has done a good job of focusing on what to teach and how to teach, but we have lost sight of who we teach—the students. To help us refocus on the most important aspect of teaching—our students—we present the voices of students in grades 5 through 12 throughout this book, as well as the stories, experiences, and challenges of their teachers and parents.

We wrote this book to accomplish several purposes:

1. To present a list of ten rights as a framework for teachers to think about and use to guide discussions related to student engagement, learning, and achievement in literacy education.
2. To offer practical suggestions and resources to help teachers consider how to make the rights a reality in their classrooms and schools.
3. To pose difficult questions, issues, and challenges for teachers to consider as they strive to reprioritize their teaching so the focus is where it belongs—on the students.

Like most long-term projects, this book has an interesting life history. The seed for this book comes from Daniel Pennac's book, *Better Than Life* (1999). That seed was planted by Jerry Johns, Distinguished Teaching Professor Emeritus and former President of the International Reading Association, who asked several of us to read the book and participate in a Problems Court Session on Readers' Rights at the American Reading Forum in 1998. After that first session, we added other colleagues to our team, and the group continued to take shape over the next several years as we surveyed and interviewed teachers, students, and parents about the notion of Readers' Rights and discussed our findings with our colleagues during the annual meetings of the American Reading Forum (ARF). As we listened to the compelling stories of teachers, students, and parents and heard the advice from ARF members who often encouraged us to share what we were learning with a larger audience, we became convinced that this book had to be written.

Each member of the author team contributed chapters, ideas, talents, and insights to this book. Because of the ongoing collaboration we experienced during the research studies that laid the foundation for this book and the recursive approach we took to drafting and revising the chapters, we decided to list author names in alphabetical order rather than listing them by the degree of contribution since that would have been impossible to determine.

We would like to thank those who reviewed the manuscript and made valuable comments: Heidi Davey, Hoffman Estates, IL; Judith Romanchuk, Campbell High School, Smyrna, GA; and Molly Williams, Still Middle School, Aurora, IL.

As you read this book, we hope that our representation of the concerns and recommendations of those we surveyed and interviewed impact you as they did the five of us. We are grateful for the voices of the students, teachers, and parents presented in this book. Their words provided the momentum we needed to commit six years to this project. When we asked one of the high school students we interviewed what he wanted teachers to take away from this book, he said, "I want them to think about having a different kind of relationship with their students." When asked to elaborate, he said, "They should have a more personal relationship with their students, one that shows they care about them." The Rights of Readers identified in this book provide guidance for how to develop this different type of relationship that can energize all of us to reclaim our commitment to the children and adolescents in our schools.

Introduction

Investigating Rights of Readers

We wrote this book primarily for teachers, including reading specialists and curriculum leaders, who teach students in grades 5 through high school. But as we shared the following rights of readers with teachers across grade levels, we have learned that our examples and recommendations apply to a much broader audience. For at the heart of these rights is the goal to engage all students in reading practices that are meaningful and self-motivating, that build positive attitudes about reading and learning and about their own capabilities as readers and learners, and that foster independence and self-directed learning. Every teacher wants to reach that goal for students regardless of their age or grade placement.

We became interested in rights of readers while collaborating with Jerry Johns, Professor Emeritus, Northern Illinois University and former president of the International Reading Association, who introduced us to the writings of Daniel Pennac. *Better Than Life* (1999), written by Pennac, inspired our journey investigating the rights of readers. Pennac's personal accounts of his son's literacy development captured us from the beginning; we saw in his son the faces of many children and adolescents we—as teachers, literacy researchers, parents, family members, and/or friends—have known.

> How amazing that those tails and circles and little bridges joined together formed real letters! And that those letters could make syllables, and those syllables, one after the other, words. He couldn't believe it. And that some of those words were familiar to him—it was magical! (Pennac 1999, p. 44)

That is the way Pennac described his son's first attempts to read—reading was viewed by his young son as a magical and enjoyable activity. Unfortunately, this excitement was not long-lasting. By the time Pennac's son reached his adolescent years, he struggled to complete the reading material assigned by his teachers and had lost interest in reading.

> Now he is a reclusive adolescent in his room, faced with a book he cannot read. His desire to be elsewhere creates a smeary film between his eyes and the page.

He is sitting in front of the window, the door closed behind him. Stuck on page 48. He can't bear to count the hours it took him just to get to this forty-eighth page. (Pennac 1992/1999, p. 20)

Pennac's experiences with his son, coupled with his reflections on how adults read books, led him to create his Reader's Bill of Rights, rights that he believed all readers, including young readers, should be granted. Those ten rights are:

1. The right to not read.
2. The right to skip pages.
3. The right to not finish a book.
4. The right to reread.
5. The right to read anything.
6. The right to escapism.
7. The right to read anywhere.
8. The right to browse.
9. The right to read out loud.
10. The right to not defend your tastes. (Pennac 1992/1999, pp. 170–171)

Our Investigations

Intrigued by Pennac's discussion of readers' rights and our interest in knowing how teachers, students, and parents may view these rights, we decided to ask these groups if they agreed with Pennac's perspective. Are these rights valued by teachers? By students? By parents? In the following paragraphs, we describe a series of research studies we conducted to examine these questions, and we discuss what we learned.

Procedures and Instruments

We developed surveys and interview questions based on the ten rights identified by Pennac. The initial survey was for teachers to determine if they agreed with the ten rights and if these rights applied to their own reading. The second survey (administered to teachers, students, and parents) was divided into two sections. The first ten statements assigned the rights to students' recreational reading and the second ten assigned the rights to students' academic reading. On each part, the respondents rated on a Likert-type scale (A = Strongly Agree, B = Agree, C = Not Sure, D = Disagree, and E = Strongly Disagree) their extent of agreement with the use of Pennac's rights during either recreational or academic reading. A copy of the parent, teacher, and student surveys appear in Appendices A, B, and C, respectively.

On the student survey (for students in grades 5 through 12), our first set of questions asked them about their beliefs about their reading habits (e.g., Do you think you are a good reader? Do your teachers think you are a good reader? What makes reading easy or difficult for you?). We then asked them to respond to Pennac's rights when applied to academic or pleasure reading (e.g., When reading an assignment, is it OK to choose not to read something?) and to explain their responses.

The Questions We Asked and the Answers We Heard

Across six investigations, we asked teachers, students, and parents to respond to the Reader's Bill of Rights and judge its usefulness for describing what they believed are "appropriate" reading habits. From our data analysis, we derived three patterns of agreement within or across our groups of participants.

* Teachers agreed with the rights when they were used to describe their own reading habits.
* All three groups believed these rights are appropriate for students' pleasure reading but less applicable to their academic reading.
* All three groups agreed on the value of rereading for academic reading.

More specifically, we learned the following from the teachers, students, and parents who responded to our questions.

TEACHERS   For our initial teacher study, we administered our first survey to ask a group of 131 prospective teachers and practicing teachers ($n = 16$ and 115, respectively) two questions *Do you agree or disagree with the rights?* and *Do you as prospective teachers and practicing teachers believe these rights describe you as readers?* Participants represented teachers who either taught or planned to teach in elementary grades ($n = 86$), middle or high school grades ($n = 9$), in special education settings ($n = 7$), or other settings ($n = 9$) and 20 teachers who did not indicate their grade-level choice. While over two-thirds of the 131 teachers agreed with all the statements (with one exception: only 51 percent of the 131 teachers agreed with the "right to not read"), only one-third indicated that their own reading practices were represented with the rights to "not read, skip pages, and not finish" (what they were reading). Two-thirds or more of all respondents agreed that the rights to "reread, read anything, read for escapism, read anywhere, and browse" represented their own reading habits. There were no patterns that differentiated between practicing and prospective teachers (Elish-Piper, Matthews, Johns, & Risko, 1999).

In our second teacher study, we asked a group of prospective ($n = 160$) and practicing teachers ($n = 108$) to respond to our second survey that focused on two main questions, *How do you view the Reader's Bill of Rights for yourself as a reader?* and *How do you view the Reader's Bill of Rights for your students?* These 268 teachers represented those with experience or interest in teaching elementary grades ($n = 168$), in a middle school or high school ($n = 44$), in special education settings ($n = 28$), or in other placements ($n = 29$). These teachers supported for themselves and their students the rights to "reread" and "read out loud." On all remaining rights, the teachers indicated their agreement with these rights as they applied to their own reading practices but were less supportive of those same rights for their students (Elish-Piper et al., 2000).

STUDENTS   We conducted two investigations to determine how students value these rights. In the first study we asked the students, *Does the Reader's Bill of Rights describe you when you are reading for pleasure?* and *Do these rights describe you when you are reading to complete school assignments?* Two hundred sixth-grade students responded to our survey. For all ten rights, these students indicated stronger agreement with the use of these rights when they read for pleasure than for academic reading. With additional analyses of their responses, we learned that these students had strong reactions (either positive or negative) to seven of the rights. Three rights for which there was *strong agreement* were the "right to reread" during both pleasure and academic reading, the "right to not defend their tastes" when reading for pleasure, and "the right to read anywhere" when reading for pleasure. Conversely, they did *not agree* that they had the "right to skip pages" when reading for pleasure and they *disagreed strongly* with three rights that applied to academic reading: the right to "choose not to read," "not finish when they read," or "skip pages" (Matthews et al., 2001).

Next, we asked 157 fifth- and sixth-grade students to respond to the same survey used in the 2001 study. As with the previous study, students indicated that they could apply more rights during pleasure reading than academic reading. These students indicated that the right to "reread" and "read aloud" could apply to both academic and pleasure reading and that "skipping pages" was a low priority for both forms of reading.

When we asked students about the reasons for some of their responses, students explained that they identified with the right to escapism because reading took them "to another place" or they "imagine they are there or someone else, like Harry Potter." They described pleasure reading as getting "sucked into it . . . if you don't get sucked in, you don't really like the book." Further, students explained why some rights had limited use for academic reading. They explained that they couldn't skip pages or not finish the reading because they would "miss the questions that are at the end of the book" or "not learn the information on those pages." One student indicated, "My teacher told me every page is important." On noting the importance of the right to reread, students indicated that rereading was important to aid memory (of facts), achieve good scores on book tests, "pass from one grade to another," and help comprehension (Bass et al., 2002).

PARENTS   For this investigation, we asked 122 parents (90 parents of K–2 students, 32 parents of upper elementary and high school students) to respond to a survey that focused on the major question, *How do you view the Reader's Bill of Rights for your child or adolescent?* These parents were to differentiate the applicability of these rights for pleasure reading described as occurring during free time outside of school and academic reading that focused on school reading or homework assignments. Consistent with the feedback received from teachers and students in our earlier investigations, the parents afforded their children more rights for pleasure reading than academic reading. The parents indicated for academic reading their children should not be able to "choose not to read," to "skip pages," or "not finish what they read." Parents of children in grades 3 and above believed their children should have slightly more rights than the parents of K–2 children in both pleasure and academic reading (e.g., freedom of where to read). Given a chance to comment on their responses, one parent's statement represented explanations shared by many parents, "free time is different to us—it means you put in your opinion and pick things you might want to learn about or you enjoy. However, any time an assignment is given, we believe our child is to submit to the leadership of his teacher and do the best he can." Additionally, many parents thanked us for seeking their opinions (Risko, Matthews, Elish-Piper, Dasinger, & Bass, 2004).

Overall, we learned that teachers, students, and parents have definite views of rights readers can assume during reading for school or for pleasure. We learned that generally, students valued reading for pleasure because they could choose what to read and where and that such reading helped them escape to new places and assume the role of story characters, but students believed also that careful reading (and not skipping pages or not completing assigned readings) was necessary to achieve on school assignments and school tests.

Voicing the Rights of Readers

It was useful to hear students' reasons for their choice of Reader's Rights; the voices of students—their explanations, their concerns, and their questions—help us as teachers to understand their interpretations of reading activities, the perspectives guiding their reading habits, and how we can respond to their choices. Also, during our investigations we shared our findings with other literacy teacher educators and classroom teachers, and they shared their reactions and experiences with us. We heard about the challenges confronting youth (in particular, upper elementary/middle school and high school students enrolled in grades 5 through 12) and their teachers in our contemporary society. We heard that too often, school curriculum goals and high-stakes testing results, instead of students' individual differences, are directing educational decisions, and student and teacher voices (i.e., their concerns, interests, expressed needs) have little to no impact on instruction. Consequently, challenges confronting our youth, such as low engagement in independent reading, passive failure approaches to reading instruction, and low achievement and participation by minority students, may not be central to middle school and high school instruction.

Hearing about these challenges for our youth, we decided to examine more carefully this notion of readers' rights as it applies to the literacy instruction of preadolescents and adolescents. What are rights of readers that may be in jeopardy in our middle schools and high schools? What rights are associated with students' engagement and interest, with students' expectations and lived experiences, and with students' identity development? To answer these questions, we reanalyzed our interview data and identified teachers, students, and parents who were willing to participate in a second round of interviews. From these interviews, we identified a set of concerns that guided our listing of a tentative set of rights that students held dear to them and that went beyond those identified by Daniel Pennac—rights students believed would enable their achievement and engagement with reading. With this set of rights in hand, we read widely to determine how and if these rights were consistent with arguments generated by literacy theorists and researchers, especially those theorists and researchers who focus on the literacy development of middle and high school students. We identified research findings and referenced and cross-referenced these with our tentative list. We concluded this analysis with a set of ten rights that are significant (as supported by research evidence and the voices of our participants) for students in grades 5 through 12 to be successful, engaged readers.

In the following chapters we discuss each right as it relates to student achievement and engagement. Each right is introduced through a letter written by a student to raise issues associated with the right. A discussion of each right is followed by evidence regarding the importance of the right for students in grades 5 through 12. Next, each chapter presents specific suggestions for how educators can put the right into practice in their classrooms and schools. Finally, each chapter concludes by re-examining the issues from the opening letter and presenting questions and ideas to help educators move forward with addressing the right in their teaching.

We believe this book will help you, as educators (i.e., upper elementary, middle school, and high school classroom teachers, reading specialists, literacy coaches, literacy curriculum leaders and supervisors, and teacher educators) keep students in the forefront of your teaching even as schools work to implement federal and state policies that focus on accountability and high-stakes testing. As educators we face increasing demands for high test scores, but we must also address the personal characteristics and changing demographics of the students we teach. We hope this book will be a useful tool to examine your instruction, methods, classrooms, and schools to ensure that all students receive the instruction they *rightly* deserve.

Identifying Our Readers' Rights

We begin this second part of our book introduction with a letter from Al, one of the students we interviewed. We include this letter to illustrate the format of letters that will begin each of our ten chapters and because we believe Al's concern about a lack of respect and caring represents a concern expressed widely by our student informants, a concern that became a catalyst for this book.

Dear Teacher,

The teacher has all the power in the classroom. What you say and do affects me—not just today, but possibly forever. When you say, "Come on, Al, we're waiting . . ." or other things like that, I feel stupid, embarrassed, and angry. It hurts and it makes it hard for me to learn from you.

When you just use the lesson plans in the book, it's boring so I tune out. I feel disappointed when you can't answer a tough math problem or a question about the Civil War without the book. I get mad when it feels like you are only one page ahead of the class. I think the other kids and I deserve better.

If I could change something about my school, I'd create enjoyable, respectful classrooms where the teacher uses her power in a positive way. In this classroom the teacher would trust the kids and honor their talents and ideas. This type of teacher would help prepare kids for later stages in life. This is the type of teacher all kids need and deserve.

Yours truly,

Al, grade 9

Who is Al? Is he a student in an urban area, or does he live in the suburbs or in a rural community? Is he a high-achieving student, does he struggle in school, or does he fall somewhere in between? Is he a native English speaker, does he speak in a nonstandard dialect, or is he an English language learner? Are his teachers experts in their subject areas and skilled with teaching methods, or does he encounter unqualified teachers and poor instruction in his school? What are his hopes, dreams, goals, and challenges? What are his talents and interests? What are his family and community like? Just who is Al? or for that matter, who are the other students who sit in your classroom Monday through Friday? We pose these questions to illustrate just how complex teaching is. That complexity encompasses choices teachers must make about content, methods, and materials for instruction, but the most important consideration in understanding teaching and learning is to know the students we teach. We believe that students are as unique as snowflakes, but they can easily lose their identity when we think about them only as part of a group. By sharing Al's voice, we want to illustrate the point that we teach individual students, not just classes or subject matter.

Education, and specifically literacy education, has been the focus of a great deal of public scrutiny, federal and state mandates, and reform efforts during the past two decades. During all of the debates about education, changes in federal and state laws, and requirements for increased accountability and testing, we have observed that one essential consideration has often been overlooked—the consideration of students' interests, capabilities, and personal knowledge. While all decisions about curriculum, standards, and assessment in education affect students directly, it is the students' voices that have been absent from much of the debate and decision making. We want to put the focus of this book, and hopefully the field of literacy education, back where it needs to be—on the student. Furthermore, we argue that in order to teach our students well and to assist them to become fully literate, certain conditions, beliefs, and practices must be in place. These ideas form a declaration of readers' rights that we present in the remainder of this book. Prepared with information supporting these rights, we urge all teachers to take proactive stances in defense of their students and their own teaching decisions.

Readers' Rights

Based on the work of Pennac (1992/1999); our own investigations; our examination of theoretical and research literature; and our conversations with teachers, students, parents, and teacher educators across the United States, we offer the following readers' rights that are essential for supporting and effectively teaching students in grades 5 through 12.

Within the last two decades, literacy researchers have provided very specific directions for educating older children and adolescents that focus on *instruction* that is responsive to students' capabilities *and instructional contexts* that support meaningful and engaged activity. Our ten rights draw attention to the contributions of this research and the importance of instruction that is personalized, caring, and supportive of students and their families. And while some of our ten rights relate more directly to students as learners, others are directed toward the learning climate of the

A Declaration of Readers' Rights

All children and adolescents have the right to:

1. be taught by a caring, competent, highly qualified teacher
2. be treated as competent individuals who are capable of reading and learning
3. culturally relevant literacy instruction
4. instruction that is individually appropriate
5. access to a quality literate environment
6. choose reading materials
7. reading experiences that create a passion for reading
8. appropriate reading assessments
9. schools that create a climate for all to learn
10. an education that involves families and communities in meaningful ways

classroom and the school and connections to the community outside the school walls. Central to our ten rights are the complementary goals of *shaping curriculum to maximize student engagement and purposeful learning* and *making connections between teachers and their students*.

Achieving these ten rights, we believe, takes the *commitment* of educators. These rights point to ways to make good education's promise to help every student achieve, and they build on the premise that all students have promise. We fear that reform efforts put in place since the early 1990s may have distracted educators from the mission of helping every student achieve. Darling-Hammond and Falk predicted in 1997 that:

> Depending on how standards are shaped and used, either they could support more ambitious teaching and greater levels of success for all students or they could serve to create higher rates of failure for those who are already least well served by the education system. (p. 191)

Unfortunately, schools and recent reforms are failing our students. More than 1.2 million students did not graduate from U. S. high schools in 2004, and researchers report that dropout rates continue to rise in the United States (Alliance for Excellent Education, 2006). Exit reports indicate students were bored, felt a lack of connection to their teachers and the curriculum, and received little or no academic support in schools when they were failing. Fifty-nine percent of the respondents could not identify someone in their high school who cared about them and their problems. This finding reminds us of the concerns expressed by Greg, a twelfth grader interviewed by Pamela Mueller (2001), who recalled: "In seventh grade I couldn't keep up with the work. They thought I was slacking off. They told me to get glasses. I had to cry in front of the class before the teacher figured out I needed help" (p. xiii). The findings in the dropout exit reports remind us, too, of Al's letter that introduced this section and his expressions of disappointment with his teacher.

Profiles of students who drop out of high school counter the stereotypes (e.g., students who don't care, who sleep in class) often advanced in popular media. Analyzing data from focus groups and interviews, researchers indicated that many of these students were "hardworking" and could have succeeded in school if they had received support (both in school and at home) specific to their capabilities and needs (Civic Enterprises, 2006). Similarly, we read that many teachers are leaving their classrooms because they, too, feel disconnected from their students and their families. Prescribed curricula, single pathways to raise test scores, learning activities that lack authenticity and connections to out-of-school experiences, and other, similar reforms are increasingly distancing students and their teachers from meaningful engagement with school activities. As Edelsky argued in 2002 and Santa reminded us in 2006, educators must make public their concerns about reforms that do not support their students' literacy development and offer research-based alternatives, such as those expressed in our rights and those that include firsthand reports of what students are saying about their own education.

In the chapters that follow, we discuss each right separately and provide suggestions for applying each right to teaching practices and changing learning contexts. We begin the book with a *big picture* view of issues related to readers' rights. These first four chapters (i.e., the right to a caring competent teacher, the right to be treated as competent learners, the right to culturally relevant instruction, and the right to individually appropriate instruction) focus on broad principles and important frameworks that establish the foundation for teaching suggestions in the remaining chapters. From these foundational chapters, we move on to rights that relate to specific classroom and school contexts and instructional considerations (i.e., the right to a rich, literate environment, to choose reading materials, to instruction that creates a passion for reading, and to appropriate assessment). The final chapters also focus on instruction but they move beyond the classroom level to consider school-level issues and the contexts that frame the school (i.e., the right to a positive school climate and the right to education that involves the family and community). The book ends with the epilogue that summarizes major ideas of our chapters and urges the reader to engage in action related to the rights presented in the book. We discuss each right separately to minimize overlap of content across the chapters. Yet we recognize that the ten rights are part of a whole; they are mutually enabling and reciprocal. As a set they provide a vision of exciting learning events for both teachers and their students— learning events that are principled and balanced, as we discuss in the next section of this introduction.

Guiding Principles

Several principles guided our thinking as we examined readers' rights and prepared this book. First and foremost, we view teaching as a relationship based on respect and caring (Freire, 2000). We regard education as a cultural, social, and political process. Within this process, teachers have a responsibility to take an active role in promoting democratic ideals and social justice (Ayers, Hunt, & Quinn, 1998). We believe that all students have rights that must be used to guide the decisions we make about the instruction we deliver, the materials we use, and the roles we provide for students in their learning. Furthermore, whether called best practices or research-based approaches, we argue that high-quality instruction is essential to support student learning. Implementing such high-quality instruction can then lead to increases in engagement, motivation, and achievement. We argue that students need to be at the forefront of all teaching and educational decisions, even before curricula are developed, materials are selected, or programs are implemented. Finally, we acknowledge that teaching in today's schools presents both challenges and opportunities. Thus, we offer suggestions for teachers to work within constraints such as large class sizes, limited access to materials, high-stakes testing, federal and state mandates, increased diversity, lack of instructional leadership, and busy schedules that they encounter in their schools and classrooms (Cochran-Smith, 2004).

As we wrote this book, we envisioned it as a vehicle for having conversations with many teachers. We hope that the ideas we present within these pages will resonate with your experiences. We aim to provide provocative ideas to help you reflect on your teaching and your students' learning. As you read this book, we anticipate that some ideas will ring true to you, but others may make you feel uncomfortable or uneasy as you examine your assumptions, your teaching, your stance as a teacher, and the rights of your students as readers. We look forward to sharing this process with you. We truly hope that this book can contribute, in some small way, to helping you become "the type of teacher all kids need and deserve," as Al wrote in his letter.

All Children and Adolescents Have the Right to Be Taught by a Caring, Competent, Highly Qualified Teacher

Dear Teacher,

I remember how great reading was in my class last year. My teacher loved to read, and she made me love reading too. She was nice and funny, but she was also a good teacher who taught me a lot. I became a better reader last year because my teacher was so good at helping me understand what I read and make connections from my life to the books I was reading. This year, when you just tell us to read the stories in the anthology and answer the comprehension questions, I feel like you don't really care about us or about reading or books. I wish you would let us talk about the stories we read so I could hear the ideas others have. It makes me think you don't care about teaching or about me either when you get out old worksheets that look like they've been copied year after year. You never sit with us to talk about what we are reading or to recommend good books to us. You just assign the chapter and tell us to answer the questions at the end. It just feels like you don't care about us or about teaching. You seem bored about teaching, and it makes me bored about learning.

Sincerely,

Bailey, grade 6

2

....

CHAPTER 1

*All Children
and Adolescents
Have the Right
to Be Taught
by a Caring,
Competent, Highly
Qualified Teacher*

*J*ust as Bailey described in her letter, we believe that all children and adolescents have the right to be taught by caring, competent, highly qualified teachers. What does it mean for a teacher to be caring and why is this important? What must a teacher know and be able to do to be classified as competent and highly qualified, and how is this related to student learning and achievement? As our schools face reform efforts, high-stakes testing, increasing public scrutiny, decreases in school funding that result in large class sizes, and limited resources, how can we make this right a reality in our schools? We offer the following insights and ideas about the right of all children and adolescents to be taught by caring, competent, highly qualified teachers.

Caring

Caring teachers know, respect, understand, and enjoy their students. They work hard to support their students as individuals and do whatever it takes to help each student learn (Gilligan, 1982; Noddings, 1984, 2004). This type of support is described by Mueller (2001) as connectedness, which is taking the time to help each student learn and responding to their needs in ways that are individualized and helpful. Palmer (1998) explains, "good teachers possess a capacity for connectedness. They are able to weave a complex web of connections among themselves, their subjects, and their students so that students can learn to weave a world for themselves" (p. 11). We agree with these educators that teaching is a relationship (Freire, 2000) where respect forms the foundation for all teaching and learning. In his analysis of extraordinary teachers, Stephenson (2001) concluded that effective teachers care deeply about their students and approach teaching as a human endeavor that is reliant on communication, respect, and compassion. During a conversation with Bailey, she shared, "My

Caring teachers build strong relationships with their students.

teacher sometimes jokes around, which is cool, but she sometimes hurts my feelings when she says things like, 'earth to Bailey' when I'm just thinking or trying to get an idea clear in my head." As this example demonstrates, a teacher's words are powerful and can contribute to building a caring relationship or creating a distance between teacher and student (Johnston, 2004). Former teacher-of-the-year Sharon Draper describes good instruction as "teaching from the heart" that forges caring relationships between teachers and students (2000).

Caring teachers foster student engagement and effort that support student achievement in school (Osterman, 2000). In general, "when students have a secure relationship with their teachers, they are more comfortable taking risks that enhance learning—tackling challenging tasks, persisting when they run into difficulty, or asking questions when they are confused" (Stipek, 2006, p. 46). This active stance and engagement with learning facilitates academic achievement.

Beyond this broad definition of caring in teaching, research by Short (1996) indicates that adolescents tend to divide the characteristics of caring teachers into two categories: personal and academic. Both personal and academic aspects of caring have been correlated to student self-confidence and engagement in literacy learning (Dillon, 1989; Dillon & Moje, 1998). Personal characteristics of caring teachers focus on the teacher's openness to talk with and listen to students, as well as a willingness to help them with personal problems. This type of caring was most often cited by female students as important. Academic characteristics of caring pertain to the teacher's ability to help students understand their assignments, to tutor students when they need extra instruction, to work with students to set goals, and to talk to students about their behaviors and work habits as they relate to the classroom and school. Male students most often identified academic dimensions of caring as important to their success and engagement in school. By emphasizing three main messages to their students, teachers can help students understand that they are both cared for and supported in the classroom. These messages are "First, 'You can do this!' Second, 'I'm here to help.' And third, 'I'm going to take great pleasure in your success!'" (Sparks, 2003, p. 45).

When Bailey felt her teacher from the previous year knew and cared about her, she was more engaged and interested in learning and in books. When she felt her current reading teacher didn't care about teaching or the students, she found reading to be less enjoyable and meaningful. Clearly, Bailey values the personal aspects of caring that her former teacher possessed. She also explained aspects of the academic dimension of caring when noting, "My math teacher is great. He has study groups after school to help us review for tests. He explains everything so clear that it makes sense. He really cares if we learn." While we agree wholeheartedly with Bailey that caring, both in the personal and academic sense, is an essential characteristic of effective teaching, it alone is not enough. Teachers must also be competent and highly qualified.

Competent and Highly Qualified

The National Commission on Teaching and America's Future (NCTAF) (1996) states that every child has an "educational birthright" to have a "competent, caring,

4
....

CHAPTER 1

*All Children
and Adolescents
Have the Right
to Be Taught
by a Caring,
Competent, Highly
Qualified Teacher*

qualified teacher" (p. 6). The No Child Left Behind Act (U.S. Department of Education, 2001) requires that all K through 12 teachers be highly qualified as defined by having full certification, a bachelor's degree and demonstrated competence in subject matter knowledge and teaching. While such reports and mandates can raise awareness of the need for competent, highly qualified teachers, they are not sufficient for understanding the many dimensions of the terms "competent" and "highly qualified." The necessary knowledge to be an effective teacher is multidimensional and encompasses several categories as outlined in Figure 1-1.

These dimensions of teacher knowledge and skills are explained by the National Commission on Teaching and America's Future in the following quote. "To be effective, teachers must know their subject matter so thoroughly that they can present it in a challenging, clear, compelling way. They must know how their students learn and how to make ideas accessible so that they can construct 'teachable moments.' Research confirms that teacher knowledge of subject matter, student learning, and teaching method are all important elements of teacher effectiveness" (NCTAF, 1996, p. 6). In addition, standards also exist that delineate what teachers should know and be able to do in specific areas of the curriculum (e.g., *Standards for Reading Professionals*, International Reading Association [IRA], 2003a). Such standards outline the knowledge, practice, and reflection that are necessary for teachers to be effective (see Figure 1-2).

One promising new practice to help all middle and high school teachers become competent to teach literacy skills and strategies across the curriculum is the use of literacy coaches (IRA, 2006; Sturtevant, 2003). These coaches work with teachers to help them use instructional strategies to improve their students' ability to read, write,

*C*ompetent, highly qualified teachers possess:

- *Content Knowledge*—Academic knowledge
- *General Pedagogical Knowledge*—How to plan and provide instruction; classroom management and organization
- *Curriculum Knowledge*—Programs and materials for teaching
- *Pedagogical Content Knowledge*—How to teach the specific content so it is understandable to students
- *Knowledge of Learners and Their Characteristics*—Understanding intellectual, social, and personal development of all students
- *Knowledge of Educational Contexts*—Understanding the classroom, district, and community
- *Knowledge of Educational Ends, Purposes, and Values*—What should be taught? What is the goal of instruction and education in general?

Source: Shulman, 1987.

Figure 1-1
....

*Dimensions of
Teacher Knowledge*

and achieve in their classes. By providing this type of ongoing, onsite professional development for teachers, schools are able to increase the likelihood that all of their teachers are prepared to support their students' content literacy needs.

We believe it is essential for teachers to be well prepared before entering the profession. We agree with the International Reading Association's stance that teacher education programs must be rigorous and contain supervised field experience components to prepare teachers to be highly qualified (IRA, 2003b). In their review of research on teacher preparation, Darling-Hammond, Wise, and Klein (1999) concluded that teachers who completed programs that contained rigorous course work in content and pedagogy and included supervised field experiences were more successful in the areas of teaching methods, classroom management, and differentiating instruction to meet the needs of diverse learners than teachers who were prepared in less demanding programs. Furthermore, this review of research concluded that student achievement, especially in math and science, was correlated to the quality of teacher preparation.

Many teachers, however, do not complete traditional teacher education programs prior to entering the classroom. According to the National Center for Education Information (2005) an average of 35,000 teachers enter classrooms each year through alternative certification programs, and many others receive emergency licenses to allow them to teach while they are completing certification requirements (NCTAF, 2003). Darling-Hammond, Wise, and Klein (1999) argue that any alternatives to traditional teacher preparation programs must be rigorous and include supervised field experiences. Unfortunately, many alternative certification programs are delivered in very short time frames, such as during a single summer, and others

1. **Foundational Knowledge**: "Candidates have knowledge of the foundations of reading and writing processes and instruction" (p. 10).

2. **Instructional Strategies and Curriculum Materials**: "Candidates use a wide range of instructional practices, approaches, methods, and curriculum materials to support reading and writing instruction" (p. 12).

3. **Assessment, Diagnosis, and Evaluation**: "Candidates use a variety of assessment tools and practices to plan and evaluate effective reading instruction" (p. 14).

4. **Creating a Literate Environment**: "Candidates create a literate environment that fosters reading and writing by integrating foundational knowledge, use of instructional practices, approaches and methods, curriculum materials, and the appropriate use of assessments" (p.16).

5. **Professional Development**: "Candidates view professional development as a career-long effort and responsibility" (p. 18).

Source: International Reading Association, 2003a.

Figure 1-2

Standards for Reading Professionals

6
....

CHAPTER 1

*All Children
and Adolescents
Have the Right
to Be Taught
by a Caring,
Competent, Highly
Qualified Teacher*

place teachers in classrooms prior to the completion of coursework in teaching methods, materials, content, and human development (NCTAF, 2003). We argue that such alternative programs are insufficient to prepare teachers to instruct children and adolescents in our schools. When students are taught by teachers who are underprepared to educate them effectively, the students are shortchanged in terms of quality of instruction and opportunity to learn.

Based on the research, theory, and educational standards described previously, we conclude that by connecting the elements of caring, competence, and qualifications, teachers can be truly effective—what each and every child and adolescent in our schools deserves.

Why Is the Right to Be Taught by a Caring, Competent, Highly Qualified Teacher Important for Children and Adolescents?

In a national survey, 90 percent of Americans stated that the best way to improve student achievement is to provide a qualified teacher in each classroom (Haselkorn & Harris, 1998). Recent studies have identified a positive correlation between teachers who possess certification in their teaching field and student achievement (Ingersoll, 2001; Wayne & Youngs, 2003). In other words, when a seventh-grade language arts teacher is certified to teach language arts at that grade level, her students are more likely to have higher achievement than a similar class of seventh-grade students who are taught by a teacher who does not possess the corresponding certification. Furthermore, even if a teacher holds the appropriate initial certification, continued professional development is necessary for her to learn about new strategies and current research to continue to build and refine her practice.

The importance of this right is supported by research; however, it is not a reality in many public school classrooms (NCTAF, 2003). Unfortunately, many low-income schools in urban and rural areas have large numbers of teachers who are not certified and therefore lack the knowledge and skills necessary to teach students well (NCTAF, 2003). We argue that unless we address this concern and make the right to caring, competent, highly qualified teachers available to all students, regardless of socioeconomic status, our educational system will be undemocratic and unequal. Such inequality can lead to cultural reproduction resulting in a caste system where the "poor stay poor" and the "rich stay rich" (Bourdieu, 1991). In other words, if poor children and adolescents in inner-city or rural areas are consistently taught by unqualified teachers who lack the knowledge and skills to teach well, those students will be denied access to opportunity, higher education, and power over their lives. Such outcomes are tragic not only for these students but for all of us. As the National Commission on Teaching and America's Future noted, "Teacher quality will make the critical difference not only to the futures of individual children but to America's future as well (1996, p. 2).

7

CHAPTER 1

*All Children
and Adolescents
Have the Right
to Be Taught
by a Caring,
Competent, Highly
Qualified Teacher*

Ongoing professional development is important for highly qualified teachers.

How Can the Right to Caring, Competent, Highly Qualified Teachers Become a Reality in Today's Schools?

Caring

Teacher dispositions such as caring are important, but they are difficult if not impossible to teach. There are, however, conditions that support teachers so they can work toward promoting care in the classroom (Weiner & Cohen, 2003). The issues of teacher burnout, increasing demands coupled with decreasing resources, rising class sizes, high-stakes testing, and the stress of balancing teaching and personal life are all challenges faced by today's teachers that sap the energy necessary to implement an ethic of care in the classroom. What, then, can we do to help teachers approach their students with an ethic of care? First, we must provide support and nurturing for all teachers so they have the "energy to teach" (Graves, 2001). In addition, we believe that teachers and students benefit greatly when their building and district leaders are visionaries who serve as instructional leaders so teachers do not feel alone, unsupported, or unappreciated in their teaching. As Graves (2001) argues, if teachers feel supported, connected, and appreciated, they are more likely to have the "energy to teach" in the ways they want, including being a caring presence in the lives of their students. This idea is borne out in the old proverb, "You can't get blood from a turnip,"

8

CHAPTER 1

*All Children
and Adolescents
Have the Right
to Be Taught
by a Caring,
Competent, Highly
Qualified Teacher*

meaning that if teachers are exhausted, depleted, frustrated, and isolated, it is unlikely that they can demonstrate caring for their students. They must first care for themselves in order to be able to interact with their students in a caring manner.

What can you do as a teacher to implement caring in your teaching?

- Examine any biases or prejudices you may bring into the classroom. Ask yourself questions such as, "Are there particular groups or types of students I have lower expectations for? If so, why?" By reflecting on your own biases and prejudices, you can examine the impact that these may have on your ability to be a caring teacher for all of your students. Acknowledging biases and prejudices is the first step in addressing and overcoming them in your teaching.
- Take time for yourself by doing things you enjoy. You will be refreshed and find that you have renewed energy to teach.
- Create an informal support network with other teachers so you can share your experiences and nurture and energize each other.
- Keep a journal of the good things that happen in your teaching to lift your spirits and encourage you to keep trying when you are facing a challenging situation.
- Reflect on the teachers in your life who made the greatest impact on you. Think about what they did that made a difference for you. Record your ideas on paper and read the list from time to time to remind yourself of the importance of teachers in the lives of their students.
- Consider how you can embody the three messages that underlie true caring in the classroom: "You can do this!" "I'm here to help" and "I'm going to take great pleasure in your success!" (Sparks, 2003, p. 45). Monitor what you say and how you say it to students to ensure that your messages and style of delivery reflect a caring attitude.
- Think about the type of caring teacher you would like your own children to have. If you don't have your own children, think of a special child or adolescent you know, and envision the type of caring teacher this youngster deserves. Strive to be that type of teacher.
- Use the "2 by 10" approach to talk informally with a student or several students for two minutes for ten days in a row. Ask open-ended questions such as, "How are you doing?" or "What is going on in your life right now?" to invite students to open up and connect with you (Curtis, 2005). Doing so will begin the process of building a caring relationship.
- Develop norms for interaction in the classroom that support a caring relationship among all class members. For example, one of us invites students to say "ouch!" if something said in the classroom hurts their feelings. Then a discussion can take place so the teacher and students can understand how their words affect others and how to be more caring in the classroom.
- Analyze your instructional methods to ensure that you are teaching content, skills, and processes in ways that are clear and accessible to all students. Ask students to offer anonymous feedback on the aspects of your teaching that are most helpful so you can target your instruction toward what works best for your students.

- Explore ways to offer one-on-one or small-group instruction to students who need additional support. Study halls, homeroom periods, advisory periods, and after-school programs are options that may work in your school.
- Demonstrate your passion for your subject matter and teaching. Let students know that you care about them and also the content, skills, and processes you are teaching.
- Make connections with students and the curriculum (Mueller, 2001). By interviewing students and gathering information about their goals and needs, you can demonstrate personal and academic caring for students. By making connections in the curriculum, you can teach skills, strategies, and content in ways that are meaningful and applicable to the real world.

Competent and Highly Qualified

Teachers must be fully prepared and ready to succeed as educators before they are placed in their own classrooms. High-quality teacher-education programs are critical to making this a reality (IRA, 2003b). While alternative certification programs appear to be "quick fixes" for placing certified teachers in classrooms, this process begs the question about whether such teachers have really demonstrated the knowledge, practice, and dispositions to teach well (NCTAF, 2003). We must strike a balance between the need to place certified teachers in classrooms with the demands that today's classrooms present. In other words, we must advocate for sound certification policies and strong induction and mentoring programs for new teachers so they can make a successful transition into professional teaching.

What can you do as a teacher to promote competence and high qualifications in teaching?

- Share your insights, experiences, and ideas with local teacher education programs to help them understand the realities of teaching in today's schools so they can continue to refine their preparation of new teachers.
- Volunteer to be a cooperating teacher for a student teacher to help her understand how to plan, teach, and inspire students to learn.
- Serve on hiring committees for new teachers at your school so you can ensure that new teachers have the preparation and potential to be caring, competent teachers.
- Be a mentor for a new teacher in your building to help him become the type of caring, competent teacher that all students deserve. If your school doesn't have a mentoring program, offer to serve on a committee to create such a program.
- Advocate for literacy coaches in your school so that onsite professional development is available for all teachers regarding content literacy instruction (IRA, 2006).
- Engage in professional development to hone your craft as a teacher. Share your new knowledge, skills, and ideas with your colleagues. You can accomplish this by taking courses, attending workshops, reading professional books and journals, participating in professional education organizations,

10

CHAPTER 1

*All Children
and Adolescents
Have the Right
to Be Taught
by a Caring,
Competent, Highly
Qualified Teacher*

joining a teacher book club, observing your colleagues' teaching, and talking about your practice with peers.

- If you are a seasoned teacher, get involved in offering professional development in your department, school, or district. This may take the form of organizing a teacher book club, doing a short professional presentation at a faculty meeting, or facilitating a study group on a topic of interest to you and other teachers in your school. Doing so will allow you to promote learning for other teachers, as well as allow you to move your own knowledge base up to a new level through leadership roles and experiences.

Putting Ideas into Action

Think back to Bailey's letter at the beginning of the chapter. If we could see ahead to the next school year, we would be optimistic that Bailey's letter might document the impact of a caring, competent, highly qualified teacher. We hope that her letter would detail a strong relationship with a teacher who knows, appreciates, and supports her both personally and academically. We anticipate that she might describe innovative teaching where she is actively engaged in her own literacy learning. As you look back at Bailey's letter, imagine what she might write about your classroom and your teaching.

As you reflect on the right of every child and adolescent to have caring, competent, highly qualified teachers, what ideas from this chapter do you plan to put into action in your own classroom and school? You may want to write your plans to record the progress you make toward reaching your goal and to document the challenges you encounter on your journey. As Bailey said, "A good teacher makes a huge difference. I wish every teacher could be like that!"

CHAPTER 1

*All Children
and Adolescents
Have the Right
to Be Taught
by a Caring,
Competent, Highly
Qualified Teacher*

1. If you were Bailey's teacher, what would you do and say to reflect a caring attitude in your practice and interactions? How do these ideas apply to your own teaching situation?

2. What concerns or worries do you have about adopting a caring stance in the classroom? Why do you feel this way? What can you do to address these issues so that caring can become a foundation for your teaching?

3. Think of a student that you were unable to connect with in your teaching. What techniques did you try to build a relationship with this student? Why do you think these techniques did not work? Based on what you read in this chapter, what new ideas do you have about building a caring relationship with this student?

4. What prejudices or biases have you seen evidence of in your school? What assumptions underlie these prejudices or biases? What steps can you and your colleagues take to address these prejudices or biases in your school?

All Children and Adolescents Have the Right to Be Treated as Competent Individuals Who Are Capable of Reading and Learning

Dear Teacher,

I've noticed that you don't call on me as much as the other kids when we read aloud in class. When we read the story in our books this week, you called on all the other kids to read out loud, but you didn't call on me to read. After we finished reading, you asked a lot of questions, but you only called on the kids that always give you the answer you want to hear. You never called on me.

You put my desk in the back of the room, and I feel like you want to forget about me. I know lots of the kids in the class are smarter than I am and better readers than I am, but I hate being treated like an idiot. I can read, but I stumble over my words because I get so nervous when I have to read out loud in front of the class. I know I don't always remember the exact words the author used when you call on me to answer questions, but I think I understand what the story is all about. Sometimes it seems like you want me to say the answer that you have in your head. I have my own way of saying things, and I don't see why you say my answer is not "exactly right" and then call on another student to "help" me answer the question.

I just wanted to let you know that I feel like you don't think I am very smart or a very good reader. I don't like being left out and wish you would try to include me in lessons.

Sincerely,

Austin, grade 8

13

CHAPTER 2

*All Children
and Adolescents
Have the Right to
Be Treated as
Competent
Individuals Who
Are Capable of
Reading and
Learning*

*A*s teachers, we may not be aware of how our words and actions are affecting our students. When we form reading groups or track students based on ability, we send a message to the ones in the "low" group that they are not competent and capable. Likewise, when a student gives an incorrect answer and we immediately call on another student to answer the same question, we show that we have given up on the first student. Although the students in these two examples were not ignored as Austin was, the students could develop feelings of incompetence that might have a bearing on their achievement.

We are well aware that individual differences are present in every classroom, but when we interviewed students in one of our research projects, we found that even "high-ability" middle school and high school students said they did not know if their teachers thought they were good readers. We strongly believe that all children and adolescents have the right to be treated as competent individuals who are capable of reading and learning. Students should *know* that their teachers believe they are competent individuals, so teachers should communicate their beliefs to students in an explicit manner. In this chapter, we will answer the following questions that focus on *the right for all children and adolescents to be treated as competent individuals who are capable of reading and learning:* What does it mean to treat children and adolescents as competent individuals who can read and learn? Why is it important for teachers to convey their beliefs of competence to the students they teach? How can teachers communicate their beliefs of competence to children and adolescents in their classrooms?

Treating Students as Competent Individuals Who Are Capable of Reading and Learning

As with the other rights presented in this book, the right to treat students as competent, capable individuals has several dimensions. It includes teacher beliefs and expectations, goal setting, strategy instruction, student self-assessment, and student demonstrations of competence. What do children and adolescents experience in classrooms in which teachers treat them as competent individuals who are capable of reading and learning?

Children and adolescents who are treated as competent individuals have teachers who truly believe that they can continue to develop as readers and learners as they progress through middle school and high school. For example, Ladson-Billings (1995) found that "exemplary" teachers of African American students in classrooms where she was a participant-observer "believed that all the students were capable of academic success" (p. 478). In a study of teachers' beliefs, Rosenthal and Jacobson (1968) described the Pygmalion Effect. Teachers were told that identified students were likely to "bloom" and make gains that would be above those of the "nonbloomers" in their classes. The designated "bloomers" did, in fact, outperform the "nonbloomers," even though the students had been randomly assigned the "bloomer" and "nonbloomer" labels. "The caring teacher who believes that students can succeed can have a positive Pygmalion Effect—whereby believing in potential creates potential—on adolescents" (Learning Point Associates, 2005, p. 7). In short,

CHAPTER 2

*All Children
and Adolescents
Have the Right to
Be Treated as
Competent
Individuals Who
Are Capable of
Reading and
Learning*

"successful reading, then, begins not with procedures, but with creative, perceptive teachers who believe children want to learn" (Deeds, 1981, p. 81).

Children and adolescents who are acknowledged as being competent have teachers who couple their belief that students can learn with high expectations. Stipek (1988) stated, "students expect to learn if their teachers expect them to learn" (p. 137). In the Ladson-Billings (1995) work mentioned earlier, the "exemplary" teachers did not allow students to choose to fail, but insisted that the students "work at high intellectual levels" (p. 479). When Ruddell (1995) studied the characteristics of teachers who were identified by former students as having "a major influence" on students' "academic or personal life" (p. 454), he found that holding "high expectations for learning" (p. 463) was one characteristic of influential teachers.

While high expectations on the part of teachers are desirable, children and adolescents who are treated as competent are guided by their teacher's high expectations and knowledge of individual students to decide jointly on realistic reading goals for learning. Alderman (1990) indicated that setting goals for performance is the first step toward success. Because students are involved in setting the goals, they accept more responsibility in making plans and decisions that will lead to reaching the goals (Learning Point Associates, 2005). They keep a record of their progress and, depending on the goal, may create a visual representation, such as a graph, of their progress.

Once realistic goals are set, children and adolescents who are in classrooms where they are treated as competent individuals have positive reading experiences as they progress through the grades. Their teachers "know that successful performances enhance students' self-perceptions of competence," and they know that it is important for students to begin "with a successful experience to bolster these perceptions of self-competence, which can positively affect their success at more difficult literacy tasks" (Sweet, 1997, p. 97).

When teachers believe the children and adolescents they teach are capable of reading and learning, they teach their students effective word identification, fluency, comprehension, and study strategies for dealing with various types of text, and they teach the students when and how to apply the strategies. Students in the middle grades and secondary schools encounter many polysyllabic words that "often carry most of the content" (Cunningham & Allington, 2007, p. 76), and their teachers teach them to use morphemes, common spelling patterns, and syllabication to decode these words (Bear, Invernizzi, Templeton, & Johnston, 2004; Cunningham & Allington, 2007; Readence, Bean, & Baldwin, 2001). The ability to recognize many words automatically and decode words quickly provides a foundation for fluent reading because the reader does not have to stop reading to figure out words (Chard, Pikulski, & McDonagh, 2006). Teachers in the middle grades and high school assess their students' fluency and use "systematic, long-term, explicit" (Chard et al., 2006, p. 43) instruction in the four components of fluency—speed, accuracy, appropriate expression, and comprehension (Chard et al., 2006; Johns & Berglund, 2002). Fluency contributes to comprehension because fluent readers are able to attend to meaning, rather than having to decode words, and comprehension contributes to fluency because readers who understand the text and the author's purpose are able to read with appropriate expression (Walker, Mokhtari, & Sargent, 2006). Middle school and high school students are able to go deeper into their reading because their teachers teach them comprehension strategies that they can apply on their own at the appropriate time (Harvey & Goudvis, 2000; Pressley, 2000; Pressley & Harris, 1990). Preteens and teens also are taught study strategies for organizing and remembering the concepts presented in reading material (Moore, Bean, Birdyshaw, & Rycik, 1999; Readence, Bean, & Baldwin, 2001). Strategy instruction is consistent with the recommendations of the position statement developed by the Commission on Adolescent Literacy of the International Reading Association (Moore Bean, Birdyshaw, & Rycik, 1999) and is recommended by other researchers in middle grades and adolescent reading (Alvermann, 2001a; Guthrie, Schafer, Wang, & Afflerbach, 1995; Harvey & Goudvis, 2000; Learning Point Associates, 2005; Pressley & Harris, 1990; Vacca, 1998).

When children and adolescents are treated as competent individuals, their teachers teach them the process of self-evaluation, which includes involving students in developing rubrics and other assessments (Learning Point Associates, 2005). Honest self-assessment is needed if students are to develop feelings of competence and success (Schunk & Zimmerman, 1997; Stipek, 1988). According to Schunk and Zimmerman, some research has shown that instruction in self-evaluation is effective as early as third grade. Schunk and Zimmerman also stated that "positive self-evaluations lead students to feel efficacious . . . because they believe they are capable of making further progress" (p. 40). Although one might expect negative self-evaluations to have a detrimental effect on self-efficacy, they do not "diminish self-efficacy . . . if students believe they are capable of succeeding but that their present approach is ineffective" (p. 40).

Children and adolescents who have teachers who treat them as competent individuals have opportunities to demonstrate their competence. In the Ladson-Billings study (1995) in which she observed "exemplary" teachers, "all of the teachers gave students opportunities to act as teachers" (p. 480). Students regularly stood before the class and explained concepts, and they served as "classroom experts" (p. 481), with each student expected to be an expert in some area. Alvermann (2001a)

15

CHAPTER 2

All Children and Adolescents Have the Right to Be Treated as Competent Individuals Who Are Capable of Reading and Learning

A teacher helps her students develop competence in reading by teaching them word identification, fluency, comprehension, and study strategies.

16

CHAPTER 2

*All Children
and Adolescents
Have the Right to
Be Treated as
Competent
Individuals Who
Are Capable of
Reading and
Learning*

described "participatory approaches" (p. 21) in which students interact with peers and with someone who is more knowledgeable, and she indicated that these approaches "support adolescents' academic literacy development" (p. 21). In a study by Tatum (2000) that involved African American eighth graders who were assigned to a "low-level track" (p. 52), these students helped each other with vocabulary activities, listened to each other read and identified miscues, and collaborated on comprehension questions.

In summary, children and adolescents who are treated as competent and capable of reading to their highest potential have teachers who believe they can succeed, hold high expectations for students, collaborate with students to set goals, teach students instructional strategies needed for success, engage students in self-evaluation, and give students opportunities to show they are competent. (See Chapter 1 for additional information on high-quality teachers.)

Why Is the Right to Be Treated as Competent Individuals Who Are Capable of Reading and Learning Important for Children and Adolescents?

The right to be treated as competent, capable individuals is important because teachers' beliefs and expectations are manifested in teacher behavior. Whether they realize it or not, teachers transmit their beliefs and expectations to their students "through a complex series of verbal and nonverbal cues" (Feldman, 2006, p. 381) that "can actually bring about positive or negative performance from their students" (p. 383).

Rosenthal (as cited in Stipek, 1988) gave examples of ways in which teacher beliefs and expectations are transmitted to students for whom they hold high expectations and to those for whom they hold low expectations. The teacher

1. Smiles and nods at high-expectation students more than at low-expectation students
2. Is friendlier toward high-expectation students
3. Seats low-expectation students farther from the teacher and interacts with them less
4. Gives high-expectation students more information to learn, or more problems to complete
5. Gives more difficult and more varied assignments to high-expectation students
6. Calls on high-expectation students more often
7. Gives more clues and repeats or rephrases the question more often for high-expectation students
8. Waits longer for high-expectation students to answer
9. Provides high-expectation students with more detailed and more accurate feedback
10. Criticizes low-expectation students for incorrect responses
11. Praises high-expectation students more frequently for correct responses

17

CHAPTER 2

All Children and Adolescents Have the Right to Be Treated as Competent Individuals Who Are Capable of Reading and Learning

12. Praises low-expectation students more for marginal or inadequate responses
13. Expresses pity toward low-expectation students when they perform poorly and anger toward high-expectation students (pp. 139–140)

The right of children and adolescents to be treated as competent individuals is significant, too, because common practices in schooling are powerful ways of conveying expectations. These practices convey different expectations to high achievers and low achievers, and they tend to convey lower expectations for minority and disadvantaged students. Willis (1991) reported that Rhona Weinstein of the University of California-Berkeley noted that the curriculum is structured to give high achievers "enriched" materials and low achievers "barren remedial" materials (p. 4). Ability grouping "implies lower expectations for lower-track students" (p. 4), with poor and minority students most likely placed in the lowest tracks (Ladson-Billings & Tate, 1995). The motivational techniques used in schools, likewise, are very different for high achievers and low achievers, with high achievers being allowed "to pursue their own interests" while low achievers are subjected to "rewards and punishments" (Willis, 1991, p. 4). High achievers are sometimes permitted to take "responsibility for their own learning," but low achievers usually have "little input or self-direction" (p. 4). Lastly, high achievers are typically the ones who "gain schoolwide recognition" and "assume leadership roles" (p. 4).

This right also is important because children and adolescents tend to seek out and participate in activities in which they feel competent. As Alvermann (2001a) stated, "adolescents' perceptions of how competent they are as readers and writers, generally speaking, will affect how motivated they are to learn in their subject area classes" (p. 6). Smith and Wilhelm (2004) supported the previous statements in a study involving forty-nine middle school and high school boys from different backgrounds, ethnicities, social classes, and levels of academic achievement. All the participants read "in contexts in which they could demonstrate competence" (p. 458) such as tutoring for a service project, organic gardening, rap music, sports, cars, history, video games, movies, TV shows, music videos, and wrestling. They tended to reject school literacy activities for which they lacked competence.

How Can the Right to Be Treated as Competent Individuals Who Are Capable of Reading and Learning Become a Reality in Today's Schools?

* Ask yourself if you believe all the students you teach are capable of making progress. Look at each name on your class roster and ask yourself that question. Notice the students at whose names you hesitate because you don't fully believe they are capable. Did you hesitate because of the students' socioeconomic status, their gender, their behavior, or their past performance on class work and tests? Try as we may, we will never be totally free of bias, but we can become aware of our biases and try to keep them from having a detrimental effect on students.

18
....

CHAPTER 2

*All Children
and Adolescents
Have the Right to
Be Treated as
Competent
Individuals Who
Are Capable of
Reading and
Learning*

- After analyzing your beliefs about the competence and capability of your students, go through your class roster again and ask yourself if you are holding high expectations for each student. Teachers sometimes form "theories" about students, and their expectations are based on these theories. "Information contrary to a teacher's theory is frequently not noticed, even if it is present" (Stipek, 1988, p. 138). To avoid holding inaccurate expectations, ask yourself if your expectations include *all* the "valid and reliable information" (p. 145) at your disposal. Did you dismiss "irrelevant information, such as race, social class, or sex" (p. 145) when you formed your expectations? According to Stipek, "expectations should be flexible" (p. 146). Do you need to revise your expectations for some students based on a reexamination of the information you have? "In general, expectations for students in compensatory and remedial programs are very low" (Anderson & Pellicer, 1990, p. 13). Do you need to increase your expectations for these students? Have you given up on some students? If so, evaluate the information that led to your hypothesis and create new expectations that will give the students a chance to succeed. Finally, tell your students that you expect *all* of them to read and learn to their highest potential.

- Show your students that you think they are capable by collaborating with them to develop goals for reading and learning. Locke (as cited in Alderman, 1990) indicated that goals should be "specific," "attainable," and "proximal" (p. 28). Canfield (1990) suggested creating time lines and deadlines for achieving goals. He also suggested letting students share their goals with fellow students so they can support each other and celebrate when goals are met. Alderman (1990) used a form for goal setting that can be adapted for different ages and abilities. It included a weekly goal, possible interferences with achieving the goal, sources of help for achieving the goal, and a rating of the student's confidence in reaching the goal. There also was a small section for evaluation. Students rated their satisfaction with attaining the goal and then gave reasons for attaining or not attaining the goal.

- Assess your students to determine their stage of spelling development because "there is converging evidence that reading, writing, and spelling development are integrally related" (Bear et al., 2004, p. 21). Bear and colleagues developed

A student reflects on how well she achieved the learning goals she set.

spelling inventories for use in kindergarten through high school. They found that many middle schoolers are in the syllables and affixes spelling stage. In this stage, students examine "how consonant and vowel patterns are represented in polysyllabic words, what occurs when syllables join together, . . . how stress or lack of stress determines the clarity of the sounds in syllables," and "how simple affixes (prefixes and suffixes) change the usage, meaning, and spelling of words" (p. 221). They also found that many middle school students and high school students are in the derivational relations spelling stage, which means they are ready to learn words that are related in meaning and spelling, have Greek and Latin word elements, and contain predictable spelling changes in consonants and vowels.

- Teach children and adolescents word identification strategies so they will feel that they are competent in figuring out unknown words and will be able to identify words quickly, an important component in fluency. Harmon (2000) stated that "by the time they reach middle school, these learners have developed ways to cope with unfamiliar words that are unproductive and self-defeating" (p. 525).
  - Use word study instruction. Whenever possible, group students according to the results of the spelling inventory that you administered, which means that secondary teachers might have "students in at least two different stages of word knowledge" (Bear et al., 2004, p. 87). Use contracts or individualized assignment plans with secondary students where they agree to sort words into categories, write the sorts, and hunt through their reading material for additional examples of words that fit the categories under study. Use worksheets for the word sorts and word hunts and have students keep the sheets in a binder or have students write the sorts and words found in hunts in a spiral notebook (Bear et al., 2004).
  - Teach students in middle grades and secondary school fifty morphemes that can be used to decode many words. Cunningham and Allington (2007) refer to these as the "Nifty-Thrifty-Fifty" (p. 80). They suggest introducing a few of the morphemes each week. Introduce the prefix or suffix and give an example of a word containing the prefix or suffix. Present and discuss other words that students should be able to decode and spell by applying their knowledge of the prefix or suffix. Discuss spelling changes that occur in words when the prefixes or suffixes are added to the word. Practice the words frequently until students can read and spell them automatically (Cunningham & Allington, 2007).
  - Teach your students to use the analogy method for decoding words, which requires students to look at the unknown word and then compare it to words they know (Gunning, 1995). Tatum (2000) taught the students in his study the analogy method through direct instruction and then transfer to reading and writing. Each day the students began the language arts period by decoding independently in writing five words that were written on the chalkboard. After this activity, students chorally chanted the spelling of the words by syllables. Dictation followed the syllabication activity, with students writing verbatim a dictated paragraph of two to four sentences and underlining selected words that emphasized common spelling patterns or were in the day's reading selection. At the

19

CHAPTER 2

All Children and Adolescents Have the Right to Be Treated as Competent Individuals Who Are Capable of Reading and Learning

CHAPTER 2

*All Children
and Adolescents
Have the Right to
Be Treated as
Competent
Individuals Who
Are Capable of
Reading and
Learning*

end of the year, twenty-five of the twenty-nine students, who had all been several years below grade level at the beginning of the year, had earned the required score on the achievement test and were promoted to high school.

• Teach your students to apply all the strategies for decoding words, including phonics generalizations that were taught in earlier grades. Bass (2005) developed the READ IT strategy that combines the strategies of context clues, morphemic analysis, analogy, and phonics to decode an unknown word. The R in READ IT stands for READ to the unknown word, look at the letters from left to right, and read to the end of the sentence. The E stands for EXAMINE prefixes, suffixes, and base words in the unknown word. The A stands for ANALYZE the unknown word for word families and common spelling patterns. The D stands for DISCOVER any sounds and phonics rules that can be applied to figure out the unknown word. Once students think they know how to pronounce the unknown word, they cross-check with the steps in IT. The I stands for INCLUDE the decoded word in the sentence where it was found and read the entire sentence. The T stands for THINK. Here the students ask themselves if the word they decoded makes sense in the sentence, if it sounds right in the sentence, and if it looks right. These steps may be posted in the classroom to remind students of strategies they can use to decode words they don't know.

• Assess your students regularly to determine their reading rate, their accuracy in reading words orally, their expression, and their comprehension.

 • Assess reading rate and accuracy by selecting a passage that the majority of your students can read orally in one or two minutes with 85 to 90 percent accuracy. Ask an individual to read the passage orally as you mark reading miscues such as insertions, omissions, and substitutions. Mark the place where the student was reading at the end of one minute. Count the total words read in one minute and subtract the number of miscues to determine the reading rate. Plot each student's reading rate on a chart or graph for future reference (Johns & Berglund, 2002). To assess expression, create a checklist or rubric containing items pertaining to phrasing, expression and emphasis, observance of punctuation, overall voice quality, and comprehension (Johns & Berglund, 2002). Reflect on the student's oral reading of the passage and mark the checklist or rubric accordingly. Ask students to retell briefly what they read as you note strengths and weaknesses in comprehension. Share the results of the fluency assessment with students privately and store the results where they can be accessed easily for comparison after future assessments are completed. As students see their progress, their self-efficacy and competence will be enhanced.

 • Model fluent reading and provide systematic, explicit instruction in the components of fluency. Read to your students using appropriate phrasing, emphasis, and observance of punctuation while maintaining good voice quality and rate. Discuss each of the characteristics of fluent reading and, if necessary, provide contrast by demonstrating undesirable oral reading. Tompkins (2007) suggested writing a sentence on the board, showing students how to chunk it into phrases, and then letting students read the sentence using correct phrasing. Later, make copies of material and guide your students in marking the text into phrases and reading it with appropriate phrasing. Teach your students what punctuation marks mean and how to pause, stop, and change intonation accordingly. When teaching students to read with expression, use both stories and nonfiction so your students can learn to use expression that matches the "tone and intent of the author" (Zutell, Donelson, Bevans, & Todt, 2006, p. 269).

- Promote fluency by providing opportunities for your students to read orally with guidance and feedback. This means that the traditional oral reading method known as round-robin reading is not appropriate for developing fluency because round-robin reading typically does not involve oral reading instruction by the teacher or feedback on students' progress. The National Reading Panel (2000) indicated that guided oral reading procedures such as repeated reading, paired reading, neurological impress, and radio reading were found to be effective in research studies dealing with fluency. For repeated reading, make copies of the passage to be read. Ask the student to read the passage aloud as you mark errors and note the rate. Chart the results on a graph. Let the student practice reading the passage silently and, at a future date, repeat the process with the same passage (Gipe, 2002). Tatum (2000) found that his eighth graders "became more conscientious in their reading habits and were willing to work toward improvement" (p. 61) when repeated readings were implemented and discussed. In paired reading, two students or a student and an adult work together. At first, pairs read aloud together, with the tutor adjusting to the tutee's rate and correcting the tutee's errors. When ready, the tutee reads alone, while the tutor monitors and corrects errors. Simultaneous reading resumes after an error is made (Topping, 2006). Heckelman (1969) described the neurological impress method, which was cited by Gipe (2002) as a useful strategy for fluency building. In this method, the teacher sits slightly behind the student and on the student's right side (so the teacher is reading into the student's right ear) while the two of them choral-read a passage. The teacher may track the print with a finger to help the student follow along. If the student stumbles, the teacher is to continue reading. With the fluency activity called radio reading, students work in groups of four to six. The teacher assigns the reading passage and group members. Once students are in the groups, let each student select a section to read. Allow time for students to practice reading the section silently and to write discussion questions. When the group is ready, one student reads as the others listen with their books closed. When finished, the group discusses the readers' questions. Reading continues until everybody has had a chance to read. One student in each group may be the designated secretary and record the number of questions answered correctly by each student (Vacca & Vacca, 1989). Tompkins (2007) suggests that the reading material selected for fluency instruction be slightly below the student's instructional reading level and be of interest to the reader.
- Teach students comprehension strategies that good readers use as they try to understand what they are reading. Harvey and Goudvis (2000) suggested

21

CHAPTER 2

All Children and Adolescents Have the Right to Be Treated as Competent Individuals Who Are Capable of Reading and Learning

22

CHAPTER 2

*All Children
and Adolescents
Have the Right to
Be Treated as
Competent
Individuals Who
Are Capable of
Reading and
Learning*

teaching the strategies of making connections, questioning, visualizing, inferring, determining important ideas in text, and synthesizing information. Pressley (2004) reported that relating prior knowledge, mental imagery, questioning, and summarizing were "validated as effective in improving comprehension in students in grades 4 through 8" (p. 139).

• Use scaffolding for teaching comprehension strategies. Both Pressley (2000, 2004) and Harvey and Goudvis (2000) agree that comprehension strategy instruction begins with the teacher explaining the strategy and then modeling or thinking aloud while using the strategy in reading a passage aloud. Once students understand how the strategy can be implemented, the teacher scaffolds practice opportunities by gradually releasing responsibility for using the strategy. Guided practice consists of the teacher and students practicing the strategy together. This type of practice allows students to receive feedback from the teacher and peers as they tell how they applied the strategy in their reading. Independent practice follows guided practice, with students working on their own as they apply the strategy. As before, the teacher and peers give feedback to students on their use of the strategy. The last step in the teaching process is application. Here students have a chance to apply the strategy with different, more challenging texts (Harvey & Goudvis, 2000).

• Combine comprehension strategy instruction with literature circles. Lloyd (2004) taught sixth graders from a variety of backgrounds who attended a suburban school. As with typical literature circles, students identified the novels they preferred to read, and the teacher placed the students in groups based on their preferences. Each group decided the number of pages to read each time they met, but the group activity differed from literature circles in two ways. The students were not assigned roles to perform, and they focused their discussions on how they applied the comprehension strategy under study as well as comprehension strategies taught previously.

• Teach online comprehension strategies. Kymes (2005) suggested that the teacher think aloud and model comprehension strategies while reading online text. The students notice how the teacher implements the comprehension strategy, and later they practice the strategy with teacher and peer guidance.

• Once students are observed implementing comprehension strategies effectively, teach them when to use the strategies. The teacher may prompt students to use specific strategies with narrative text, expository text, poetry, and other genres. By using the strategies in all content areas, teachers demonstrate the appropriate time to use the strategies (Pressley & Harris, 1990).

• Teach children and adolescents study strategies for remembering and organizing important information in their reading material, but remember that "no single study method is going to be effective in all study circumstances" (Brozo & Simpson, 1991, p. 213).

• Teach students a general study method for use with expository texts. Robinson (as cited in Reutzel & Cooter, 2004) developed SQ3R, which stands for survey, question, read, recite, and review. Following is a modification of SQ3R that incorporates some of the comprehension strategies presented earlier. Model how to do each step with a short chapter in a content-area textbook that students are required to read. Show them how to survey the chapter by reading aloud the headings, subheadings, captions, highlighted vocabulary, and inserts throughout the chapter. As you read, demonstrate how to make connections to personal experiences, other texts, and your knowledge of the world. Then go back to the beginning of the chapter and model how to generate questions that will guide your reading of the chapter. Headings, subheadings, and other features that you read in the survey step may prompt questions. Next, demonstrate how to read the text and answer the questions you posed before reading. Some answers may require the comprehension strategy of inferring. When you have answered the questions, model how to read the questions again and answer them from memory. Finally, show students how to write the answers to the questions or write a summary of each section of the chapter for use when reviewing the material. Cue students to use the comprehension strategies as they engage in guided practice and independent practice with the study method.

- Teach students to monitor their comprehension as they read and study. Harvey and Goudvis (2000) suggested teaching students to
  - Track their thinking through coding, writing, or discussion
  - Notice when they lose focus
  - Stop and go back to clarify thinking
  - Reread to enhance understanding
  - Read ahead to clarify meaning
  - Identify and articulate what's confusing or puzzling about the text
  - Recognize that all of their questions have value . . .
  - Develop the disposition to question the text or author
  - Think critically about the text and be willing to disagree with its information or logic
  - Match the problem with the strategy that will best solve it. (pp. 19–20)
- Provide students with opportunities to evaluate themselves and their implementation of word identification, fluency, comprehension, and study strategies. Earlier in this chapter, goal setting was discussed. Teach students to consider how well they achieved the learning goals they set. Let them explain in writing or orally if they met, partially met, or did not meet their goals. Ask them to explain why they rated themselves as they did and to identify "reasons for attaining or not attaining" their goals (Alderman, 1990, p. 29). Finally, ask them how you can help them achieve future goals.
- As students attain their goals and demonstrate their competence to you, give them opportunities to demonstrate their competence to others. Let them lead the literature circles and discussion groups in class. Have them share their thinking as they implement the strategies that you have modeled and coach their classmates in strategy implementation. Arrange for them to tutor a younger child who is struggling with word identification, fluency, or comprehension.

23

CHAPTER 2

All Children and Adolescents Have the Right to Be Treated as Competent Individuals Who Are Capable of Reading and Learning

Putting Ideas into Action

CHAPTER 2

*All Children
and Adolescents
Have the Right to
Be Treated as
Competent
Individuals Who
Are Capable of
Reading and
Learning*

Think about what Austin said in his letter. If you were his teacher, would you move his desk closer to the front of the room? Would you call on him to share his personal experiences and his prior knowledge of the topic being studied so he could be included in lessons more often? Would you become accepting of reasonable answers instead of thinking there is one right answer to questions? Clifford (1990) summed up our beliefs about treating students as competent individuals when she wrote, "we must emphasize error tolerance, not error-free learning; reward error correction, not error avoidance; ensure challenge, not easy success" (p. 25).

DISCUSSION QUESTIONS FOR STUDY GROUPS

1. Reread the ways that Rosenthal said teachers transmit their beliefs and expectations to students. Analyze your teaching. Which things on the list do you find yourself doing from time to time? Which things do you seldom do? What can you do to change the way you interact with some students?

2. As a middle school or high school teacher, you are expected to "cover" the essential content in your teaching area. What challenges would you face if you decided to help your students set personal learning goals and evaluate themselves on the achievement of the goals that they set? Is there room for both content and goal setting with self-evaluation in your teaching?

3. Suppose you are Austin's teacher and, after reflecting on your teaching, realize that you have not been treating Austin as though he is competent and capable of reading and learning. Consider the questions in Putting Ideas into Action. Would you move his desk closer to the front of the room? Would you call on him to share his personal experiences and his prior knowledge of the topic? Would you accept reasonable answers instead of expecting Austin to repeat the exact words from the text? What else would you do to show Austin that you think he is competent? What ideas and insights can you draw from Austin's situation that you can apply to your own teaching?

All Children and Adolescents Have the Right to Culturally Relevant Literacy Instruction

Dear Teacher,

Today when you asked me to read aloud in class I was embarrassed. I know you want me to practice and correct my mispronuncements but I can't always do that. I am glad you meet with me after school on Mondays to help me learn how to say the words correctly. I want to sound like you when I read aloud.

I know I read poorly in class today but I really like this Shakespeare play. I understand most of the words but I can't always pronounce them and the names of the people and places are funny to say.

Some of my friends laugh about Shakespeare and joke in Spanish and tell me no sabe!!! that means they do not understand. I think I comprehend too much!!! Comprehendring is my problem!! When I read I think about what the words mean. And I say them in Spanish before I say them in English. When I do this I use both sounds sometimes to say the words in my head and I don't have time to change the words to correct English before I read aloud.

My mother loves Shakespeare's plays and she tells me to think about what the words mean and the musica of the lines. I think I should think about pronouncing instead. What do you think?

Carlos, grade 10

CHAPTER 3

*All Children
and Adolescents
Have the Right
to Culturally
Relevant Literacy
Instruction*

*P*erhaps you can identify with Carlos because you, too, have learned English as a second language. Or maybe you remember when you learned a second language while in high school or college when you tried to transition from English to the new language. You may remember how you relied on your knowledge of English to help you pronounce words or make sense of what you heard or the texts written in another language. Perhaps you are thinking of the second language learners in your own classroom. Perhaps these students speak Spanish, Farsi, or Mandarin Chinese.

We learn from Carlos that he reads for meaning and that he is drawing on his literacy experiences with his mother to use strategies (e.g., think about what the words mean and the rhythm of Shakespeare's writing) to support his reading comprehension. We learn, too, that Carlos seems to be interested in reading Shakespeare and he may even be defending this interest when talking with his friends. We fear, however, that he is learning from his teacher that accurate pronunciation may be more important than comprehension.

You may be thinking about Carlos' goal to achieve "accurate" pronunciation of words: "I want to sound like you" and "I should think about pronouncing." That goal concerns us for at least two reasons. First, we are reminded of the variations represented in the language of the five of us; growing up in three different regions of the United States, we often notice how we pronounce some words differently from each other (e.g., the words "want" and "won't" sound very similar when pronounced by southeastern United States speakers) or use regional or slang expressions in our daily speech (e.g., We "redd up" the room instead of "clean the room" is a Pennsylvania Dutch expression commonly used in western Pennsylvania). Even with practice, it would be difficult for us to "sound" alike—nor would we want to, since our language is an integral part of who we are. We have a long history of using our forms of syntax, phonology, and semantic referencing. These were influenced by the language patterns of our family, friends, colleagues, students, and neighborhood communities, and vary according to our audience and contexts for interactions. As educators, we have learned to adjust our regional forms of expression or home vernacular to enhance communication with our family and friends and with more formal audiences. Yet specific characteristics of our language continue to go with us and define us. For example, after speaking to a group of teachers in Ohio, an audience member told one of us, "You are from Pittsburgh! I can tell by the way you pronounce certain words." We have learned what Delpit (Delpit & Dowdy, 2002) made explicit "language plays . . . a pivotal role in determining who we are" (p. xvii).

Second, we worry that both Carlos and the teacher in this classroom have a vision of language and literacy learning that is counterproductive. Word pronunciation may develop long after meanings are attached to words. You may recall words that were part of your "reading vocabulary" before they became part of your oral language; you may know what a word means but only later learn that its pronunciation is quite different from the one you had in your head during reading. Word pronunciation can occur after multiple exposures to hearing the word in various contexts. Often, word pronunciations develop with use in oral exchanges (that are meaningful) with peers and others. And sometimes word pronunciations and word meanings are learned simultaneously. Seldom do we remember how to pronounce words that don't have meaning for us. With Carlos' misconception about the importance of pro-

nunciation, we fear that Carlos' attention to meaning will be lost if accurate pronunciation is both his goal for reading and the means to achieving this goal.

In this chapter we discuss issues related to the *right of all children and adolescents
to have access to culturally relevant instruction*. We describe forms of literacy instruction
that are both *responsive* to diversity in ways that capitalize on students' cultural and
linguistic knowledge and *transformative* in ways that place diversity at the center of
the literacy curriculum when building new knowledge, strategies, and skills.

27

CHAPTER 3

*All Children
and Adolescents
Have the Right
to Culturally
Relevant Literacy
Instruction*

Culturally Relevant Instruction

Literacy instruction that is *culturally relevant* (Ladson-Billings, 2005) is designed ex-
plicitly to build on children's and adolescents' knowledge; language; beliefs, attitudes, and interests; conversational and group participation styles; experiences; and
the social events of the communities they represent (Gutierrez, 2005; Heath, 1983;
Ivanic & Moss, 1991). It requires connections to families and communities (as discussed further in Chapter 10). And in the classroom, it requires respect for differences; respect that is constantly displayed when teachers and students actively listen
to each other, engage in dialogic conversations, learn new concepts, and ask questions that genuinely interest them.

You may be thinking that the above description should apply to all classrooms,
and we agree. Cultural relevancy as it relates to instruction can be defined broadly;
for the concept *culture* represents the practices and activities of "virtually every human
activity" (see Figure 3-1).

Every student brings a culture and language variations to the classroom; the right
we discuss in this chapter, however, focuses specifically on those students who may
feel disconnected from the school curriculum because their cultural experiences and
knowledge and/or language are not *appreciated* or *appropriated* (made visible) in the
school context. And in that context, we advocate for instruction that is both respectful and responsive to these differences. We advocate, too, for instruction that appro-
priates these differences, using these as resources for making connections between
what students know and their learning of new academic knowledge, strategies, and
skills. Delpit (1995) reminds us that we can further marginalize diverse students if we

*C*ulture as a construct of importance for learning is most often invoked when the
person or activity under question is seen as different from what is expected. However,
culture is characteristic of virtually every human activity—it is part of every teaching and
learning encounter in every classroom . . . the key point in thinking about culture and
literacy is that appreciating culture is not the same as appropriating cultural practices
and knowledge for instructional purposes.

Source: Rueda, 2005, pp. 307–308.

Figure 3-1

*Culture Guides
Learning*

28

....

CHAPTER 3

*All Children
and Adolescents
Have the Right
to Culturally
Relevant Literacy
Instruction*

fail to teach them mainstream content and skills. Too often students identified as struggling readers or English language learners (ELLs) receive "remedial instruction" that does not provide access to academic content. Conversely, the use of multiple materials (different genre and multimedia) and invitations for multimodal representations of meanings (drawings, writing, multimedia, oral discussions) can help students, especially English language learners, access prior knowledge and make academic content more comprehensible (August & Hakuta, 1977; Montecel & Cortez, 2002).

Researchers have identified characteristics of children's and adolescents' cultural practices and language patterns that may not be appreciated or appropriated in some classrooms, the language characteristics of white Appalachian children (as described by Purcell-Gates, 1995), the African American vernacular or multiple interactive styles of urban African American students (as described by Obiddah, 1998), the differences between the home talk of children from urban and rural communities (as described by Heath, 1983), or the expectations about genre and text language displayed by children of working class families (as described by Hicks, 2004). Similarly researchers have documented how instruction fails to accommodate English language learners' different levels of language proficiency in ways that provide high-quality interactions during instruction (Doherty, Hilberg, Pinal, & Tharp, 2003). Language patterns and understandings about the use of language, developed through multiple interactions with others, are the cultural tools students use to *mediate (or support) their learning* and *communicate with others,* both in and out of school.

As educators, we need to understand how our students use oral and written language in their daily routines, how they interact with others, and how they interpret those interactions. We need to understand what expectations families have for their own and their children's reading and writing activities (e.g., Do they write letters to communicate with others or participate in instant messaging? Do they tell stories in a plot development format or by episodes that are not necessarily sequential? Do they participate in "group talk" by starting and finishing each other's sentences?). These are only some of the questions that we can ask to identify characteristics of cultural communities, but once identified we must remember that identifiable characteristics of cultural communities are situated and vary across individuals; they cannot not be generalized to others and they are not static. Instead, these practices can and do change according to expectations associated with audience, contexts, and interactions with others.

In Carlos' letter at the beginning of this chapter, we learn that the feedback he is receiving from his teacher and mother provides conflicting influences on Carlos' reading of Shakespeare. First, there is the culture of the classroom and what seems to be an expectation of speaking English "correctly." Carlos is desperately trying to "fit" into this classroom, to "sound like" his teacher. Yet he brings with him a rich appreciation for these readings, influenced by his mother's interest and attention to the rhythm and meanings of Shakespeare's language. Carlos expects that texts should hold meaning; thus, his search to "comprehend." Conversely, Carlos' teacher provides a powerful audience for him, and an unfortunate consequence of her feedback on reading accurately, while well intended, could divert his attention from the meanings of texts he is reading. This situation poses a serious dilemma for Carlos and requires attention to his knowledge and literacy goals.

A careful analysis of students' knowledge, experiences, and expectations for literacy is essential for designing appropriate and responsive literacy instruction. And once known, we must determine if the routines and expectations of our students (and their families) are similar or different from our own. That they may be different is not a reason to worry; that instruction does not capitalize on these differences is.

We provide one example of culturally responsive instruction to help us identify some of its attributes. When Luis Moll (2003) visited Vanderbilt University he described how he and his colleagues approach such instruction within a school located in a large Hispanic community. His approach to culturally relevant instruction is well documented (e.g., Moll, 2000; Moll & Greenberg, 1990; Moll, Tapia, & Whitmore, 1993; Moll, Saez, & Dworin, 2001). This instruction occurs in an Arizona bilingual school where Moll and his colleagues collaborate with teachers and community leaders. Students attending this school learn literacy initially in Spanish (even those students who come to school with English as their home language) and then gradually during the early school years learn English and literacy in English. When he traced students' progress over time, Moll concluded that these students met all established expectations—they performed well on norm-referenced achievement tests and on other (and perhaps more important) school and community measures (e.g., they enjoyed reading and writing, they read independently, and they were becoming literate in both languages). Noting that their scores on the high-stakes tests across the early grades moved both forward and backward before reaching a steady upward climb, Moll called for a kind of "educational patience" that allows educators to stay the course once they have carefully planned and implemented instruction that aligns with students' capabilities and culture. Such a focus rewards long-term progress instead of imposing sanctions against those schools that are not meeting short-term goals.

Specifically, Moll described several characteristics essential to culturally responsive instruction. These include: *educational sovereignty* (power and agency for decision making is shared by the school district, teachers, and community); *highly qualified and caring teachers; language sovereignty* (Spanish is protected and given status in the schools he describes); *instruction that represents community values and culture; instruction that encourages collaborative and shared learning among students, teachers, and community members;* and *teachers' close observations of students' literacy development.* Their methods for "appropriating" students' culture to facilitate new learning and supporting students' "language rights" (Perez, 2004) provide a powerful example of instruction that is possible for all students who are typically marginalized by schools because of their cultural and/or linguistic differences.

Culturally responsive instruction in Moll's example focuses on the four types of knowledge identified by Perez (2004) as essential for attaining literacy achievement: *cultural, linguistic, content,* and *text.* In Chapter 4 we discuss literacy knowledge and cultural and social provisions students possess to support their learning (Matthews & Cobb, 2005). In this chapter, we return to our goal of identifying what students know and do as literacy learners and users. To do so, we draw on the work of Perez (2004) to illustrate another way to describe students' *funds of knowledge* [*home and out-of-school knowledge*], as discussed by Moll, Amanti, Neff, and González (1992). Perez's work provides a perspective complimentary to the Matthews and Cobb (2005) perspective. Taken together they help us elaborate on the importance of rec-

30

CHAPTER 3

*All Children
and Adolescents
Have the Right
to Culturally
Relevant Literacy
Instruction*

ognizing characteristics of students' knowledge so that we can teach to this knowledge; a concept basic to our rights framework.

Cultural knowledge develops from numerous opportunities to observe and interact with others; typically, family and community members. For example, cultural knowledge relevant to literacy instruction is influenced by how families and communities talk about and use reading and writing and oral communication in their daily lives (to read aloud to family members, to discuss problems with others, to pay bills, to order food ingredients or clothes from catalogs, to read menus, to write music). In the school Moll described, out-of-school reading and writing activities were incorporated into the curriculum (e.g., one inquiry project led to a study of community texts, such as menus and advertisements used in Hispanic businesses—their purpose, language use, word choice, and audience).

In their study of Vietnamese high school students in New Orleans, Zhou and Bankston (1998) describe a close association between their families' spiritual beliefs and respect for school learning. Thus families were interested in their children's academic work and provided space and support in the home life for talk about school projects and activities. Understanding these beliefs and forms of home support provides a way for teachers to initiate communication with parents and learn about their home literacy activities.

McCarthey (2002) describes how teachers in her study of upper elementary and middle school students regularly held conferences with their students to learn about the influence of their students' cultural knowledge on their writing. One student was Ella, an African American fifth-grade girl who lived in New York City and whose mother was a proofreader in a publishing company and whose father was a university professor. Ella brought her rich writing history, including her particular interest in fiction, to the classroom, having written at home and school for many years. Multiple meetings with her teacher enabled Ella to negotiate the use of fictional aspects into the writing assignments that had previously excluded any fictional writing.

Linguistic knowledge represents the knowledge of structure, phonology, and language rules that continues to develop from infancy through adulthood. Moll's school privileged Spanish oracy and literacy because almost all students attending that school spoke Spanish at home, and those whose home language was English lived within a Spanish-speaking and -literate community. Numerous restaurants, banks, and other neighborhood businesses used Spanish as their primary language for communicating with the community. English-speaking children and adolescents were acquiring some Spanish in their daily interactions with their neighbors and other community members and this knowledge was further developed in the school setting along with their literacy development in English.

As Moll described, students learning to use their home language to make connections to sounds and meanings in English texts, similar to the meaning-oriented process Carlos describes in his letter, maximized English language learners' transition to English oracy and literacy. Similarly, Carol Lee (2004) and others discuss characteristics of African American vernacular and how teachers can facilitate connections between the systematic nature of linguistic and phonology characteristics of African American language and texts read in school, starting with texts that are culturally familiar, that are written in the African American vernacular (e.g., perhaps selecting lyrics from pop music or texts such as *The Color Purple*, by Alice Walker), and that pre-

31

CHAPTER 3

*All Children
and Adolescents
Have the Right
to Culturally
Relevant Literacy
Instruction*

Collaborating on song lyrics two boys are writing to accompany the digital text they generated.

sent universal writing styles (e.g., irony, satire) or themes (e.g., lost love, oppression). These text experiences serve as bridges to reading and comprehending similar (and complex) writing styles and themes in texts written by authors who use language in multiple ways, including different forms of Standard English. Teachers who draw attention to these multiple ways that language is used to convey meaning can help students appreciate its richness and power in different contexts and for different audiences.

Content knowledge represents the world knowledge and rich array of concepts students bring to and learn in school. The world knowledge of many students attending Moll's school came from families where fathers, uncles, and brothers were house-builders. Inquiry projects in the classroom and school helped students use this knowledge *while learning new knowledge*, as students examined ways to build small and large objects, applied math concepts to create wood projects, learned science concepts about soil conditions and land formation to examine sites for building houses, and applied what they were learning about architectural styles to the architecture in their communities. Parents and community members, viewed as resources for the school, taught in classrooms to extend students' knowledge by helping them identify questions, pose problems, and evaluate strategies for solving these problems.

Similarly, Snipp (2004) describes knowledge that teachers of Native American children and adolescents can draw on in their teaching. For example, many Pueblo families are contributing to the recent renaissance of Pueblo pottery, tribal arts such as basketry and wooden crafts, or decorative arts such as beading and jewelry; children and adolescents from these families may have developed rich concepts about

32

CHAPTER 3

*All Children
and Adolescents
Have the Right
to Culturally
Relevant Literacy
Instruction*

soil selection for pottery or design and measurement decisions for crafts and decorative arts, which can be related to math, science, and the arts in school.

Text knowledge comes from experiences with texts in multiple formats and organizations. Students come to school with expectations about structure and content—text purposes, how texts are read, and how information is presented. In Moll's school texts were chosen to support Spanish and English literacy and to both "match" content with students' cultural and existing knowledge *and* build new knowledge. As Perez (2004) explains, multiple forms of texts, including multicultural texts, fiction, and nonfiction, can be especially useful for deriving connections between disciplinary knowledge (e.g., solar system) and cultural knowledge (e.g., fables of heroes who live in the earth's solar system). When we think back on Carlos' letter, we wonder if his teacher is drawing connections between the students' lived experiences and the events in the Shakespeare play.

Similarly, teachers and students can read Native American spirituals or folktales or artwork as texts in their classrooms—texts that become pivotal for connecting students' world knowledge to concepts studied across the curriculum (e.g., study of Native American writers, trace history of religions and spiritualism in the United States). Texts central to students' history and experiences then become central to the school curriculum instead of left at the doorstep of the classroom (Nieto, 2000).

The works of Moll and his colleagues, Perez, Lee, and Snipp, among others, provide vivid descriptions of what is possible if we are going to move students from the margins to the center of an educational process in which both our students and we as teachers can thrive. Application of these works to our own classrooms will vary depending on our students and literacy goals; what can be held constant, though, are the educative constructs of culturally relevant instruction, as we described earlier.

Why Is the Right to Culturally Relevant Literacy Instruction Important for Children and Adolescents?

The issue of equity lies at the heart of this right to culturally responsive literacy instruction. Banks' (2004) use of the term "equity pedagogy" (instead of "culturally relevant pedagogy") underscores the importance of culturally sensitive instruction to increase the academic achievement of low-status or marginalized students. Providing literacy instruction that is responsive to individual's differences is a goal central to principles of democratic education. Early in this twenty-first century, both policy makers and educators are focusing on equity, too, in their calls for closing the "achievement gap" between students from culturally dominant homes (e.g., traditionally in the United States this has been white, middle- and upper-income families) and minority students (e.g., in the United States, second language learners, African American and Native American students, students living in poverty). We argue, however, that mechanisms designed to "close the gap" instead follow a tradition and authority that have been largely ineffective, and not supported by scientific evidence. In the following paragraphs, we discuss problems we encounter and possible ways to overcome these problems. We acknowledge that the problems we describe are situated within U.S. contexts, but believe these same issues confront educators world-wide (e.g., Heather Bell in New Zealand, 2005, personal communication).

33

CHAPTER 3

*All Children
and Adolescents
Have the Right
to Culturally
Relevant Literacy
Instruction*

How Have We Failed Our Students?

Unfortunately, the traditions associated with deficit views of minority students, norm-referenced standardized testing, fixed time lines and expected "stages" for achieving stated goals, and narrowly defined literacy goals and curricula have disadvantaged culturally and linguistically diverse students. And it has allowed us to maintain a culture of disability in U.S. schools, as described by McDermott, Goldman, and Varenne (2006). As Mann (1987) argued almost two decades ago, we must take a hard look at these school traditions and place the problem on the instructional design and traditions instead of the teachers and students who are working so hard (with inappropriate tools) to make schooling better. McDermott and his colleagues (2006) would add that we as teachers must constantly seek evidence of the knowledge and skills students possess and that exceed (the limiting) expectations of schools.

For decades, home and out-of-school literacy practices and language use that are different from practices of mainstream families have been viewed as *deficient* instead of as resources for school literacy learning (Lee, 2004; Lopez, 1999; Perez, 2004). Lee (2004) and Ball and Farr (2003), for example, describe how teachers evaluate negatively African American's episodic storytelling style because it differs from white students' topic-centered style or assume inferiority of language development because their language use differs from Standard English. In many classrooms, students with differences are "muted" (Devine, 1994); the tools they use to support their learning are viewed as inferior and not allowed in the classroom of English-only schools (such as those in California and Arizona, where legislation has prohibited dual-language teaching) or schools where students' language use is constantly corrected.

The *high-stakes testing* of students is particularly problematic for culturally and linguistically diverse students. Contrary to claims that nationwide testing practices, such as the National Assessment of Educational Progress (NAEP) and other standardized, norm-referenced tests, are scientific and objective, "test items are contrived, skills and knowledge are tested in isolation, and content selection is arbitrary and representative of the values, culture, and experience of the [white, male, middle-class] authors" (Gipps, 1999, pp. 360–361). And as Au (2000) and Solano-Flores and Trumbull (2003) argue, norm-referenced tests will always place minority students at a disadvantage because the items do not account for out-of-school literacy learning or students' language diversity. Even test items translated to students' home language are inadequate because they do not provide accurate or meaningful semantic and syntactic representations of that language. The awkward wording or loss of context often confuse students. Conversely, when researchers changed test items in more authentic ways, such as choosing vocabulary to represent the experiential and content knowledge of a group of African American students, these students scored as well as their white peers (Williams & Rivers, 1972 as cited in Lee, 2004).

Fixed time lines and expected stages of development of skill sets prerequisite to subsequent skill sets are not supported by literacy researchers. And these notions for ensuring progress are particularly biased against individual differences and trajectories

34

CHAPTER 3

*All Children
and Adolescents
Have the Right
to Culturally
Relevant Literacy
Instruction*

for learning (e.g., episodic storytelling may develop earlier for some African American students than topic-centered storytelling represented in skill time lines), and for students who may need more time to acquire an academic language (e.g., English language learners may learn conversational English in two years but require five to seven years to become fluent in the academic language of English (Solano-Flores & Trumbull, 2003). This issue is further exacerbated by a push in some states for early exit (e.g., after one to two years) from language support classes.

Rigid adherence to *narrowly conceived curricula* and *too few teachers of color* are additional factors contributing to inequitable instruction. Classrooms are becoming increasingly more culturally and linguistically diverse. In the United States, for example, it is expected that by 2020 there will approximately 6 million students with a home language other than English (as compared to 2.5 million in 1992). Large school districts, such as the Los Angeles Unified School district reported that in 2003 there were fifty-five distinct languages in their district, 72 percent of students are Spanish speaking; only 9.5 percent are white. And while our classrooms are becoming more diverse, our teacher population remains the same. Approximately 90 percent of U.S. teachers are of European American ancestry, primarily women, who speak English only (Howard, 1999). Teachers are teaching children and adolescents from cultural and language groups different from their own (Dillworth, 1994).

Rather than acknowledging differences across individuals according to knowledge, culture, and language, policy makers and curriculum leaders continue the tradition of what Bartolome (1994) called a "methods fetish," the goal to find the "best" method for teaching *all* students (i.e., all students on the same page at the same time).

Taken together, this set of factors inhibits a cultural view of literacy instruction. There are few goals more important for reform than the provision of instructional contexts that are equitable, excellent, and responsive to students' knowledge, background, and experiences. Without such reform Jimenez (2003) warns us "far from advancing the academic achievement of marginalized groups, these mainstream definitions of literacy will serve only to legitimate and exacerbate current inequities" (p. 122).

Our inability to respond to cultural issues and teach academic knowledge in ways that are culturally relevant to our students has produced serious and negative consequences. One consequence is students' disinterest and rejection of academic literacy. We learned about this consequence firsthand when we interviewed middle and secondary students. Repeatedly, students told us that they were not "connecting" with their school texts—frustration was expressed by Chris, the high school student who told us that "books are highly overrated"; by Jessica, a fifth-grade girl, who told us that her teacher made reading difficult by not telling her "all the stuff [you need to know] about the story"; by Sam, a sixth-grade girl who told us that all the required biographies just "don't stick." A similar finding was reported on the High School Survey of Student Engagement (2005), a national survey administered to 180,000 students from 167 high schools in twenty-eight states. Eighty percent of high school seniors reported that they spent three hours or fewer a week reading assigned materials for all their classes, even though 66 percent or more of these seniors indicated they had good grades and had already been accepted into a college after graduation. Eighteen percent indicated they spent no time on assigned readings. Across all four years as high school

35

CHAPTER 3

*All Children
and Adolescents
Have the Right
to Culturally
Relevant Literacy
Instruction*

students, 55 percent of the students reported little effort on school readings and read assigned readings for all classes three or fewer hours a week.

A second consequence, strongly related to the first, is an alarming increase in dropout rates of middle and high school students and a rise in incarceration of minority individuals. A recent report generated by the Civil Rights Project at Harvard University (2005) indicated that students in large urban California school districts, consistent with national data, have dropout rates that exceed 50 percent and, among these dropouts, African American and Hispanic students were more likely to be represented than most other racial and ethnic groups. Using data compiled by the National Center for Education Statistics (NCES), Balfanz and Legters (2005) report that nearly 50 percent of African American students and nearly 40 percent of Latino students across the nation do not graduate from high school, with the largest percentage of dropouts occurring in Southern and Southwestern high schools. Noting schools' inability to make connections to students' lived experiences and provide agency for their own learning, Hicks (2004) argues that resistance to academic assignments (discussed earlier) and choosing to drop out of schools may be the only way minorities can exercise any power over their learning.

Third, despite decades of reports by researchers and policy makers, the problem of overrepresentation of culturally and linguistically diverse students in special education persists (Artiles, Klingner, & Tate, 2006; Risko, 2005; Utley, Obiakor; & Kozleski, 2005). Sadly, we believe this tradition will continue until we step away from beliefs that equate differences with deficits and disability.

We Must Do Better

Literacy researchers who have provided us with alternate instructional visions for culturally and linguistically diverse students propel us to move forward in ways that are sensible and responsive to students. In the following paragraphs, we describe research evidence that supports culturally relevant pedagogy—different practices across different settings have produced high achievement and engagement when taking a cultural approach to literacy instruction. For example, Gutierrez, Baquedano-Lopez, and Alvarez (2001) described how students' "hybrid practices" (i.e., shifting from English to Spanish to facilitate comprehension of English texts; using both English and Spanish to communicate orally or in writing) facilitated their active participation and literacy learning within a classroom that was designated as English-only. Creating opportunities for code switching and confirming meaning in a home language encourages students to make sense of written and oral communication and worry less about surface skills (e.g., pronunciation of words) that may not enhance comprehension.

Carlos' letter demonstrates his use of a hybrid construction (using both English and Spanish words) to help him communicate more clearly his intended message. This hybrid practice is an example of how he used his knowledge and language as *cultural tools* to explain his thinking. Understanding the meaning of his message, a culturally appropriate response from his teacher would focus on Carlos' concerns and reinforce his desire to read for meaning. Such a response signals to Carlos that he is a competent writer, one who conveys meaning clearly, and that comprehension is the primary goal for reading.

CHAPTER 3

*All Children
and Adolescents
Have the Right
to Culturally
Relevant Literacy
Instruction*

Similarly, Delpit (1992, 1995; Delpit & Dowdy, 2002) drawing on her research, describes how rich, interactive discussions that are open to students' natural switching from African American and Standard English languages provide respect for students' home language and a receptiveness to learning new forms of their oral language. These findings correspond to research reported by Perez (2004) indicating that when matching school and text discourse(s) more closely to community and home discourse(s), students had higher participation and were viewed as "competent" literacy learners. And Zentella (1997), after studying the literacy learning of nineteen Puerto Rican high school students (and their families) in New York City, concluded that the highest literacy achievers were those students who were fluent in both their home language and English and who were involved in literacy instruction that supported use of both languages.

Numerous researchers describe how oral and literacy skills associated with a first language can facilitate oral language and literacy development of a second language. For example, Pappas described students' use of Spanish sounds to facilitate acquisition of English sounds in words (Pappas, 2002). Similar connections were made between phonology and rules of language for French-speaking children learning English (Bruck & Genesee, 1995), children who spoke Mandarin Chinese learning English (Bialystok, 1997) and Hebrew-speaking children learning English (Geva & Wade-Woolley, 1998).

Other researchers have traced high levels of achievement of culturally and linguistically diverse students to instruction that is "authentic." Authentic pedagogy, as defined by these researchers who examined its effect on the learning of students within twenty-three restructured urban schools, focuses on active participation in real-world and complex problems, higher-order thinking, extended reading and writing opportunities, and authentic audiences for students' work (e.g., government officials, local newspapers, parents, other students) (Newmann, Marks, & Gamoran, 1995; Lee, Smith, & Croninger, 1995). The instruction they describe corresponds to the principles of culturally responsive instruction we present in this chapter. Such instruction sets content learning and higher-order thinking at the center of its curriculum; lower-level skills (e.g., word pronunciation, mechanics of grammar) are embedded in the context of this instruction as a means to acquiring deep understandings of complex concepts.

Similarly, Torres-Guzman (1992) describes vividly the active engagement of inner-city, linguistically diverse high school students who used their experiences to aid their learning about toxic waste in New York City; their project led to a city investigation and the cleanup of polluted property in their neighborhood. These students, known as the Toxic Avengers, received an award from the Citizen's Committee of New York. Active learning around important issues produced agency, engagement, and deep learning.

And Landis, Kalieva, Abitova, Izmukhanbetova, and Musaeva (2006) taught their students (in grades 1, 5, 8, and 11) in Kazakhstan to conduct ethnographic interviews with community members to learn about the history of their town and community. As they analyzed data from their interviews, students constructed Venn diagrams to present comparisons of their own knowledge and viewpoints with those of their informants and responded to their field notes in double-entry journals. They then worked in groups to compare and analyze the information they collected and to generate writings representing what they were learning. Through this process, the students not only learned about their community but also strategies (e.g., conducting follow-up interviews to probe information more deeply, how to cross-reference different perspectives and sources) that helped them form reasonable conclusions and justifications for their arguments.

Once again, we are drawn to Carlos' letter as we think about ways to apply this research to instruction that may be appropriate for him and other students in his classroom. Making connections between his experiences and language seems to be a central recommendation for Carlos' teacher.

37

CHAPTER 3

*All Children
and Adolescents
Have the Right
to Culturally
Relevant Literacy
Instruction*

How Can the Right to Culturally Relevant Literacy Instruction Become a Reality in Today's Schools?

Responding to cultural and linguistic differences requires advocacy and implementing assessment and instructional methods that break with the inhibiting traditions we describe earlier.

How Can I Get Started with Changes?

- *Join or organize a teacher-administrator-parent-community action committee.* We have two goals for this committee. One is to involve parents and the community to form educational plans, and the second is to take action by making changes that are recommended by this committee and to take action by advocating for the students and their rights as literacy learners. In this committee, discuss and identify common goals for your students, distinguish what can be accomplished short term and long term, and identify projects to accomplish goals, such as
  - Study high-stakes test manuals to determine whether students attending your school are represented in the testing sample to establish norms and test items and advocate for alternative tests.
  - Communicate with the public (through editorials and community meetings) about inequities in tests and funding.
  - Create opportunities to describe to the public (e.g., newspaper editorials, community papers) and families the positive accomplishments of your students.
  - Determine ways to build collaborations with families and community to bring their talents into the school.
  - Identify ways parents and community members can participate in students' learning.
- Make connections between state and district curriculum goals and the goals you have for your students. Even within highly prescribed curriculum plans,

38
....

CHAPTER 3

*All Children
and Adolescents
Have the Right
to Culturally
Relevant Literacy
Instruction*

theme- and issued-based projects can meet several curricular goals simultaneously, integrate disciplinary content, and provide access to multiple literacies (e.g., Damico with Riddle, 2006).

- Discuss diversity in your school and how to involve parents and community. (See Chapter 10 for specific suggestions about involving parents and community members.)
- Identify ways parents and community members can participate in students' learning, both in and out of the classroom.
- Identify community events that are important to the students and families of the school; plan to join these events to demonstrate respect for the families and to learn about their interests, jobs, hobbies, and life out of school.

What Changes Can I Make in My Teaching and Interactions with My Students?

- Form teacher study groups and investigate the languages represented in your school, including African American vernacular and regional dialects.
- Respond to multiple languages represented in the school.
  - If there are English language learners, consider implementing a school-wide dual-immersion program, as described by Luis Moll (2003), especially if there is a large second-language group in your school. Discuss this possibility with the action committee described earlier and weigh advantages and disadvantages.
  - Advocate for teachers and/or teacher aides who speak the community languages represented in your school to team-teach with or support teachers who have a different language history.
  - Encourage hybrid language and code-switching practices. Prepare students to collaborate with and act as peer tutors for each other, using their shared language and experiences during reading and writing activities. For example, Carlos could join a peer group to discuss, and perhaps dramatize, meaningful elements of the Shakespeare play. Learning from each other by drawing connections to their personal experiences and perspectives can deepen learning and facilitate use of cultural and linguistic knowledge.
  - Encourage students to use their language for learning. Using home languages helps students mediate new learning.
- Make connections, connections, connections. Choose texts that have a strong connection to students' cultural, content, linguistic, and text knowledge (their funds of knowledge). Introduce texts that extend these forms of knowledge by making connections between novel concepts and prior knowledge.
- Engage students in active participatory forms of learning and listen to what students are saying and how they are participating. Borrow from their "youth culture" (Lewis, 2001), which could include readings about popular musical

39

CHAPTER 3

*All Children
and Adolescents
Have the Right
to Culturally
Relevant Literacy
Instruction*

Teachers identifying strategies for representing their students' home languages in the school curriculum.

groups or popular magazines, to make connections to their interests and experiences.

- Implement shared and interactive reading and writing instruction, in which you share the pen with your students to cowrite drafts of papers, think aloud, and share your reading and writing strategies using explicit language and descriptors of the processes you use (e.g., "I organized this first sentence in the paragraph to introduce the topic of my paper"; "In this sentence, I used the word *problem* to tell my reader that my main character has a problem she is trying to solve"), and/or participate in Readers Theatre to dramatize text readings, poetry, and plays.
- Expect and encourage multiple modes for representing what students are learning, such as dramatic presentations, illustrations, and creating blogs on the Internet. Inviting multiple ways to make sense of information (hearing different explanations, observing enactments of concepts, acting out or using art to express interpretations) provides multiple encounters with concepts (and thus enriching understandings) and can increase chances for success in school (Delpit, 1995) because this approach invites students' use of their own social and learning practices.
- When possible, choose texts in students' home language. Is it possible, for example, that Carlos' mother has a Spanish version of Shakespeare's plays that could be used in the classroom as an alternate text?
- Remember to respect differences, but also to teach to them (Delpit, 1995). Referring to Rueda (2005) again, appreciating cultural differences is insufficient. Culture must be appropriated in ways that support new learning.

CHAPTER 3

*All Children
and Adolescents
Have the Right
to Culturally
Relevant Literacy
Instruction*

- Build academic knowledge, strategies, and skills. For example, when engaging students in inquiry projects, be certain that students have access to and are learning academic concepts and content, and the strategies and skills they need to succeed in academic areas. Access to more difficult texts can be accomplished with audiotapes, videos, peer tutoring, collaborative group learning, and community members as translators for ELLs.
- Teach skills and strategies needed for comprehending complicated texts and for making connections across the curriculum and to prior knowledge.
- Teach vocabulary and comprehension (and word pronunciation) within contexts that are meaningful for the students. Schools that beat the odds (Langer, 2001) integrate skills and strategy teaching within meaningful content units. Make use of first-language connections when possible for word pronunciation and provide multiple and authentic ways for students to use information they are learning, especially applications to real-life events out of the classroom.
- Study forms of cultural modeling described by Carol Lee (2004). Such instruction includes use of issues or problems to initiate reading widely (both culturally relevant and extended texts), to build oral and written participation that uses both community norms of "talk" and socializes students to forms of Standard English, to embed skills and strategy learning and practice, and to draw connections between skills and strategies and everyday routine literacy practices.

How Can I Assess My Students' Reading and Writing Knowledge? Progress?

Implement forms of responsive assessment (Henning-Stout, 1994) that are appropriate for your instructional goals. These could include:

- Multiple opportunities for tracing students' reading and writing performance. Rather than relying on more formal tests that may be administered infrequently, organize ways to collect daily (or almost daily) data on students' performance (e.g., comprehension of text segments, written analyses of text characters, use of vocabulary to convey text interpretations).
- Document students' funds of knowledge. Keep notes about students' language expressions, references to outside of school and home activities.
- Develop learning goals *with* your students and establish methods for students to evaluate their own learning. Recall how much we learned about Carlos' strategies from the brief letter he wrote to his teacher.
- Plan to conference with students during class time, conducting conferences as frequently as possible so that students can discuss their reading and writing assignments.
- Accept oral and written miscues; use these as indicators of strategies students are learning to use and as points of discussion during conferences.
- Avoid labeling students' performance (as deficient); discuss students' progress in the context of their strengths and next steps in learning new in-

formation. Then set goals with your students for new skills and strategies to be learned, areas that require further development.

- Observe how your students (and their parents) participate in group discussions and other opportunities for interactions. Take cues from them for leading discussions and assessing their participation in the classroom.
- Assess the "alternate literacies" students bring with them, such as translating rental documents, paying bills, called *treasure troves* by Gregory and Williams (2000), and use these as bridges and ways to forge connections with the curriculum.
- Evaluate assessment data by its situatedness, recognizing that students' cultural and language knowledge constantly changes as they appropriate new customs, ideas, and language information.

Additional suggestions for assessment are provided in Chapter 8.

Putting Ideas into Action

Rueda (2005) tells us that cultural ways of learning affect every human being. We believe it is important for teachers and prospective teachers to understand their own cultural practices, expectations they have for reading and writing, and how these practices and expectations affect the way they teach. Talk with your colleagues about your cultural practices and expectations and how these impact your instructional choices. What can be learned from a study of your own culture and language? How does your culture and language contribute to who you are? What do you learn about the culture and language of your colleagues? What could the teacher learn about Carlos' home culture and language and how would this affect her teaching? Imagine how a rich discussion of Shakespeare's language and purpose for writing his plays could involve Carlos and his peers in lively debates and a classroom community that is constantly striving for comprehension and connections between lived experiences and text ideas. Facilitating those connections lies at the heart of culturally responsive teaching.

DISCUSSION QUESTIONS FOR STUDY GROUPS

1. James Damico, a college professor, and Ruthie Riddle, a first-year teacher, describe in their article (2006) how they supported Ruthie's fifth-grade students' use of multimedia to develop a CD with a content emphasis on freedom and slavery. Students read multiple texts, watched movies, and wrote about what they were learning. Their final products were to demonstrate this learning through multimodal formats that included dramatizations, news broadcasts, editorials for the local paper, and video or pictorial collages. Damico and Riddle observed high engagement and deep learning about content and issues. Discuss the role of multiple literacies or multimodal involvement and how these might affect learning and engagement.

42
....

CHAPTER 3

*All Children
and Adolescents
Have the Right
to Culturally
Relevant Literacy
Instruction*

Identify a unit of study where you could engage students in similar ways to study complex issues affecting the history of our country. What connections could be drawn to students' contemporary life?

2. Discuss your cultural practices and how these influence your own learning and teaching. Examine how they might impact your interactions with your students.

All Children and Adolescents Have the Right to Literacy Instruction That Is Individually Appropriate

Dear Teachers,

As we prepare to enter tenth grade, we must admit to thinking about our years in school. We remember events that have influenced how we think about school and ourselves.

I (Rashad) recall that elementary school was really hard for me. The teachers expected us all to work on our own. We were assigned the same reading workbook pages. We studied the same spelling words. We wrote on the same topic. Now that I think about it, it was just boring! What was my reward for this boredom and apathy—straight A's. There is another reason elementary school was hard. I was the only student of Indian decent, I felt alone; so I just tried to be like everyone else. It now seems strange that none of my teachers seemed to recognize what was so obvious to me—that I am Indian. That changed when I went to Sagamore Middle School and then Westwood High School, which represented many cultures. I no longer felt alone, and I could just be myself. Middle school is when I began to feel like my teachers believed in me and that I had potential. Mr. Douglas, my honors English teacher, was great. He let us choose our own writing topics because he said we should write about things that are important to us. For the first time, I felt challenged, and he made me feel accomplished. Because of that, I really tried. He made every student feel like part of the class. It was obvious that he wanted us to understand what he was teaching. He held before- and after-school tutorial sessions and made us comfortable with asking questions in class.

44
....

CHAPTER 4

*All Children
and Adolescents
Have the Right
to Literacy
Instruction That Is
Individually
Appropriate*

The most influential teacher, I (Sam) ever had is Mr. Brian, my ninth-grade English teacher. The most important thing I learned from him was that I'm a good writer. Whenever I write I remember the advice he gave me, "Sam, take a stand in your writing. Let your audience know how you feel." The real turning point for me though was when he wrote on one of my papers, "You are one of my favorite contributors [to the Newsletter]. You have proven time and time again, that you have a very sharp wit and a knack for the comedic. You are a wise young man and more sophisticated than most your age as a thinker and a writer." No one had ever said anything like that to me. He called me a writer, and that changed how I feel about myself. His comments made me work harder because I wanted to live up to his expectations. I enjoyed his class for other reasons too. We got to discuss current events and most importantly he treated me like a normal kid. We could joke around with him, and he joked around with us. He treated us like we were equal with him. As we think about the upcoming year, we wonder if there will be teachers like Mr. Douglas and Mr. Brian. We hope so.

Sincerely,

Rashad and Sam, grade 10

What do these young men value in the teachers who influenced them? Comments such as, "He had confidence in me," "He called me a writer," "You have a sharp wit," and "He treated us like we were equal with him" suggest that for these boys the criterion for being influential is when teachers recognize them as individuals.

These two boys were interviewed the summer prior to their entry into tenth grade. Rashad, a first-generation Indian American whose parents had been in the United States approximately twenty years, spoke of being the only Indian student in his elementary school, a fact never acknowledged by any of his teachers. Rashad said he "tried to be like everyone else" and spoke of the relief he felt when he moved to the middle and high schools, which "represented many cultures," including many who shared his Indian heritage. Rashad then said, "I could just be myself." This adolescent boy's statements reflect the need for teachers to notice rather than ignore the differences in their students. Delpit provides some insight into why this is important, especially for children of color, "[I]f one does not see color, then one does not really see children. Children made 'invisible' in this manner become hard-pressed to see themselves worthy of notice" (1995, p. 177). Perhaps, if Rashad tried to "be like everyone else," he would become visible to his teachers for, as he inferred, as a student of Indian origin he was invisible. Fortunately, Rashad later entered a school where he no longer had to be like everyone else and as he said, "I could just be myself." We adopt, yet expand, Delpit's claim to state that efforts must be made to ensure no child or adolescent is made to feel invisible in the classroom.

Rashad's classmate, Sam, is a member of the mainstream culture, meaning he is white and middle class. This adolescent boy provides a different example of the importance to recognize what's unique about the children and adolescents in your classroom. In Sam's case, his teachers' vision was obstructed by a label.

In fifth grade Sam was diagnosed with attention deficit hyperactivity disorder (ADHD). Although his teachers considered him bright, his penchant for calling out answers, interrupting class with a humorous comment, and slouching in his desk annoyed many of them. Rather than being invisible to his teachers, Sam was made clearly visible by the label ADHD. Teachers expected Sam to behave in certain ways and they responded to him accordingly, and as often happens, Sam's behavior reinforced their expectations. This brings to mind a well-known phenomenon in education—the powerful influence teacher expectations can have on a teacher's behavior as well as that of students. In Sam's case, it was difficult for many of his teachers to see the individual behind this label. Not surprisingly it was Sam who said Mr. Brian influenced him because he treated him as "an equal." But Mr. Brian did more; he recognized Sam's strengths. He encouraged him to write and spoke of how his writing reflected his "sharp wit and [his] knack for the comedic." He gave Sam specific advice to strengthen his writing, advice Sam said he thinks about each time he writes. He told Sam he was "a wise young man and more sophisticated than most your age as a thinker and a writer." Until that time, he had not been recognized as a writer and certainly the words *wise, sophisticated,* and *thinker* had never been used to describe Sam. This transformed him: "His comments made me work harder because I wanted to live up to his expectations." In contrast, other teachers punished Sam by removing him from the classroom, turning his desk away from the other students, or embarrassing him in front of his peers with comments like, "Oh that's just Sam in his slacker position." These teachers failed to see the individual behind the label of ADHD. We might suggest that not only did the label prevent Sam's teachers from seeing his capabilities but their lack of recognition prevented Sam from seeing them also.

The comments and reflections of these two adolescent boys provide a fitting introduction to this chapter on *the right of children and adolescents to literacy instruction that is individually appropriate.* Both boys spoke of how being recognized as an individual made them "feel accomplished." They also spoke of the consequence, "I really tried," and "I wanted to live up to his expectations." We suggest that these two boys are not unique. Like their peers from different cultures, with different capabilities, with different strengths, they thrive when others recognize their individual gifts and use their strengths to address their needs. In this chapter we further explain why we believe each child and adolescent not only deserves but, in order to thrive, requires literacy instruction that is individually appropriate.

Individually Appropriate Instruction

Position statements of several professional organizations list variations of the right to individually appropriate instruction as a principle evident in effective literacy environments. For example, the International Reading Association's *Standards for Reading*

46

CHAPTER 4

*All Children
and Adolescents
Have the Right
to Literacy
Instruction That Is
Individually
Appropriate*

Professionals (2003a) includes "Candidates use a wide range of instructional practices, approaches, and methods, including technology-based practices, for learners at different stages of development and from differing cultural and linguistic backgrounds." And the position statement *Supporting Young Adolescents' Literacy Learning*, constructed by a joint committee of the International Reading Association and the National Middle School Association (2001), contains "To support young adolescent learners, schools should provide instruction that is appropriate for each individual student" (p. 2). And the position statement for adolescent learners composed by the Commission on Adolescent Literacy of the International Reading Association (Moore, Bean, Birdyshaw, & Rycik, 1999) lists as one of its principles, "Adolescent learners require teachers who understand the complexities among individual adolescent learners" (p. 8).

We believe it's essential to remind ourselves that the children and adolescents who attend our schools are individuals from different cultures, of different abilities, and with different strengths and needs. This fact, we believe, is often not acknowledged in the current environment of high-stakes testing and scripted literacy programs, and in middle and high schools where teaching content seems to take precedence over teaching students. Such lack of consideration is evident when scripts are followed to present the same skill to all students, when each teacher on a grade level is expected to follow the same pacing chart, and when administrators walk into a classroom to make sure the teacher is teaching according to a predetermined plan. Practices such as these imply that literacy teaching and learning proceed via a one-way path in which information contained in a set of materials is mediated through the teachers' actions and then absorbed in its original form by the students (Bloom, 2000).

Teachers feel constrained by such practices, as evidenced in comments like, "I have to move on to the next lesson even though I know some of my students haven't learned what I'm teaching," and "If I'm not teaching what I'm supposed to be teaching at the time I'm supposed to teach it, then I get in trouble and I get written up." One particularly revealing example of how constrained teachers feel occurred in one of our classrooms. Mona was meeting with a group of twenty elementary teachers, students in a fifteen-month-long master's program, for their first literacy class. To introduce the year-long theme of their work, "How to empower your students as literacy learners," the group viewed a short clip of a classroom teacher. After viewing the clip and discussing how this teacher empowered her students, the teachers worked in small groups to generate lists of ways they can empower their students as literacy learners. Four teachers, who work in schools with high populations of struggling readers and with many restraints on how to present their content and time frames for presenting that content, were stumped. Initially, they expressed doubts that empowering their students was even an option in their restricted teaching environments. After spending several minutes discussing their shared struggles, they chose to focus on ways to empower their students that could be implemented during brief moments such as a transition from one activity to another. The title they chose for their chart was "Ways to Empower Students as Literacy Learners When You Teach with Your Hands Tied." The metaphor of teaching with your hands tied aptly reflects the constraints many teachers feel. These restrictions appear in more subtle ways. For example, high school English teachers feel constrained when required to use literature from the Western canon instead of more contemporary texts to which their students could more readily relate.

We suggest, however, that while teachers feel constrained, perhaps the children and adolescents who are the recipients of a one-size-fits-all literacy program feel as Rashad stated in his interview: "None of my teachers realized my potential or really the potential of anyone . . . The teachers expected us all to work on our own. We were assigned the same . . . workbook pages . . . studied the same spelling words . . . wrote on the same topic. . . ." As suggested by Rashad's comments, students absorb much more than the lesson objective. From the students we surveyed and interviewed, we learned what they were thinking as the teacher taught and as they sat in the classrooms: Do you think I'm worthy of being in your classroom? Do you care that I can't read the textbook? Do you know I feel physically ill when asked to read in front of the class? Do you think I'm competent?

We believe, and research supports, that effective literacy instruction builds on what students know rather than focusing solely on what they don't know. Teachers successful in differentiating instruction to accommodate the wide range of needs of the students in their classrooms are able to see the differences of the individuals in a class group. Tomlinson (2001) states that these teachers are able to "peel back first impressions, to look beyond actions, and to erase stereotypes" (p. 17).

One strategy teachers can use to *peel back* first impressions to reveal the uniqueness of their students is to identify the *provisions* that accompany each student into the classroom (Matthews & Cobb, 2005). These *provisions* function similarly to what hikers might take on a hiking trip to support them as they travel, in that they are what children and adolescents take into the classroom to support their literacy development. Although there are numerous ways children and adolescents can vary—for example, in physical ability, interests, personality, or learning styles—we focus on three categories of provisions that many consider to be the foundation on which formal, school-based literacy knowledge should be built: literacy knowledge provisions, cultural provisions, and social provisions. These provisions are compatible with the view of literacy as a social process learned within cultural contexts presented in this book's introduction.

What Are Literacy Knowledge Provisions?

Literacy knowledge provisions refer to what children and adolescents know about communicating, sharing, and constructing meaning. There are two sources for this knowledge: (1) informal, outside-of-school experiences with families, communities, peers, media, and (2) formal, inside-of-school experiences with teachers, peers, books, and curriculum. Informal understandings incorporate what individuals learn about sharing, constructing, and communicating by observing others in their home and community. This includes the print available in these contexts as well as the ways family and community members use these materials. For example, some families may read television guides, newspapers, church bulletins, and the print on board games (Purcell-Gates, 2002), while others have rich oral traditions, such as the call-and-response form of telling stories and inviting audience participation that occur in African American churches.

48

CHAPTER 4

*All Children
and Adolescents
Have the Right
to Literacy
Instruction That Is
Individually
Appropriate*

Although all cultural groups develop ways of sharing, constructing, and communicating that are unique, teachers should not generalize common cultural practices of a particular demographic group to all members of that group. Therefore, the interests, values, and ways of interacting can't be assumed to represent all members of a group (e.g., urban African Americans, suburban European Americans). The ways of using and interacting with literacy events that students observe in their homes and communities provide the core meaning-making practices that should be used to support students' acquisition of more formal, school-based literacy knowledge.

Typically, the more formal, school-based literacy knowledge is what's listed in content standards and curriculum guides. However, for our purposes, Patricia Alexander's lifespan model of reading development (2003) is useful for identifying core elements of formal, in-school literacy knowledge. She identifies three core elements of literacy learning: (1) knowledge of reading (e.g., how to create a summary of a text) *and* knowledge of content topics (e.g., Industrial Revolution); (2) interest in reading; and (3) ability to process (apply strategies) while reading. To identify students' school-based literacy knowledge provisions, teachers might ask questions such as:

Knowledge of Reading: "Readers' knowledge of language and . . . content domains are critical forces in developing competence" (p. 7).

- What is the reader's knowledge of vocabulary and high-frequency words?
- What does the reader know about topics related to reading; e.g., sound symbol relationships, text genres?
- What topics does the reader know a lot about; e.g., space travel, sports?

Interest in Reading: "Readers' personal interest in reading becomes a driving force in their development" (p. 9).

- Does the reader enjoy reading? At home? At school?
- What topics are of personal interest to the reader?
- How does the reader respond when he or she must read about a topic of little personal interests?

Strategic Processing: Readers' advancing knowledge of strategies for comprehending text enables them to process increasingly complex texts.

- What strategies—e.g., rereading a sentence or the previous section—does the reader apply when surface-level comprehension problems arise?
- What deep-processing strategies that involve personalizing or transforming what is read—e.g., cross-text comparisons—does the child or adolescent apply when comprehension problems arise?

All children and adolescents come to school with knowledge about how meaning is created, constructed, and shared within their home community. This knowl-

49

CHAPTER 4

*All Children
and Adolescents
Have the Right
to Literacy
Instruction That Is
Individually
Appropriate*

edge provides the foundation on which more formal, school-based literacy knowledge should be built. For instance, Arnetha Ball (2000) used her high school students' knowledge of rap music to teach figurative language and metaphor. These inner-city high school students knew what figurative language and metaphor were in a context familiar to them—rap music—and Ball used this known form of musical language to teach the formal, school-based literacy concepts. (For an in-depth description of Alexander's lifespan model of reading development, see Alexander, 2003, 2005.)

Mrs. Middleton, a middle school teacher described by Tomlinson (2001), uses an activity that could easily be adapted to identify students' school-based literacy knowledge (pp. 39–42). Students in Ms. Middleton's classroom create an individual line graph that describes their perceptions of their strengths and weaknesses. Along the vertical axis are descriptors, identified by the students, which represent the students' perceptions of themselves (examples: *awesome, dismal, dead meat*). On the horizontal axis of the graph are components of school-based learning—spelling, reading, and writing. Students then mark the perception of themselves that best describes their knowledge of each school-based component. When completed, the graphs are placed on a wall. Each day, two or three students present their graphs to the class. Once all have presented their graphs, the teacher discusses the differences evident within the group, which then leads to a discussion of ways the teacher and students can work together to support everyone's learning. Mrs. Middleton's ultimate goals are for her students to believe her classroom is a comfortable place to learn and is a place where differences are respected.

To adapt this activity to gather students' perceptions of their specific literacy knowledge, change the descriptors along the horizontal axis to correspond to goals you define for your students. Sample descriptors for reading knowledge could be *reading big words, reciting poetry*. Sample descriptors for reading interest could be *reading novels, reading about history*, and sample descriptors for strategic processing could be *can get unstuck when reading, ask myself questions as I read*. This activity could provide useful information to assist teachers' instructional planning. This activity could also help students recognize that all individuals have strengths in some areas and needs in others.

What Are Cultural Provisions?

The cultural provisions children and adolescents bring to school can provide additional information that can be useful when planning classroom literacy activities. Culture, for our purposes, are "shared knowledge, customs, emotions, rituals, traditions, values, and norms" (Ogbu, 1988, p. 11). All children and adolescents come to school as members of cultural groups and therefore possess valuable cultural provisions. One way teachers can identify their students' cultural provisions is to visit the communities in which their students live. How does the community celebrate special events? What do the individuals appear to value during these events; for example, storytelling, music, or physical movement, such as dance? Teachers may also want to learn what activity settings are common in their students' homes; for example, are there family dinners, book reading, reading of a religious text, or family reunions?

50
....

CHAPTER 4

*All Children
and Adolescents
Have the Right
to Literacy
Instruction That Is
Individually
Appropriate*

For older students, such as preadolescents and adolescents, their cultural contexts expand to include their peers, so you might ask: How do these young people spend their free time? How do they use different symbol systems while with peers; for instance, music, physical movement, visual or print media, the Internet? What do they read for fun? Take the example of one adolescent we interviewed. Sean talked about how he and his friends enjoyed reading comic books and wondered why teachers never allowed them to bring them to class. He said, "Believe it or not, reading comic books increased my vocabulary."

What Are Social Provisions?

There is a close relationship between social provisions and cultural provisions. Whereas cultural provisions develop from the routines and contexts valued by the students' family and community, social provisions are the ways students learn to interact with others within these routines and contexts. To illustrate this relationship, suppose a middle school boy from a rural community enters an urban middle school classroom. Now imagine that prior to entering this school the boy lived on a poultry farm where his parents raised chickens for a large wholesaler. He grew up observing and eventually participating in such routines as rising early with his sister to care and feed the chickens. These experiences are different from those of an urban middle school student who spent these same years observing and participating in different routines such as riding a metro train with friends downtown to eat chicken fingers in a favorite fast-food restaurant. One set of experiences is not more important than the other; they're just different. Yet from these different experiences, each learned valu-

Doing homework with a friend is an important out-of-school practice for many teens.

able ways of interacting with others (social provisions) that enabled him to interact successfully in his home community. The social provisions each boy possesses can be useful to the boys' teacher. The teacher might use the rural boy's (social) knowledge of collaborating with his sister learned in their morning routine (source of cultural knowledge) of caring for and feeding the chickens, to introduce the boy to collaborative literacy projects or readings on distributed and collaborative work assignments in industry. The teacher might use the urban boy's (social) knowledge of coordinating with friends to ride the metro train system (source of cultural knowledge) to eat at a favorite restaurant to illustrate the need to create a schedule to plan the completion of a multiphase project.

To identify children or adolescents' social provisions, teachers might observe how these students interact during literacy instruction. During such observations, questions such as: How does the student interact with classmates? Teachers? What roles does the student assume when in groups which require him to use his literacy knowledge? How do other students respond to the student? How are the student's interactions related to what you know about the student's community or home? Observations guided by such questions can reveal patterns of interactions that are unique to the student.

Another source for identifying social provisions is to consider the age of the child or adolescent. For example, often eleven-year-olds have a strong need to belong, so cliques, typical of this age, are emotionally challenging. Being included or excluded in an activity involving a specific peer group can result in an intense emotional response for learners this age. Perhaps that is why many teachers find that preadolescents enjoy reading to younger children, which minimizes the fear of rejection, and participating in small-group book discussions, which satisfies their growing need to be with peers (Wood, 1997). While variations exist within any age group of learners, there are general patterns that might be useful when designing literacy experiences.

To summarize, all students enter their classrooms with provisions that can be used to support their literacy learning in school. The young, from their first days of life, observe and then participate in events and interactions with significant others; this leads them to absorb critical insights about creating, sharing, and communicating meaning with others. Later, as they expand their world to include peers, the media, and technologies, their understanding of meaning making also expands. When these meaningful experiences are ignored, a key resource for students' literacy development goes untapped. In contrast, when teachers appreciate the value of their students' literacy knowledge provisions, cultural provisions, and social provisions, they can tap into a very valuable resource.

Why Is the Right to Literacy Instruction That Is Individually Appropriate Important for Children and Adolescents?

No single pathway to literacy development can assist all children and adolescents to develop as effective literacy users. If there were, this book would be moot. We agree

52
....
CHAPTER 4

*All Children
and Adolescents
Have the Right
to Literacy
Instruction That Is
Individually
Appropriate*

with Carol Santa (2006), the former president of the International Reading Association and an advocate for adolescent literacy, that there is a wealth of information available that informs us of about what contributes to effective literacy learning and instruction. And, we believe that the focus of this book—*the student* and *the rights* that organize the book's contents—are excellent sources for a lot of this information.

Knowing the information, however, is not sufficient; it's what we do with that information that makes the difference. Gerald Duffy (1997), a literacy scholar with a long-term interest in effective literacy instruction, offers one suggestion. He refers to literacy professionals who successfully help their students become engaged and effective readers as entrepreneurial literacy educators. Entrepreneurial literacy educators understand the complexity of literacy learning. They use this understanding to guide their decision making about what they teach and how they teach. Most important, what they teach and how they teach matches the needs of their students. So entrepreneurial literacy professionals have a cache of tools available, and they select the tools they believe are the most appropriate for the students they are working with at the moment.

This sounds good in theory, but how does it work in reality? One example is revealed by Judith Langer (2000). She examined middle and high school English programs in urban high-poverty areas, where students consistently outperform students in schools with similar populations. What makes this noteworthy is that the teachers in these "beating-the-odds" schools exhibited six distinguishing features:

1. Students learn skills and knowledge in multiple lesson types.
2. Teachers integrate test preparation into instruction.
3. Teachers make connections across instruction, curriculum, and life.
4. Students learn strategies for doing their work.
5. Students are expected to be generative thinkers.
6. Classrooms foster cognitive collaboration.

Most likely the teachers in these beating-the-odds schools possess the traits consistent with Duffy's concept of entrepreneurial teachers. They used approaches proven successful with the students they taught, such as presenting skills, strategies, and knowledge in multiple ways *and* connecting what's learned in school to the students' lives outside of school. Whereas the less-successful teachers, in comparable schools with similar students, used strategies known to be less effective—such as using a single approach, teaching skills or strategies in isolation, and focusing on covering content rather than making connections of students' experiences to their learning. One brief example from a middle school English class demonstrates how one beating-the-odds teacher designed the vocabulary component of her English curriculum:

Gail Slatko teaches vocabulary skills within the context of literature and writing. Students perform a variety of exercises, including completing workbook exercises designed to increase their vocabularies and creating "living dictionaries" of unfamiliar words they encounter in books, magazines, and newspapers. To teach analogies, she requires students to discuss and explain their responses to examples she provides. As a culminating activity, students create vocabulary mobiles to display in the room (Langer, 2000, p. 6).

We believe Duffy would describe Gail as an entrepreneurial teacher. The variety of experiences acquired across school and home contexts demonstrates her understanding of the complexity of literacy learning and her use of cultural and literacy knowledge provisions. Gail's consistent success with students with whom others have had less success suggests she's able to apply her understanding in flexible ways to meet the different needs of her students. And the numerous strategies used suggest she possesses a substantial cache of tools (e.g., strategies, activities, materials) so she can select the ones most likely to meet the unique needs of her students.

Unfortunately, not all children and adolescents have teachers like Gail. According to data released by National Assessment of Educational Progress (NAEP) (USDE, 2005), 31 percent of fourth-grade students and 31 percent of eighth-grade students scored at or above the Proficient level, the level at which students represent "solid academic performance" (p. 2). From these data it appears that approximately one out of three students is operating with only partial knowledge of skills or strategies required to perform basic grade-level work. When the scores are compared across race/ethnicity for whites, blacks, and Hispanics, the scores paint an even bleaker picture. The average achievement score for eighth graders performing at or above the Proficient level are: whites, 41 percent; blacks, 13 percent; and Hispanics, 16 percent. Far too many students are working below the capacity needed for the jobs these young people will be asked to fill (Alvermann, 2001a).

Many find statistics like those from the 2005 NAEP assessments alarming. Recently, concern for older children and adolescents who struggle with reading has, as mentioned throughout our chapters, garnered the attention of commissions and professional organizations. In 2004, *Reading Next: A Vision for Action and Research in Middle and High School Literacy* (Biancarosa & Snow) was released and represented the work of literacy scholars charged to make recommendations for how to address the unique needs of these older readers. The literacy skills required of these readers are, "more complex, more embedded in subject matters, and . . .multiply determined; [further,] adolescents are not as universally motivated to read better or as interested in school-based reading as [younger readers]" (p. 2). The *Reading Next* panel made fifteen recommendations; the two that follow challenge the status quo of most middle schools and high schools—extend teaching blocks and create intradisciplinary teams.

Extend Time for Literacy. For students who struggle with reading, minimal gains will be made if literacy-focused instruction is provided in thirty- or forty-five-minute blocks. Two to four hours are what this panel of experts recommended. Additional time can be gained by reconceptualizing the middle or high school schedule. Such rescheduling would require language-arts and subject-matter teachers to work together to provide the students who struggle with the literacy instruction they need. Increased time would also make it possible for teachers to consider how to adapt instruction to meet the needs of all their students.

Create Interdisciplinary Teaching Teams. To bring coherence, consistency, and clear oversight to the literacy program in middle and high schools, interdisciplinary teams of teachers should be formed as described in the *Reading Next* report (Biancarosa & Snow, 2004). Their charge would be to meet regularly to ensure that students, who advance through their classes do not slip through the cracks because of a lack of individualized instruction.

The NAEP statistics that introduced this section, as well as those presented in other chapters, certainly alarm many educators. The lack of broad-based literacy

CHAPTER 4

*All Children
and Adolescents
Have the Right
to Literacy
Instruction That Is
Individually
Appropriate*

growth in our middle and high school students, as reflected in these statistics, is troublesome and viewed as a crisis (Biancarosa & Snow, 2004). This crisis is evident not only in those students considered to struggle as readers but also in the growth of those whose performance is characterized as average or above average. Although these students may not struggle, many, such as Biancarsoa and Snow (2004), would say performance is stunted by literacy instruction too often perceived by students as uninspiring and irrelevant. All students need the opportunity to fulfill their promise as effective oral and written language users. Designing instruction informed by knowledge of students' provisions (literacy knowledge, social, and cultural) is one strategy we suggest for creating those opportunities.

How Can the Right to Literacy Instruction That Is Individually Appropriate Become a Reality in Today's Schools?

We anticipate a question that, undoubtedly, many of you are asking at this time: "How can I vary my instruction to meet the individual needs of my students, when I don't even have the time to teach all I must teach each day?" Instruction that meets individual needs doesn't mean one-on-one.

- *Identify the literacy knowledge provisions, social provisions, and cultural provisions of your students.* Return to the earlier sections of this chapter and consider how Arnetha Ball (2000) used her students' out-of-school interests to teach more formal, school-based literacy knowledge. Review how the line graphs created by Ms. Middleton's students enabled her to learn valuable information about her students' perceptions of their literacy knowledge. Both teachers, through their actions, demonstrated respect for what their students brought to the classroom. Consider how you might do the same. Perhaps students could create murals or posters representing their outside-of-school interests. Once this information is gathered, think of how you might adapt your school literacy lessons to incorporate these interests.
- *Differentiate your instruction to meet the unique reading needs of your student population.* Differentiated instruction is an approach many teachers use to address the varied needs of their students. Organizing classroom space and instructional time are key factors to such differentiation. Space is designed for individual work, small-group work, and learning centers. Yatvin (2004) recommends small round tables over desks because of the intimacy tables provide when working with a small group of students. Teachers find that breaking instructional time into blocks and then the blocks into activity segments provides more opportunities to interact with different students in different ways (confer, instruct, monitor). Teachers in differentiated classrooms often work with small groups of students while other students work independently and in project groups. Students in these classrooms must be able to manage their own behavior and work without direct supervision.

In addition to Yatvin (2004), Tomlinson (2001) provides a useful guide to differentiated instruction.

- *Examine the beating-the-odds studies.* Download reports, case studies, and additional references describing these studies from http://cela.albany.edu. These materials provide specific useful information.
- *Ask your students to create a line graph to identify their provisions.* Follow the procedures used by Mrs. Middleton. These graphs could be a springboard for discussions and a useful way to get to know your students. Such discussions could also help demonstrate to your students your interest in creating an environment where all can learn.
- *Review Patricia Alexander's (2005) lifespan model of reading development.* This model, which she refers to as a womb-to-tomb view, provides an excellent resource for teachers in middle and high school to consult for how to address the unique needs of their older readers. She describes how students develop their reading competence throughout a lifespan. As students progress through middle and high school, much of this competence occurs as students work in content area classes. Collaborate with your content-area colleagues and share strategies to enhance students' interest and comprehension of content material. You may find numerous strategies you already share. For example, many content area teachers use graphic organizers to introduce content to students; reading teachers also find these useful. *Classroom Strategies for Interactive Learning* by Buehl (2001) is an excellent resource to review and share with your colleagues. Buehl identifies numerous

Students benefit when teachers collaborate.

CHAPTER 4

*All Children
and Adolescents
Have the Right
to Literacy
Instruction That Is
Individually
Appropriate*

strategies to encourage interactive learning. As an example, we share one idea, the Sequential Roundtable Alphabet, which Buehl recommends to introduce a topic and to quickly assess students' knowledge of the topic. To illustrate, prior to beginning a unit of study on British literature, divide students into small groups of four. Give each group a legal-sized piece of paper with the letters of the alphabet printed on it. Instruct the groups to identify a word or phrase for each letter of the alphabet that relates to British literature. When time is up or the charts are complete, discuss the groups' entries. To add excitement to the activity, impose a time limit for completing the chart.

- *Gaze into the eyes of each student in your classroom(s).* Identify one gift that each student brings to school. Go further and ask: Does that student believe I see an individual with strengths? How would that child or adolescent describe my views of him as a reader? Writer? Will that student be able to perform the activity prepared that day? And finally, ask what can I do today to let each student know I am pleased that student is in my class?

Putting Ideas into Action

The letter that opened this chapter suggests the reason many of us go into education. We want to make a difference. This is true whether we work in a school with all the needed resources and with students whose test scores are above the national average, or in a high-needs school where we struggle each day with limited administrative and material resources and with students whose scores are well below the national average. Whatever the teaching situation, we must make our interactions with students count.

When you teach your last class and walk out of your classroom for the last time, what do you want your legacy to be? Remember, your legacy is established one student at a time. What will your students take with them as a consequence of spending a year with you? Will they say you recognized their individual strengths? Perhaps, if you are a reading specialist, a student might recall that he learned to read in your classroom when he had struggled the previous years. If you are an upper elementary teacher, perhaps a young girl might recall when she shared with you her first written story. You encouraged her to submit it to the school's literary magazine. She did. It was accepted and, from that point forward, "writer" was part of her growing identity. If you are a middle school teacher, the boy who read twenty-two books in your semesterlong independent reading course might recall that it was in your class he first learned that reading could be a source of personal enjoyment. Or maybe, if you're a high school teacher, one day there will be an adult like Mona (one of the authors) who, as a student in your tenth-grade literature class, recalls when you recognized that a quiet D student understood Shakespeare when others in the class struggled. To this day, she remembers when you stopped by her desk and said, "You know you're capable of doing so much better in school than you have." That young girl earned her only B in high school in that class because no other teacher in her thirteen years in public school ever suggested, in actions or words, that she was "capable." A teacher's legacy is earned one student at a time. What will your legacy be as a literacy educator?

CHAPTER 4

*All Children
and Adolescents
Have the Right
to Literacy
Instruction That Is
Individually
Appropriate*

1. How is the scheduling of courses determined in your school or school system? Explore alternative scheduling patterns to see if changes can be made to allow more time for literacy instruction. Some have tackled the scheduling challenge by combining two courses together, such as social studies and English, to gain more time. What possibilities might exist in your school?

2. What social, cultural, and literacy provisions do your students bring to your classroom? How could you use your students' provisions to support their learning of school-based, formal literacy skills and strategies?

3. Gerald Duffy refers to effective literacy educators as entrepreneurial teachers. One characteristic of these teachers is their ability to match their literacy instruction to the needs of their students. Teachers who can do this have a large cache of ideas and materials, or a rich literacy tool kit. What's in your literacy tool kit?

All Children and Adolescents Have the Right to Access to a Quality Literate Environment

Dear Teacher,

I sat in your class today, but you know what, it was like every other day. You lectured, we took notes; we began the assignment that was written on the board; the bell rang, and the class ended. All I needed was a sheet of paper and a pencil.

There was one time, though, that was different. It was when we were reading The Odyssey and you wanted us to discuss whether we thought Odysseus was a hero. You asked us to bring in whatever materials we could find that were examples of people we thought were heroes. Jennifer googled the word hero on her computer. She said she found over 4 million Internet site options. She brought in one that talked about everyday heroes. Caleb, the skateboarder, brought in one of his skateboard magazines to show us a story about his favorite skateboarder. Jamal brought in a rendering (by the way, a new word for me) of his dad's most recent drawing of a hospital he's designing. I brought in a collage that I made of females I admire who play sports. All of those things made our small-group discussions very interesting. We each had such different ideas about heroes; it was very cool. Our discussions were open, and all who wanted to, could butt in and talk. After we shared our ideas, we knew what a hero is. We all didn't have the same idea, and we decided that was cool. It was just neat having that new way of learning. It made our discussion about whether Odysseus was a hero or not a lot more interesting because we each had thoughts about what makes a person a hero. That was fun. Could we do that again?

Cameron, grade 9

59

CHAPTER 5

*All Children
and Adolescents
Have the Right
to Access to a
Quality Literate
Environment*

*C*onsider the contrasting learning experiences described by Cameron—using paper and pencil where the students sit and listen versus using a variety of materials, both print and nonprint, where students examine and then share their individual ideas with others. What differences might occur in what the students learn in these two contexts, not just about the topic but about the value of their ideas? How might access to the different materials influence their attitudes toward examining whether Odysseus is a hero or not? How might access broaden their understanding of the concept of *hero?* Why might adolescents like Cameron prefer to have access to a variety of materials, including digital and online ones?

Now let's consider the teacher. Why might lecture be her predominant instructional method? What pressures might she experience from others to teach in this way? What policies within or outside the classroom might weigh on the teacher's decision of how to teach? What if her students are from a rural area? An affluent area? What if their high school is a high-needs school? What challenges might this teacher face in these different situations?

What about Cameron? As real as the constraints her teacher might face are, let's consider that this is Cameron's only time to be in high school. To what materials does she deserve to have access? How might the available materials influence her future plans? How might the ways she's asked to use these materials influence her overall perception of literacy and the role of literacy in her life? If the materials in class resemble materials she has access to at home, how might that influence her motivation to participate in literacy experiences? None of these questions has a simple answer, but the quality of the learning environment children and adolescents have access to determines many critical outcomes. It's this significance that prompted us to identify the right of access to a quality literate environment as one of ten rights that children and adolescents should be afforded. For our purposes, a quality literate environment for children and adolescents provides a variety of materials, including new technologies, and affords interactions with materials and classmates that are instructive as well as authentic.

Access

For decades literacy educators have asked questions about the importance of students' access to a quality literate environment. Does such access enhance students' literacy achievement as well as their interest in and ability to relate to the teaching that takes place? Consistently, answers to such questions confirm that the quality of the literacy environment does matter. Access to a quality literate environment helps weak readers excel (Langer, 2001). Access to a quality literate environment enables students in high-need areas to achieve at levels comparable to peers in more affluent areas (Knapp, 1995). Access to a quality literate environment creates excitement in learning (Langer, 2001). And access to a quality literate environment creates depth in children's and adolescents' ability to use oral, written, sound, and visual texts to create, construct, and communicate (Leu, Kinzer, Coiro, & Cammack, 2004).

Even though there is a long-standing interest within the literacy community to consider what access to a quality literate environment means for children and

60

CHAPTER 5

*All Children
and Adolescents
Have the Right
to Access to a
Quality Literate
Environment*

adolescents, our surveys and interviews of young people like Cameron gave personal meaning to this right's importance. Their statements confirmed for us that the materials they use and the ways they are asked to interact with those materials influence not only what they learn but also their attitude and engagement in school.

What Materials Create a Quality Literate Environment?

The answer to the question, what materials create a quality literate environment, is—it depends. It depends on the literacy needs of the learner. It depends on how the learner spends time outside of school interacting with print, oral, sound, and visual texts. It depends on the personal interests of the learner. It depends on the desired outcomes of the experiences. And, perhaps most important, it depends on the characteristics of the target learner. (See Chapter 4 for a discussion of how to use the construct of *provisions* to identify unique characteristics of each learner.)

During the past decade, there have been calls to attend more to the unique characteristics of the preadolescent and adolescent learner. In response, the International Reading Association (IRA) formed a Commission on Adolescent Literacy and charged it in part to "revitalize professional interest in and commitment to the literacy needs of adolescents" (Moore, Bean, Birdyshaw, & Rycik, 1999, preface). They identify seven principles to support adolescents' literacy development. The first of the seven principles states that, "Adolescents deserve access to a wide variety of reading material that they can and want to read" (p. 4). In *Reading Next: A Vision for Action and Research in Middle and High School Literacy* (Biancarosa & Snow, 2004), providing a variety of texts with a variety of topics at a variety of reading levels is one of fifteen elements identified to improve literacy at the middle and high school levels. Such variety enables students to gain critical content information and become active participants in the classroom learning environment.

Children and adolescent learners should have access to materials they want to read. (See Chapter 6 for a discussion of the importance of choice in reading.) These include books, textbooks, as well as more sophisticated visual and media images, and the Internet. Many teens today surf the Web. They download images from the Internet. They create their own Web pages. They instant-message. They podcast, join discussion blogs (forums), and locate information on a wide range of personally relevant topics. These young people move easily among multiple forms of print, visual, and sound media. The changes in ways information is shared and gained by children and adolescents have created new ways to interact around these multiple forms of texts as well as new social contexts in which to participate—such as online chat rooms (Leu et al., 2004).

When teachers bridge in-school reading with what students like to read out of school, students are likely to read more.

61

CHAPTER 5

*All Children
and Adolescents
Have the Right
to Access to a
Quality Literate
Environment*

Exposure to such varied information sources in the daily lives of these young people often creates a sharp contrast between what they experience in their lives outside of school and what they experience in school. Our interview with Michael, a high school sophomore, represents the views of many his age. When asked, *Do you think it is okay to use your imagination when reading an assignment?* he responded, *That question . . . goes back to my point . . . everything should be video-based. Books are overrated. With video [you] can see it, [you] have richer sources of information. The old-time way of learning is with books.* What Michael calls "the old-time way of learning" is referred to by some literacy scholars as "the institution of old learning" (O'Brien & Bauer, 2004).

Marc Prensky (2005/2006) shares Michael's view, as evident in his discussion of the gap that exists between what students experience out of school and what they experience in school. Prensky states, "schools are stuck in the twentieth century, [while their] students have rushed into the twenty-first" (p. 8). He refers to students as *digital natives,* to reflect their ability to move fluently among the "digital language of computers, video games, and the Internet" (p. 9). In contrast, he refers to those of us who find this new language less familiar as *digital immigrants.* For even if we use these new information sources, we, like someone who learns a second language late in life, maintain an "accent." Although the labels used by Prensky to describe this divide are humorous, they belie a serious challenge to today's teachers. The fast-paced introduction of new ways of accessing and sharing information and the predominance of the old ways used in classrooms place many teachers, especially those who work with preadolescents and adolescents, in an instructional bind.

The literacy field, however, is embracing these changes to accommodate the multiple ways that students like Michael gain and share information in their out-of-school lives. Such accommodations are represented in an area referred to as New Literacies, which extends what counts as literacy beyond traditional reading and written forms prevalent in the twentieth century (Street, 2003). This broader definition considers literacy as a social practice, which varies by context and form. From this view, literacy includes texts used in performance of a job, such as the reading of a car manual by a mechanic to determine the appropriate tire pressure, as well as the diagrams a football coach sketches of a play. Eisner's (2003) statement that "literacy is not limited to what the tongue can articulate but what the mind can grasp" captures the focus on meaning and how broadly such meaning can be represented—core elements of a new literacies perspective (p. 342).

As literacy teacher-educators, we embrace this broader view of literacy and believe that a critical step for teachers is to examine the practices embraced by their students in their day-to-day lives. Examples might include texts of popular culture (such as hip-hop, spoken-word poetry, rap, [maga]zines, music videos, graffiti, and Internet blogs). To illustrate, we examine a sample of literacy practices used regularly by many children and adolescents surrounding the context of the Internet. As reported in the 2005 Pew Internet report on "Teens and Technology," 87 percent of twelve- to seventeen-year-olds use the Internet (Lenhart, Madden, & Hitlin, 2005) and other current technologies to accomplish many tasks throughout their day. For this group, one important function of the Internet is to maintain social contacts. Figure 5-1 presents a sample of ways these young people use the Internet to manage their social lives.

Any parent of a teenager has witnessed such use. Recently, Evan, the seventeen-year-old son of one of the authors, was observed doing his homework. A Bob Dylan

62

CHAPTER 5

*All Children
and Adolescents
Have the Right
to Access to a
Quality Literate
Environment*

song was playing on his iPod, his cell phone was positioned between his shoulder and his ear, and he was online. Where was his book? He didn't need it; his English teacher had posted a set of questions on their homework blackboard, and he had a 10 p.m. deadline to submit the answers to these questions. Was Evan more engaged because he could multitask while doing his homework? We don't know, but we do know that he certainly represents many of today's high school students.

The prominence of technology use outside of schools requires our attention to this essential tool in school literacy programs. We can only imagine what lies ahead for the students in our schools today. Schools must establish places for students to use the multiple technologies they so fluently navigate outside of school. This is supported by the *Reading Next* report (Biancarosa & Snow, 2004), which includes a recommendation that technology be used for learning and as a topic of learning. To strengthen this recommendation, a technology component is one of fifteen elements the *Reading Next* panel identified for an effective literacy program.

What Interactions with Materials Create a Quality Literate Environment?

Preadolescents and adolescents are by their developmental nature social beings. Their interactions with others are central to their growing awareness of self and the world. Typically, during middle childhood, preadolescents become increasingly

Maintain Social Contact

Internet: A Conversational Centerpiece

"I usually check my email and I have an online journal and so I'll write in that, chat with my other friends, and if I have little things to do around the house then I can do it [while instant messaging] because unless it's somebody that responds quickly, then I can just go around and do something quick and come back" (p. 23).

Instant Messaging (IM): A Tool for Maintaining Relationships

"It's a good way to talk to people that you couldn't usually call or that live far away . . . or people that you don't know well enough. It's a good way to get to know people" (p. 24).

IM: An Efficient Social Tool

"If you only have like an hour and a half to spend on the Internet then you could talk to like maybe ten people. Whereas you can only talk to three if you were going to call" (p. 24).

aware of their social standing as they begin to make comparisons between themselves and others. This is evident in Hannah's comment when asked if she liked to write: "I'm not a good writer. Monica's writing is really good. I'm just not able to write the way she does." Older adolescents begin to develop a more complex and multidimensional view of self as implied in the statement made by Evan, currently a junior in high school, when asked if he liked writing: "I don't like structure, like when you have to have a 3-3-11 or you have to have 5 paragraphs. My writing style is more like a stream of consciousness."

Capitalizing on their interest in self and others provides a powerful tool for capturing the attention of these young people. That's why access includes not only the availability of materials but also the ways students interact with those materials and with others as they learn. If children and adolescents interact and discuss with others while learning, they also experience cognitive benefits—such as refined and expanded thinking (Fall, Webb, & Chudowsky, 2000). (For an expanded discussion of motivation and engagement, see Chapter 7.)

If we return to Cameron's letter, which opened this chapter, it's easy to see how the discussions with her classmates probably stimulated her thinking about the topic, increased her vocabulary, and added new information. This doesn't account for the synthesizing, comparing, and analyzing she likely did to create her collage. Now compare that complexity with the thinking required of her as she sat and listened to the teacher. Comments from the students we interviewed, such as, "Why should I retain boring stuff, it's a waste of [mental] space," suggest they're probably not thinking about the information presented through traditional lectures. Let's look at how one teacher, Karen Luchner (n.d.), uses her knowledge of literacy teaching and learning to design lessons for her high school students, lessons that are both engaging as well as sensitive to the characteristics of the adolescent learner. She describes the series of lessons as follows: "In th[ese] lesson[s], students use a Discussion Web to engage in meaningful discussions. Students work in groups to answer the question, 'Are people equal?' and analyze all sides of the responses, forming a consensus and presenting it to the class. Students then read *Harrison Bergeron*, by Kurt Vonnegut Jr., and use supporting details to complete another Discussion Web that looks at whether people are equal in the story. Groups form a consensus, present their position to the class, and engage in class discussion. Freewrites, a persuasive essay, computer activities, and an informal class debate help students extend and apply knowledge." These lessons, a debate rubric, participation rubrics, and a Literary Graffiti form are available at no cost at www.ReadWriteThink.org.*

Karen, through her lessons, demonstrates an awareness of the characteristics of her high school students and her role in preparing them to use oral, visual, and written language in complex ways. Even if we can't anticipate future ways today's students will communicate and create information, our charge as educators is to equip them with the competence and confidence to use increasingly complex materials

*From "The Pros and Cons of Discussion" and "A Biography Study: Using Role-Play to Explore Authors' Lives." Copyright © ReadWriteThink.org. ReadWriteThink.org. is a nonprofit website maintained by the International Reading Association and the National Council of Teachers and English, with support from the Verizon Foundation. The site publishes free lesson plans, interactive student materials, Web resources, and standards for classroom teachers of reading and the English language arts.

64

CHAPTER 5

*All Children
and Adolescents
Have the Right
to Access to a
Quality Literate
Environment*

(Alvermann, 2001a). Karen's lessons provide a useful example of how this can be accomplished.

Why Is the Right to Access to a Quality Literate Environment Important for Children and Adolescents?

We know that children and adolescents gain an understanding of vocabulary, functions of print, structures of language, and information and concepts through exposure to a quality literate environment (Guthrie & McCann, 1997). We know that a quality literate environment is a key determinant of students' short-term and long-term success in developing as literate individuals in the twenty-first century (Snow, Burns, & Griffin, 1998).

From the children and adolescents we surveyed and interviewed, we became aware of the unintended consequences when classrooms do not have a quality literate environment that reflects students' everyday literate lives. Students assume their teachers don't care about them as individuals. They assume the teacher is "just one page ahead of them in the textbook." Mostly, they're bored! They're bored with what one student called "rotating and reading," commonly referred to in elementary school as round-robin reading. (A practice, to our surprise, that many middle and high school students we interviewed said still occurred in their classrooms.) They're bored with sitting and listening. They're bored when the in-class instruction repeats what's in the textbook, implying they didn't even need to read the assigned material at all!

However, more is at stake than just making learning relevant and interesting to the students. We know that when children and adolescents find the materials and ways of interacting with the materials relevant and interesting, they are likely to be more engaged. Engaged students spend more time participating in literacy activities (Guthrie & McCann, 1997) and this increased participation results in higher levels of achievement (Anderson, Wilson, & Fielding, 1988). As reported in Chapter 4, the recent NAEP scores indicate that only 31 percent of fourth graders and 31 percent of eighth graders scored at or above the Proficient level of performance (National Assessment of Educational Progress, 2005). From these test scores, although we certainly acknowledge the limitations of such scores, we submit that if the students in these classrooms found their schooling experiences more engaging perhaps they would spend more time involved in the experiences and possibly achieve at higher rates (Anderson et al., 1988).

When teachers integrate technology while teaching, students are more engaged in the lesson.

65

CHAPTER 5

*All Children
and Adolescents
Have the Right
to Access to a
Quality Literate
Environment*

We know care needs to be exerted to ensure that the materials and routines used in a school's literacy environment don't support some learners while excluding others (Gee, 2003; Gee & Green, 1998; Lankshear & Knoebel, 2003). Some of these inequities are subtle. Take, for example, when a Caucasian teacher evaluates an African American child's retelling of a story to be less advanced than his Caucasian classmates because the retelling does not conform to the storytelling format more familiar to the teacher (Michaels, 1984). Others are more obvious; for example, when the books used by teachers don't represent the ethnicity, socioeconomic status, geographic location, or family type of the students seated before them.

We also know that for some students a quality school literate environment may be the difference between success and failure. Recall the description of Evan, who, while completing his homework, moved among several technologies. Evan is fortunate. He has the newest technologies. This is not the case for many students who live in poverty areas. The 2005 Pew Internet project (Lenhart et al., 2005) reported that although 87 percent of individuals ages twelve to seventeen use the Internet, the 13 percent who don't are disproportionately African American and generally from lower-income homes. Unfortunately, this lack of availability is not limited to technology. Books, what many literacy educators consider the cornerstone of literacy, are also limited. Children from poor environments are less likely to purchase large numbers of books (Neuman, Celano, Greco, & Shue, 2001). They are also less likely to have large numbers of books in the libraries in their neighborhoods (Neuman et al., 2001). Having access to fewer books is just one consequence of poverty. Poverty is a circumstance that warrants sustained attention by schools and teachers who seek to provide a quality literate environment for the children and adolescents who live in these areas (Haberman, 1995).

Finally, evidence suggests that high-support schools and classrooms can do much to foster students' literacy development. These so-called "beating-the-odds" studies (Langer, 2001) provide growing evidence that given access to a quality literate environment, students who traditionally fail can and do succeed at the levels of their more advantaged peers.

How Can the Right to a Quality Literate Environment Become a Reality in Today's Schools?

Today teachers face many constraints: class size, increased paperwork, fewer choices in how they teach, and limited availability of appropriate materials. Perhaps similar constraints impinge on Cameron's teacher and might explain why she teaches the way she does. Our concern is one expressed by many of the teachers we spoke with in the course of our work on this book. They lamented that the focus of many educators appears to be shifting from student learning to teaching content. We hope the suggestions that follow assist you in creating a quality literate environment with attention on your students.

66

CHAPTER 5

*All Children
and Adolescents
Have the Right
to Access to a
Quality Literate
Environment*

What Can You Do to Provide Your Students with Access to a Quality Literate Environment?

* Survey your students at the beginning of the year to identify the types of print and nonprint materials they use in their day-to-day experiences. Suggested questions are, "How is information shared in your home? What do you read? What kinds of writing happen in your home? Your neighborhood? How do you communicate with your friends? How do you use the Internet in school and out of school? Knowing how your students spend their communicative life outside the classroom provides a menu of responses to offer as options for how your students could respond to projects you assign. Meyers and Beach (2003) describe the multiple-media forms used by a group of ninth graders at State College High School. The students were asked to represent in some media form the social worlds in which they participated. One student took digital photographs of students interacting in groups. Other students used Adobe Premiere to create movies from still images, music, and song lyrics. While others used SoundEdit 16 to explore the words in songs to illustrate aspects of their social worlds (pp. 236–237). Consider the critical thinking, the writing (even though it was via visual images) and the editing they performed as they created their statements about their social world.

* Make books and other print materials available in the classroom. We are aware that some middle and high school teachers share classrooms. One middle school teacher we know pushes a cart to the five different classrooms in which she teaches. Her cart is loaded with books, magazines, and newspapers, as well as her teaching materials.

* Survey Internet use by the teachers and the students in your school. Log on to Project Tomorrow's website to read how to participate in their annual Netday Speak Up Event (www.tomorrow.org). Although the survey responses from participating schools and districts become part of their national database, participants gain free access to their aggregate school and/or district data.

* Ask students to photograph their community and home and to write about what these spaces communicate about their lives. Review their photographs to learn about your students' out-of-school lives. Then consider how you can connect your classroom learning to what you now know about your students' lives outside of school.

* Increase your knowledge about reading and the unique needs of these older readers. Start with materials available at no cost and easily accessed on the Web. Position statements on preadolescent and adolescent literacy can be downloaded from the International Reading Association (www.reading.org) website. Donna Alvermann's (2001a) *Effective Literacy Instruction for Adolescents* is available from the National Reading Conference (www.nrconline .com). Download the report commissioned by the Carnegie Corporation, "Reading Next: A Vision for Action and Research in Middle and High School Literacy." Identified in this report are fifteen elements for developing effec-

67

CHAPTER 5

*All Children
and Adolescents
Have the Right
to Access to a
Quality Literate
Environment*

tive middle and high school literacy programs. This report can be down-loaded from www.all4ed.org.

- Relinquish the talk. The literacy environment of children and adolescents is enriched when they can discuss with others. As Cameron wrote, "I sat in your class today, but you know what, it was like every other day. You lectured, we took notes; we began the assignment that was written on the board; the bell rang; the class ended." Al, whom you met in the introduction of this book, said in a written response, "The boring classroom is all too common." Mostly the classroom is boring because the teacher does all the talking. Approximately seventy-five years ago philanthropist Edward Harkness had a vision for a form of teaching, "What I have in mind is [a classroom] where [students] could sit around a table with a teacher who would talk with them and instruct them by a sort of tutorial or conference method, where [each student] would feel encouraged to speak up. This would be a real revolution in method" (Exeter Academy, n.d.). Little did Mr. Harkness know that over seventy-five years later this still would be a "revolution in method." This revolutionary method is called Harkness Teaching. This is a seminar teaching style where students sit around an oval table, "interacting with other minds, listening carefully, speaking respectfully, accepting new ideas and questioning old ones, using new knowledge, and enjoying the richness of human interaction" (Exeter Academy, n.d.). One adolescent we know participated in these discussions in his high school British Literature class. Prior to class students read assigned portions of *Sir Gawain and the Green Knight: Pearl and Sir Orfeo* and were asked to consider several questions as they read. In class they began by discussing these questions, but shortly the discussions led to the students' insights and thoughts. This male student commented on how much he looked forward to the Harkness Table discussions, and how they added interest to reading the assigned material (Exeter Academy, n.d.).

- Invigorate your literacy teaching by borrowing ideas from other literacy educators. One excellent source for such information is www.readwritethink.org. This site provides free access to complete lesson plans developed by literacy professionals for literacy professionals. Karen Luchner's lessons, described in a previous section of this chapter, illustrate the quality and completeness of these lessons.

Putting Ideas into Action

In what ways can you personalize the information in this chapter? Does the literacy environment in your classroom and your school reflect the experiences of the students who spend, on average, six hours a day in school? What challenges do you face that prevent you from providing your students with a quality literate environment? Can you work with others to address these constraints? Do you remember why you wanted to be a teacher? Was it because you wanted to make a difference? We hope considering the suggestions set forth in this chapter for how you can

68

CHAPTER 5

*All Children
and Adolescents
Have the Right
to Access to a
Quality Literate
Environment*

provide your students with a quality literate environment reinforces your belief that you can make a difference in the lives of the children and adolescents with whom you work.

*D*ISCUSSION QUESTIONS FOR STUDY GROUPS

1. For our purposes, a quality literate environment refers to the types of materials used as well as the ways the students interact during learning. How can these two components of access help you enrich your literacy program?

2. What policies within or outside of your classroom weigh on your decision of what materials you use to teach? What can you do to expand the materials you use in the classroom?

3. What media and technologies do your students use outside of school? How might you use these technologies to build more formal literacy skills?

All Children and Adolescents Have the Right to Choose Their Reading Materials

Dear Teacher,

I read and reread the first pages of the social studies chapter about the American colonies, but I just don't understand it. It's boring stuff. All those words that I don't know, all the dates and people that I can't remember; things I will never need to know. My dad told me that he loved to read about the colonial period. In fact, he remembered reading about the American soldiers who had to march and fight in the cold winter without any shoes and how their horses would slide and fall on the ice because they didn't have shoes either. Those soldiers had a hard life but won the war. He said the book he read was called "Redcoats and Rebels" [Hibbert, 1990]. Why can't we choose books that would help us understand the people who lived during the colonial war and why they were fighting the "redcoats"? We would learn who the redcoats were and other important stuff.

Jed, grade 5

CHAPTER 6

*All Children
and Adolescents
Have the Right
to Choose Their
Reading Materials*

*A*s you read this letter, what personal connections did you make with Jed and his concerns? Did you remember having similar thoughts about your middle or high school textbooks? Your college textbooks? The lack of opportunity to choose at least some of your reading material? What kinds of books interest you? Why? What are characteristics of books you choose to read? For personal reading? And for learning new information? For learning history, for example? Do you think Jed would have understood the material on the American Revolutionary War in his history textbook if he had read *Redcoats and Rebels* first? Does this letter remind you of a time when one of your teachers told your class that the textbook would not be used for a semester; perhaps instead you were given many choices of books to read—books organized around themes that your class would study and discuss?

Or perhaps Jed's letter worries you because you know as a teacher that there are some books used in school that your students do not like and/or find difficult to understand. Some books provide information about events, people, or concepts that seem far removed from the your students' experiences. Yet some of these books are required by your school district or to meet goals of the state curriculum. And you know that some of the information embedded in these textbooks will be tested on the state examination; you fear that students will be disadvantaged (e.g., fail the state test, be identified as students with reading comprehension problems) if they do not have access to this content. More important, some information presented in these textbooks may be worth knowing to broaden knowledge about the arts and sciences and/or to be informed citizens in a democracy (e.g., what can be learned from a study of the actions of U.S. colonists?).

We had similar thoughts when we first read Jed's letter. And these thoughts helped us identify issues relevant to the *right of all children and adolescents to choose their reading materials*. In this chapter we discuss what we can do to foster reading of multiple texts, including those that might seem uninteresting and unrelated to students' personal experiences.

Choice

The right of students to select what they read, we believe, is essential for developing readers who *can* read and who *want* to read (Moore, Bean, Birdyshaw, & Rycik, 1999). Unfortunately, Podl (1995), a middle school and high school teacher, describes what many teachers observe. Few of her students read for pleasure (the act of reading for pleasure she viewed as *oxymoronic* when applied to her students) because they associated reading with memorizing facts for quizzes rather than finding personal connections. Guthrie and Humerick (2004), who conducted a meta-analysis of classroom-based research, evaluated the impact of several lesson features on student outcomes, including students' reading engagement. Three factors they identified—easy access to a variety of interesting texts, opportunities for students to choose what they read, and time for students to collaborate with other students while reading—were estimated to have a significant impact on reading achievement, and as Dick Allington (2005) 2005–2006 president of the International Reading Association noted, each variable impacted reading achievement more than systematic phonics instruction, as reported by the National Reading Panel (2000).

Why is *choice* valued highly by literacy researchers and the students we interviewed? There are many reasons. One is empowerment. Having the right to choose texts for personal reading and for at least some academic reading is self-empowering—an attribute that can be especially important for middle and high school students who eagerly seek their own identities as they transition to adolescence. A second reason relates to the importance of affirming students' self-concept and ability to make good choices for their reading actions. Affording the right to choose reading materials signals to students that teachers believe they are capable readers. And third, when their choices are acknowledged (even celebrated), children and adolescents tend to read more often, adopt a competent reader identity, and with developing confidence as a reader, are less resistant to reading more challenging, complicated texts (Alvermann, 2001b; Cavazos-Kottke, 2005; Kasten & Wilfong, 2005; Smith & Wilhelm, 2004; Wigfield, 2004). Choice of reading materials, also, provides access to personal knowledge, interests, and experiences. Too often students reject school texts when their own expectations and interests are not available to them in the texts they are required to read (e.g., Barton & Hamilton, 2000; Galda,1982; Hinchman, Alvermann, Boyd, Brozo, & Vacca, 2004). Enabling students' control or agency over their own learning is central to enhancing intrinsic motivation (Shannon, 1995; Wigfield, 2004).

Recognizing the power of self-selection for children and adolescents, the board of directors of the International Reading Association concluded that students' right to choose at least some of their reading materials in schools is a highly desired attribute of high-quality instruction for children and adolescents. In two position statements, entitled *Adolescent Literacy* (Moore et al., 1999) and *Making a Difference Means Making it Different: Honoring Children's Rights to Excellent Reading Instruction* (IRA, 2000), the board of directors advocated for students' access to multiple forms of texts and the right to choose what they read for academic and personal purposes (see Figures 6-1 and 6-2).

There are several issues related to facilitating students' choice of reading materials. First, there is the issue of determining how choices are made. To address this

*A*dolescents deserve access to a wide variety of reading material that they can and want to read.

All adolescents, and especially those who struggle with reading, deserve opportunities to select age-appropriate materials they can manage and topics and genres they prefer. Adolescents deserve classroom, school, and reading materials tied to popular television and movie productions, magazines about specific interests such as sports, music, or cultural backgrounds, and books by favorite authors. They deserve book clubs, class sets of paperbacks, and personal subscriptions.

Source: Moore, Bean, Birdyshaw, & Rycik, 1999.

Figure 6-1

Adolescents' Rights

72

CHAPTER 6

*All Children
and Adolescents
Have the Right
to Choose Their
Reading Materials*

question, some researchers differentiate preferences from interests. Monson and Sebesta (1991), for example, define *preferences* as what students might like to read if given the opportunity and access and *interests* as associated with what they are actually selecting to read. We know, however, from our teaching and observations, that students may choose books based on their length (e.g., for some students, shorter is better!), their reading level, and/or the interests of their peers. We know, also, that both preferences and interests (if these are meaningful distinctions) are influenced by factors such as students' out-of-school experiences, the need to take agency for personal learning, the need to read informational texts that are useful for real-world applications, and efforts to be successful and free from anxiety that come from assigned texts that are too difficult for the reader (Rubenstein-Avila, 2003/2004). Additionally, for English language learners choices are influenced by perceptions that content is culturally relevant and that the language density is appropriate for their development (Riches & Genesee, 2006).

Yet choosing one's own reading materials can be a difficult task for some readers. Roller (1996) found that struggling readers frequently chose books they did not want to read or that were too difficult for them. Mueller (2001) interviewed adolescent girls and boys representing diverse economic backgrounds who admitted they were "not good" at choosing books and usually chose them by their length or cover or in absence of knowing how to choose books, continued to reread the same familiar books year after year. The quest to find the "right" book was challenging. As David explained to Mueller, "easy books make me love it; real hard challenging ones make me hate it" (p. 31). And when they were unable to make good choices, these students told Mueller that books were "boring," a description we heard often in our interviews. Trying to unravel what her students meant by their cries of "boring," she learned that "boring" held many meanings—for some students, it represented a lack of success in book reading, for others it meant a lack of interest in the book's topic, and for others it meant a lack of action (reading was too passive an activity). Tatum (2006), after interviewing a teenage African American boy, hypothesized that students' choice of books may be hampered, also, by their "inactivist-literacy development"—they had no history of reading books that affected their daily lives. Helping students make good choices is a responsibility of the teacher and it requires having a wide menu of texts available, including online, audio, or video texts; guidance in finding books that match ability and interest (Roller, 1996); and/or guiding students to follow advice offered by Jasmine, a teenager, (Mueller, 2001) who said that book choice improved when you "read enough pages in the book to see if you are hooked" (p. 33) or the student "Q" who told Tatum (2006) that you need to give the book "a

*C*hildren have a right to access a wide variety of books and other reading materials in classroom, school, and community libraries.

Children . . . who are allowed to choose what they read, read more for pleasure and for information.

Source: International Reading Association, 2000.

Figure 6-2

Children's Rights

chance" and keep reading because the book may start "getting good" (p. 2). Helping students make good choices can lead to increased reading and changed attitudes. As Sergio explained to the reading consultant at his high school, "I don't hate all reading now [that I can choose some of my reading materials] . . . I hate reading when I'm being told to read. I hate it and I won't do it . . . If it is a pick-your-own book and you make sure you like it, I will probably read it. And I will probably like it too" (Mueller, 2001, p. 31). These words provide powerful reasons for affording the right of choice *and* helping students make good selections.

Second, we might wonder if we should limit what students read, especially when some students hold tightly to preconceived biases about choice of topic, genre, or author. We fear that our students may never expand their reading interests. Rather than limiting choices, however, teachers often keep records of books students read to trace their choices of reading materials and the reasons for these choices. Once this information is identified, teachers can provide multiple ways to draw connections between their interests and the topics (and textbooks) under study in the classroom (Bean, 2002). Sometimes teachers choose popular culture texts, such as video games, magazines, or manga comic books (Schwartz & Rubenstein-Avila, 2006) as a way to open a discussion of concepts that are relevant to students' lives (e.g., unfair treatment of students in school, local government polices that affect curfews for children and adolescents), to bridge between interests and historical or science/ethical concepts discussed in the school curriculum to examine opposing viewpoints (Alvermann & Heron, 2001), and to extend and elaborate on information that is often greatly reduced or too abstract in school textbooks.

School literacy content then becomes more relevant and useful when applied to real-world issues or contemporary problems students face. For example, Jed's class could be asked to compare and contrast the hardships the colonists faced seeking independence and the challenges they face seeking independence as preadolescents. Similar to a study of the perspectives of the British and the colonists, Jed and his peers could discuss the different perspectives (of their parents, their teachers, their friends) about an issue that matters to them and how these perspectives might affect their own independence. Perhaps this discussion could lead to a study of the readers' rights discussed in this book; perhaps it could produce meaningful connections to literature such as *Holes* (1998), in which the author, Louis Sachar, describes how adolescents are affected by the unfair conditions of institutional authority. Connections could be drawn between these conditions and the complaints of colonists who opposed British authority over their new homeland, and thus, connections are made to the curriculum of the classroom (Barton & Hamilton, 2000).

Additionally, teachers who know what students are reading independently can organize text content around topics and ask students to share book "preview" talks with other class members; the goal of these previews is to provide connections between these popular texts and topics under study in literature, history, and science and to encourage broader reading within these content areas (Wigfield, 2004). Recommendations from others—especially others such as peers who are valued—can enhance interest, engagement, and a willingness to read texts that go way beyond their personal choices—student talk can be a primary catalyst for taking on new reading habits (Adler, Rougle, Kaiser, & Caughlan, 2004; Conniff, 1993; Gambrell, 1996; Kasten & Wilfong, 2005). And the discussions can deepen understandings of text content and build shared communication and understandings of concepts, an

74

CHAPTER 6

*All Children
and Adolescents
Have the Right
to Choose Their
Reading Materials*

Choosing to share a favorite part of a book with another student.

outcome that can be extremely supportive of English language learners, who may be attempting to understand subtle differences of word meanings within varying contexts (Riches & Genesee, 2006).

Third, there are curricular decision points that are crucial for supporting students' literacy development; the dilemmas confronting teachers are *balance and timing.* For balance, how can teachers honor students' choices *and* encourage them to read more widely? To read more complicated and challenging texts? To change genre? To read about cultures different from their own? We are reminded of a popular slogan we have seen on T-shirts, "so many books, so little time!" Considering these dilemmas, researchers who study motivation have a consistent response to the question about balance and encouraging wider reading: timing is the crucial factor. Important to the process of learning to read widely is the *time* required for students to first become "firmly and unshakably hooked on reading" (Kasten & Wilfong, 2005, p. 658.). Before broadening reading interests, students need to first *find themselves* in their readings and see that the content is relevant and/or useful for their lives.

Why Is the Right to Choose Reading Materials Important for Children and Adolescents?

As we discussed in the previous section, researchers argue that self-selection of reading materials is essential for initiating and sustaining engagement in reading, developing strategic and independent reading habits, fostering feelings of self-worth and self-efficacy, and enhancing deeper processing of text ideas (e.g., Finders, 1997; Ivey & Broaddus, 2001). Reading improves when students read and students read when they have access to books they can choose and books they can read (Allington, 2005). And as we discussed in the previous section, students tell us that they will read when they have choices and see the connections between text topics and their experiences and interests. In many classrooms, however, middle and high school students are not provided with this opportunity for choice. Instead, transmission models of teaching, prescribed curriculum and textbooks, tracking students through prepackaged leveled texts, and required lists of out-of-school reading material inhibit students' agency over their own reading selections.

Recognizing the limitations of fixed and scripted curriculum on students' learning, Csikszentmihalyi (1991) warned that such instruction often produced students who choose not to read and argued, "the chief impediments to learning are not cognitive. It is not that students cannot learn; it is that they do not wish to" (p. 115). Unfortunately, this warning has not been heeded. A decade later, in the midst of new reform movements, the goal to help "every child" pass state literacy tests is too frequently associated with higher uses of scripted and teacher-driven curriculum (Cummins, Brown, & Sayers, 2007) and fewer opportunities for student choices.

As literacy educators, we expect our students to be active and strategic learners—learners who monitor their understandings, who persist in their reading and writing efforts, who adjust their learning strategies to the demands of the text, and who make connections between their experiences and texts they read. Unfortunately, these forms of active learning and participation may not be present in all reading and writing programs. The students we surveyed, for example, told us they had few choices (for adjusting their reading habits) when asked to read for academic purposes. This finding is particularly problematic when we juxtapose it with studies that identified an increase in disinterest and passivity in reading as students progress from the elementary to middle and high school grades, a finding reported for both successful and less successful and reluctant readers (Bintz, 1993; Worthy & McKool, 1996). Too often, the gap between reading materials required for school assignments and reading materials students choose to read for their own purposes is huge (Newkirk, 2002; O'Brien, Stewart, & Moje, 1995).

Bintz (1993), Ivey and Broaddus (2001), and Worthy and McKool (1996) studied the reading habits of middle school reluctant readers and concluded that a lack of choice in reading materials and too few opportunities to read what they *were allowed* to choose contributed to students' negative attitudes about reading in school. Yet, as Bintz learned, those students described as having negative and passive attitudes in school were often highly engaged, persistent, and strategic when reading the materials that interested them outside of school. Finders (1997) described such activity as the "literate underground" of students—a place for reading success that may not be accessed by schools. These findings coincide with Deci's (1992) claim about the importance of interests to guide activity: "freely doing what interests them . . . when so motivated, their behavior is characterized by concentration and engagement; it occurs spontaneously and people become wholly absorbed in it" (p. 45).

Being "wholly absorbed" in one's reading or intentional about selections can be the catalyst that sparks interest in additional reading, deepening content and world knowledge. Analyzing the development of expert readers, for example, Alexander

This middle school student seems to be enjoying his book choice.

(2003) concluded that expertise is impacted equally by the factors of knowledge acquisition, adoption of strategic actions, *and* interest and persistence. Similarly, Schiefele (1991), a decade earlier, associated learning with interest and engagement—all necessary elements for deepening understandings of concepts under study. How can this right become a reality in today's schools?

There are multiple ways to support students' choice of reading materials in the middle and high school grades; these include the use of book clubs, core texts with links to other texts, and problem-based or inquiry-oriented projects. Some require simple adaptations of curricular formats; others require more elaborate modifications. All, however, can be implemented to support the goals teachers have for their students *and* the goals students set for their own learning and participation.

How Can Teachers Provide Choice as an Integral Part of Their Middle and High School Literacy Program?

- Initially, decide on your instructional goals and the place to include choice in your literacy curriculum. When we think about ways to design instruction with choice as *one* cornerstone of our program, we do not expect that all school reading materials will be chosen by the students. Rather, we envision literacy instruction that provides access to multiple texts, including both teacher and student selections and multiple text types, including, for example, texts written by students, popular culture texts, magazines, author sets, Web-based materials, multimedia texts, films, and musical lyrics (additional suggestions are provided in Chapter 5). The reading materials in students' backpacks or in their homes and communities, including texts in multiple languages, should be represented in the classroom and available for self-selection.
- To support both preferences and interests, students need access to multiple genres, varied content, multicultural materials, and multiple levels (both easy and more challenging) of reading materials. And casting a wide net is more likely to produce books and other materials that interest, are readable by, and are read by middle school and high school students; unfortunately, Worthy, Moorman, and Turner (1999) learned that the books we typically have in classrooms are not those that interest adolescents.
- Broaden your definition of "what counts" for reading materials. Too often, middle school and high school students, particularly boys, indicate that they don't enjoy reading but what they are referencing is school materials; often their backpacks are filled with Internet printouts, magazines, and newspapers that are obtained out-of-school (Cavazos-Kottke, 2005).

77

CHAPTER 6

*All Children
and Adolescents
Have the Right
to Choose Their
Reading Materials*

- Include texts that have potential for making connections to students' lives, cultural experiences, language differences, and who they are as individuals. For example, Tatum (2006) recommends texts that represent the voices of African American teenage males and those that can serve as "roadmap texts" (texts that help students understand the social conditions of their lives, answer questions about their identities, and determine what actions they can take to solve real-world problems). Similarly, Reeves (2004) and Mueller (2001) learned from their interviews with adolescents that it makes sense to provide access to books that connect to students' experiences outside of school, books that students recommend, and books that appeal to students' imagination and creative abilities. Additionally, Reeves advocated for asking students how they wanted to read their book choices (e.g., orally, silently, in small groups, in class, or at home).

- Include texts that represent different levels of language density for English language learners and, when possible, those representing the languages of students in your classes. If materials representing students' home languages are difficult to acquire, ask community volunteers to write and read these to groups of students, translating these throughout the sharing time. Activities that foster community involvement and attention to different cultures and languages can help students take on new understandings of world issues and lead to inquiry projects about issues, such as fair treatment of immigrants, that may affect their neighborhoods and worldview.

- Early in the process, begin to negotiate for more flexibility in requirements for reading assignments.
    - Join with teachers across disciplines to discuss texts required in your school curriculum and/or by your school district.
    - Identify and read texts that seem to be relevant to your goals (and those of your students) and major concepts you will study.

High engagement occurs when students choose and share texts that interest them.

78
....

CHAPTER 6

*All Children
and Adolescents
Have the Right
to Choose Their
Reading Materials*

- Identify texts from the required readings that will challenge and interest your students.
- Identify texts that could be eliminated to allow for texts chosen by students. Allow for flexibility and last-minute changes.
- Begin a series of meetings with district curriculum leaders to negotiate alternate book selections and to initiate a plan for tracking and evaluating students' independent reading choices and engagement.
- Collaborate with school curriculum leaders and public librarians to provide a wide range of reading materials that can accommodate your students' choices, and cultural and linguistic differences. It is difficult for individual teachers to acquire the amount of books that would be necessary to appeal to a diverse student group but collaborating with other teachers, librarians, and the community may help to achieve this goal. Doug Fisher (2004) described how teachers at Hoover High School in San Diego amassed great quantities of books by applying for a state school-improvement grant to purchase books and holding book drives in the community to seek donations of used books and magazines. Numerous books were added to their book collection (and they list books that became favorites for their high school students) plus they obtained eighty magazine subscriptions. And over one hundred newspapers were delivered to their school every day! Analysis of the outcomes of this project indicated that 88 percent of their students participated in independent reading every day.

How Can Teachers Initiate and Sustain Choice of Readings in Ways That Enhance Students' Literacy Development?

- Identify concepts that are central to your curriculum and cross disciplines, make these concepts highly visible, and build connections constantly to texts students are reading and writing.
- Initiate inquiry-based or problem-based learning. For example, at Vanderbilt University we continue to collaborate with classroom teachers who "anchor" their interdisciplinary instruction to a core text (e.g., a written text, a film, an editorial from a local newspaper); an anchor must have sufficient information to provide hooks to multiple questions and additional readings. For example, we have used the film *Young Sherlock Holmes* to invite student questions that lead to reading required texts and texts of their choice; these texts include fictional pieces, such as mysteries and science fiction, or nonfiction texts on British history, geography, science, and economics.

   Similarly, Moje, Collazo, Carillo, and Marx (2001) at the University of Michigan collaborate with teachers in Detroit, Michigan, to develop project-based science curricula to make connections between science concepts and literacy development. Within such curricula,
- Students generate many of the questions that guide instruction and additional readings.

79

CHAPTER 6

*All Children
and Adolescents
Have the Right
to Choose Their
Reading Materials*

- Students read both required texts and texts they choose to answer their own questions.
- Teachers (often across disciplines) and students collaborate to deepen each other's learning and to hook students onto additional readings for their projects or enjoyment. Similar to our anchored instruction, shared concepts develop as students collaborate with each other and different perspectives are viewed as a positive way to extend learning.
- Students are actively engaged in problem identification and problem solving; problems are solved (at least partially) by reading widely on selected topics.
- Students learn new ways of thinking, talking, and writing about information they are learning (and in turn, are finding authentic reasons for reading and referencing text information); for example, they may collect and chart data and use a text resource to help them explain their data analysis.
- Students of all levels and interests have access to multiple levels and genres of texts to help them complete their selected projects.
- Texts chosen by students to pursue their own questions and interests can provide opportunities to bridge to different perspectives and across cultural and linguistic differences (Farnan, 1996).
- Develop students' interests in analyzing different perspectives for problem solving or resolving conflict. Think, for example, how Jed's class may have been more engaged in the study of the U.S. colonial period if they had participated in a lively debate on the differing perspectives of the British and the colonists.
- Accompany choice of reading materials with choice of methods for displaying knowledge. Encourage multimodal "productions" (e.g., drama, Internet projects, Internet blogs, art, music, comics, multiple genres of written and digital texts) for students to demonstrate their reading interests and what they are learning from their readings. Altering ways to express what they are learning can appeal to students' strengths, out-of-school experiences, and cultural experiences, and encourage deeper engagement and learning. Success comes from capitalizing on their strengths.

How Can I Organize My Instruction to Accommodate Students' Choices, Especially When I Have Sixty-Minute Periods for My Language Arts and English Literature Classes?

- Use various organizational formats to engage readers in discussions of their text choices, such as forming small groups as book clubs (McMahon & Raphael, 1997). Often adolescents do not have opportunities to take active roles in text discussions at the middle and high school levels. Book clubs, as one type of small-group gathering, can provide *choice* in multiple ways, such as choice in membership, organization of group format, role of participants,

80
....
CHAPTER 6

*All Children
and Adolescents
Have the Right
to Choose Their
Reading Materials*

topics for discussion, methods for representing what they are learning, and books that are read. Initially, teachers will need to help students plan for these meetings, provide options for some of the reading materials, and continuously monitor for effectiveness. Sometimes a common theme or favorite author is the unifying factor for a group who has read different books; other times, groups form because they have all read the same book. Membership in such groups can have a positive impact on sustaining interest and engagement in chosen texts (Wigfield, 2004). And for English language learners in particular, participation in group discussions can enhance concept development, clarify misunderstandings, and develop "sophisticated" understandings of text ideas (Saunders & Goldenberg, 1999).

- Organize nontraditional group meetings for students to share their readings. For example, high schools in Nashville, Tennessee, offer after-school and evening times for groups to meet for Poetry Café sessions. Students organize these meetings and come together to read and react to poetry, often poetry that they have written. Similarly, Kasten and Wilfong (2005) describe the strong and positive responses they received when Wilfong's high school students were invited to organize their own Book Bistro sessions. For these sessions, students selected their own texts to share with each other (usually they read excerpts to each other) and often formed smaller groups within the larger group based on interest in topics or genres. And Vogt (2000) describes how she forms groups of students to role-play characters from a novel or historical account attending a dinner party. Ideas associated with a poetry café or dinner party may be a catalyst for you to expand on these suggestions. For example, perhaps you can host a pizza party once a semester for students to discuss their independent readings. Perhaps book clubs can be formed where students reading similar genres come together to share their readings.

Putting Ideas into Action

Returning to Jed's letter that opened this chapter, think of specific ways you could incorporate choice of readings into a social studies unit on the U.S. colonial period. Talk with students you teach and ask them about their choices for reading on this topic or other topics; what could help them become more enthusiastic about their reading? Ask them whether they value the right of choice and how you can work together to provide choices for some of the class readings.

Providing access to the right of choice in reading materials may be the catalyst that makes *the* difference in your students' literacy lives. The greatest danger we face as literacy teachers is students' loss of interest and engagement in reading. Think about Jed's reaction to a new procedure in his classroom—choice of some reading materials. Do you think one of his first choices for reading would be *Redcoats and Rebels*? We think Jed values his father's recommendation. We envision Jed feeling empowered, and with empowerment would come his confidence to take on additional readings. We envision new reading habits; Jed would read more widely and actively share what he is learning with his peers. From a passive and uninterested reader, Jed would become the highly engaged student we hope to meet in all our classes!

CHAPTER 6

*All Children
and Adolescents
Have the Right
to Choose Their
Reading Materials*

1. Before joining your study group, develop a list of books and other forms of texts that have impacted your life—perhaps they were inspirational, informative, memorable because of the writing style or language use, a way to escape from daily stresses, a way to communicate (e.g., letters, instant messaging, email), and so on. Perhaps these were the readings that made you think about new ideas or changed your perspective on an issue. Then list all the school reading materials (i.e., literature, textbooks, biographics, historical documents) that also made a difference in your life. When you join your discussion group, compare and contrast your lists. Are the same books and materials on both lists? How do the lists differ? What implications for teaching come from this discussion?

2. As posed by Jed's letter, identify a particular topic or content area that you know your students will study this year. Collaborate with your discussion group to generate a list of readings (including multimedia resources, pop culture texts, and texts from your local community) that are relevant to that topic. Think about ways that these texts could be grouped thematically for inquiry projects that students can pursue independently or in small groups. Develop a plan for offering choices of texts students can read to support their inquiry project and how they can report back on those readings.

3. Bring to your group meeting a selection of pop culture texts (e.g., teen magazines, comic books, song lyrics) that your students may be reading or thinking about out of school. Identify topics embedded in these materials that may provide hooks to content you are studying, current world or local news, or issues confronting your school and community. Think about how you will use these materials to lead into class discussions and/or readings.

All Children and Adolescents Have the Right to Reading Experiences That Create a Passion for Reading

Dear Teacher,

I hate the way our school puts the names of students in the hall with the number of points they have earned in the school's reading program. I hate it because I never have as many points as most of the kids in my class. I know how to read, and I make good grades in reading, but I sometimes like to read books that are not in my so-called "zone."

You know what I love to do when I go to the library or a bookstore? I love to go down the aisles and read the titles on the books. When I see a book with a title that sounds good, I read the blurb on the back of the book or read a page or two to see if I like it. Sometimes I get a book that is a little bit hard to read just because I am interested in the topic. I might even turn the book in without reading every word, but I think that's ok. I have the most fun reading when I find a really good book and get sucked into it and don't want to put it down. As I'm reading, I might stop awhile and imagine I am one of the characters in the book.

When I read the books that are in my zone, I know I'll have to take a test on the book. I'm afraid to skip pages because I might miss something important and not pass the test. If I don't pass the test, I won't get points and will be embarrassed because I don't have many points by my name in the school hall. Having to read for points is taking all the fun out of reading for me, and I just thought I'd let you know how I feel.

Sincerely,

La Shondra, grade 6

83

CHAPTER 7

*All Children
and Adolescents
Have the Right
to Reading
Experiences That
Create a Passion
for Reading*

*L*a Shondra has discovered the joy of reading and doesn't need points to encourage her to read, but her desire to read could be extinguished if she continues to have more negative feelings associated with reading for points. Other children and adolescents, however, might have positive feelings toward the point system and might read because of the points and prizes. As teachers and administrators, we must remember that what we thought would have a positive impact on *all* our students might actually have the opposite effect on some.

We believe that *all children and adolescents have the right to reading experiences that create a passion for reading* and that this passion for reading should be evident throughout the entire school. For this reason, we have included administrators in our discussion of this right and have provided suggestions for both administrators and teachers in the section on making this right a reality in today's schools. What does it mean to create a passion for reading? Why is it important for teachers and administrators to provide reading experiences that create a passion for reading when there is so much emphasis on test scores? What can teachers and administrators do to engage students in positive reading experiences that will enable them to become passionate about reading?

Creating a Passion for Reading

Creating a passion for reading is complicated. It involves attitudes, interests, self-efficacy (the belief that one is capable of performing a given task), motivation, engagement, and numerous other aspects of the affective domain. "Affective domain teaching occurs simultaneously with teaching in the cognitive domain, never in lieu of it" (Malikow, 2006, p. 36). What do children and adolescents experience in schools and classrooms where teachers and administrators create a passion for reading?

Children and adolescents who participate in school reading experiences that create a passion for reading have teachers and administrators who know that reading is an emotional as well as an intellectual experience. The teachers and administrators have shed a tear, laughed, and felt angry as they read a book, and they believe that the students in their school will be more likely to read if they have emotional connections with reading, too. Instead of simply being *educators*, the teachers and administrators are *affective educators*, who are knowledgeable of the affective domain and its power in making someone accept or reject an activity. As Cramer and Castle (1994) stated, "affective aspects of reading are equal in importance to cognitive aspects" (p. 3).

When children and adolescents are in schools that develop a passion for reading, they see their teachers and administrators demonstrate positive attitudes toward reading and express the value and importance of reading. Instead of saying their teachers and administrators *probably* like to read, as the students in a study by Baker (2002) did, they *know* that the teachers and administrators in their schools love to read. One ninth-grade student in a study by Strommen and Mates (2004) described "a teacher who spoke about books with a real passion" (p. 197). This teacher as well

84

CHAPTER 7

*All Children
and Adolescents
Have the Right
to Reading
Experiences That
Create a Passion
for Reading*

as some others "demonstrated an enthusiasm for books, had lots of books in their classrooms, let students borrow books, and read aloud in class frequently" (p. 197).

Children and adolescents who attend schools that want their students to develop a passion for reading have teachers and administrators who know their students' affective strengths and weaknesses as well as their intellectual strengths and weaknesses. They know that "students' levels of reading motivation" vary "as much as the students themselves" (Edmunds & Bauserman, 2006, p. 414). The teachers and administrators have knowledge of and access to instruments for assessing facets of the affective domain, such as attitudes toward reading, reading interests, and readers' self-concept. If published instruments don't seem to be a good match for their school and students, they create their own instruments. In addition to written assessment, they use informal means to learn about their students' affective strengths and weaknesses.

Teachers and administrators in middle schools and high schools understand that "boys are biologically, developmentally, and psychologically different from girls" (Tyre et al., 2006, p. 45). They take these differences into consideration and plan reading experiences for boys that reflect their interests, preferred teaching styles, and learning pace (Taylor, 2004/2005) as they try to rekindle a passion for reading that the boys had when they were in the primary grades.

Children and adolescents who are engaged in reading experiences that make them *want* to read have access to materials that they are interested in reading (Moore, Bean, Birdyshaw, & Rycik, 1999). In a study conducted by Scholastic, Inc. (2006), the participating students said the main reason they did not read more was because they had trouble finding books they liked. Media centers in schools that want their stu-

Boys like to read informational texts, magazines, and newspapers.

dents to be passionate about reading have an abundance of print material as well as electronic media (Alvermann, 2003; Alvermann & Hagood, 2000). In the Scholastic (2006) study, four of ten students in the study reported using a "technology device" (p. 4) to read, and that device was most often a computer. Classrooms, too, have libraries for putting reading material "within arms' reach" (Castle, 1994, p. 151), and they are stocked with a variety of print and with computers that have interesting software and Internet access. (See Chapter 6 for suggestions on helping students choose books that interest them and support their learning in school.)

Children and adolescents who develop a passion for reading are in classrooms where teachers employ a variety of reading formats that students enjoy. One format that has been found to be motivational is teacher read-alouds (Cunningham & Allington, 2007; Pflaum & Bishop, 2004.) Ivey (1999b) found that the teacher's reading of a book with expression and enthusiasm was the impetus for students wanting to read the book. Another format that is popular for sparking an interest in reading is independent, silent reading, where students select their own reading material (Cunningham & Allington, 2007). According to Moore and colleagues (1999), time available to read is often overlooked, but it is essential. Teachers know from experience that the traditional oral reading practice of round-robin reading does not have a high level of student engagement, so they use "stand-up performances" (Wasserstein, 1995, p. 41), involving the oral reading of rehearsed pieces—such as Readers' Theatre, plays, skits, and speeches—that students seem to enjoy. They use whole-class, small-group, and one-on-one instruction and find that children and adolescents enjoy collaborative work, especially literature groups or circles in which different groups read different books and group members have assigned roles (Pflaum & Bishop, 2004).

Children and adolescents who participate in reading experiences that create a passion for reading do not need incentives for reading because their teachers and administrators understand that extrinsic motivation is less effective than intrinsic motivation. Brandt (1995) interviewed noted author Alfie Kohn on human behavior and education. Kohn said that "the more you reward someone for doing something, the less interest that person will tend to have in whatever he or she was rewarded to do" (p. 14). He went on to say, "rewards are most damaging to interest when the task is already intrinsically motivating" (p. 13), as was the case with La Shondra. Teachers and administrators who want their students to be passionate about reading do not display points as they do at La Shondra's school. Displaying points humiliates struggling readers because "a low-ability student who is working hard will still not achieve a point score equivalent to her or his high-ability counterparts" (Biggers, 2001, p. 73). Further, displaying points can cause students' self-efficacy to suffer. According to Stipek, (1988), "a feeling of self-efficacy is an inherently positive emotional experience" (p. 94), but when students see themselves as incapable of performing the task of reading at a designated level, they tend to avoid reading.

When children and adolescents have school reading experiences that create a passion for reading, teachers and administrators encourage voluntary reading beyond the school. When the readers in the Strommen and Mates (2004) study were asked questions about their love of reading, all of them recalled experiences outside of school. They also had ample reading material and went to the public library and to bookstores. Teachers and administrators assist in making reading material available to students outside of school, especially during the summer months. The study

86
....

CHAPTER 7

*All Children
and Adolescents
Have the Right
to Reading
Experiences That
Create a Passion
for Reading*

conducted by Scholastic (2006) found that four of ten students reported reading *more* books for fun during the summer.

Why Is the Right to Reading Experiences That Create a Passion for Reading Important to Children and Adolescents?

In the last few years, many politicians and educators have focused almost entirely on the cognitive domain as they attempt to improve scores on multiple-choice tests that supposedly measure reading achievement, yet the 2002 National Assessment of Educational Progress (NAEP) data indicated that "approximately 68 percent of Grade 8 students and 64 percent of Grade 12 students are reading below the proficient level" (Learning Point Associates, 2005, p. 5), which is the level where students are competent with "challenging subject matter" (p. 4). Because "motivation is not measured with the high-stakes assessments currently being used in most states" (Cassidy, Garrett, & Barrera, 2006, p. 35), many politicians and educators seem to have forgotten about the affective domain. This right is important because cognition and the affect "work together in reading" (Guthrie & Wigfield, 1997, p. 8).

Because the No Child Left Behind legislation in the United States has been extended to adolescent readers (Cassidy et al., 2006), reading has become a priority in schools that have students in this age range. This right is important to teachers and administrators in middle schools and high schools who are looking for ways to generate more engagement in reading and to integrate reading into the content areas taught in their schools.

When children and adolescents develop a passion for reading, they *want* to read; therefore, they read more frequently and have more opportunities to apply word identification strategies and skills, develop reading fluency, increase vocabulary, improve comprehension, and "improve reading achievement" (Sanacore, 2002, p. 1). However, reading frequency drops off as students get older. The Scholastic (2006) study revealed that 44 percent of the participating students in the five- to eight-year-old range indicated that they read books for fun every day, but by ages fifteen through seventeen, 46 percent said they read books for fun only two to three times a month or less.

The right to reading experiences that create a passion for reading is especially important in middle schools and high schools that boys attend. Although some sources say there is no gender gap in literacy (Perkins-Gough, 2006), others think there is (McFann, 2004, Tyre et al., 2006; Viadero, 2006). Viadero reported that scores on the NAEP show that "boys score an average of 5 points lower than girls in reading" (p. 16) at age nine, and they score an average of 14 points lower than girls at age seventeen. The Scholastic (2006) study found that "girls are more likely than boys to have positive attitudes about reading and to regularly engage in reading for fun" (p. 9).

When a passion for reading is created in children and adolescents, they are more likely to become lifelong readers and learners. They add to their knowledge of the world and their knowledge of themselves. They develop insight, which means that reading can change their thinking (Harvey & Goudvis, 2000). As a result, they will become well informed, productive citizens who can think for themselves and "create visions for the future" (Taylor, 2004/2005, p. 298).

87

CHAPTER 7

*All Children
and Adolescents
Have the Right
to Reading
Experiences That
Create a Passion
for Reading*

How Can the Right to Reading Experiences That Create a Passion for Reading Become a Reality in Today's Schools?

Providing reading experiences that create a passion for reading is often a schoolwide effort. In this section, we offer many suggestions for administrators and teachers in hopes that you will be able to identify a few ideas that you can implement as you begin to make this right a reality in your school.

Suggestions for Administrators

- Reflect on the goals of your literacy program. Are the goals focused on the cognitive domain alone in an effort to improve reading test scores or is there equal emphasis on the cognitive and affective domains? If your school doesn't have a goal that addresses the affective domain, work with teachers to develop one.
- Create and participate in a study group to learn more about aspects of the affective domain that relate to reading. You might want to study McKenna's (1994) model of reading attitude acquisition, Wigfield's (1997) dimensions of reading motivation, and Rosenblatt's (1994) transactional theory of reading and writing to provide background knowledge on this right. If assessment data at your school reveal that boys' scores on reading measures are lower than girls' scores, you might choose to study what others say about the reasons for this discrepancy and how they have attempted to correct the problem. Your group might want to choose one or more of the following books to study: *"Reading Don't Fix No Chevys": Literacy in the Lives of Young Men*, by Smith and Wilhelm (2002); *To Be a Boy, to Be a Reader: Engaging Teen and Preteen Boys in Active Literacy*, by Brozo (2002); and *Misreading Masculinity: Boys, Literacy, and Popular Culture*, by Newkirk (2002). Another possibility for a study group is investigating instructional practices that are more conducive to boys—from creating single-sex classes (King & Gurian, 2006; Tyre et al., 2006; Viadero, 2006), to expanding your concept of reading to include materials boys read outside of school, to incorporating teaching methods that have been found to be effective in addressing the learning needs of boys.
- Assist teachers in reviewing published inventories for assessing facets of the affective domain. For sixth grade and below, you might be interested in the instrument for assessing reading attitudes that was developed by McKenna and Kear (1990), the interest inventory by Worthy, Moorman, and Turner (1999), the inventory to assess students' self-concept as readers by Gambrell, Palmer, Codling, and Mazzoni (1996), or the inventory to determine stu-

88

CHAPTER 7

*All Children
and Adolescents
Have the Right
to Reading
Experiences That
Create a Passion
for Reading*

dents' perceptions of themselves as readers by Henk and Melnick (1995). For high school, you could look at the interest inventory created by Brozo and Simpson (1991). After reviewing these and other published instruments, decide whether they are appropriate for your students. If not, use some of the published assessments as models and write your own interest inventory. Also, discuss informal ways to learn about your students. Teachers might observe their students as they read and complete work in class, read students' reading logs or journals, review artifacts created by students, and listen to them when they talk about reading (Brozo & Simpson, 1991; Cole, 2002/2003; Strommen & Mates, 2004). They might have students draw pictures of themselves doing school reading activities in which they were engaged and school reading activities in which they were not engaged (Pflaum & Bishop, 2004). Brozo (2006) suggested an informal strategy called My Bag for learning about students' interests. Students simply put objects in a bag that represent them and their lives and then share the objects with their teacher and fellow students.

- After you know the interests of the students in your school, work with the school media specialist to find out if materials in the media center match the interests of your students. Over 60 percent of the sixth graders in the Worthy et al. (1999) study preferred scary books, story collections, cartoons, and comics, but some of these materials were not present in the school media center. Also, encourage the media specialist to be passionate about reading.
  - Find out if the school media center has an abundance of "trade books, textbooks, magazines, newspapers, visual images, videos, CD-ROMs, music lyrics, and the Internet" (Alvermann, 2003, p. 2). It also should have the hardware and software for students to produce media texts such as songs, poems, novels, magazines, and videos (Alvermann & Hagood, 2000).
  - Check the media center for reading material that is of interest to boys. Remember that boys have individual interests and reading preferences (Taylor, 2004/2005); however, the following list of preferences based on research could be used as a starting point. Boys are inclined to read informational texts, magazines, newspapers, graphic novels, comic books, and electronic texts (Smith & Wilhelm, 2002), including "multimedia genres of digital storytelling—such as video literature (vid lit)" (Newkirk, 2006, p. 65). They like to read about things they might do or be interested in doing and tend to enjoy escapism and humor (Smith & Wilhelm, 2002). Schwartz (2003) pointed out that boys like characters who are similar to themselves, so reading "materials should feature people of different ethnicities, races, and backgrounds who live in a variety of types of homes and communities" (p. 2). The website guysread.com is a valuable resource for locating reading material for boys.
  - Work with the media specialist to make the media center an inviting place. In the Scholastic (2006) study, students who indicated they read books for fun every day identified the library/librarian as their source for ideas about books to read. Have liberal hours for students to return and check out books, such as during lunch and homeroom and before and after school. To encourage boys to read, have the media specialist conduct

programs for boys, include nonfiction when speaking to classes, encourage boys to work in the library, and put books in places frequented by boys, such as near computers, copy machines, and study areas (McFann, 2004).

- Walk through your school and evaluate the materials in the corridors and in the media center. Would a visitor know that you, your teachers and media specialist, and your students have a passion for reading? Your school might want to adopt a slogan that shows your love of reading. Have a banner made that contains the slogan and hang it in a prominent place near the front door. Purchase posters and print for the hallways and media center that promote reading. You might purchase some of the attractive reading posters with sports figures and other celebrities, including males. Display attractive book jackets in the halls, along with snippets from the books in large print that will catch the attention of students.

- Rethink your position as the instructional leader in the school. Do students see you as a role model for reading? In your daily encounters with students in the hallways, lunchroom, and other places, talk about reading. Tell students how you go to the library and the local bookstore and share interesting tidbits about something you read or are reading. Show students new books that you buy and receive as gifts and have lots of books in your office. Read to a class or group of students every day. You just might be the person who "lures" (Morrow, 2004) your students into reading!

- Work with teachers in your school to evaluate the incentives that are used in your school. Ask yourself if the "incentives are linked to the desired behavior" of reading and if they "promote engagement in the desired behavior" of reading (Gambrell & Marinak, 1997, p. 215). Ask yourself if some struggling readers might be embarrassed or feel they are not capable of reading because they are being compared to good readers. If you and your teachers decide that the present incentive program is not creating a passion for reading that will continue after students leave your school, develop an incentive program that is based on students' personal goals. Castle (1994) described a project with sixth graders that involved the students completing and signing individual contracts stating what they would do for recreational reading. She sent a letter to parents explaining the project and giving them suggestions for encouraging their child to read. Among the student-selected rewards for fulfilling contracts were "gift certificates to bookstores, opportunities to read to younger students, and extra credit on grades" (p. 160). With the high interest in electronic media that some students have, you could give them extra time to research topics of interest on the Internet, to produce electronic texts for their peers to read, and to work on projects involving multimedia.

- Invite guests, including local authors, to read to students and to share with students the importance of reading in their lives. Ask them to tell about some of their favorite reading material and to read excerpts. To provide good role models for both boys and girls, invite local business leaders, coaches, and teachers of both genders; male and female athletes at a local college or university; and parents and other relatives of students. Local service organizations often have men who are willing to be mentors for boys (Brozo,

90

CHAPTER 7

*All Children
and Adolescents
Have the Right
to Reading
Experiences That
Create a Passion
for Reading*

2006). These guests could speak to the entire student body, or they could read to individual classes and small groups. If it is difficult for role models to come to school in person, ask them to record an audiotape or a DVD that could be played to students.

• If your school doesn't have a buddy reading program where students in your school read to younger students, consider beginning one. Handel (1995) wrote about a program that involved middle schoolers reading to elementary students. The middle school students were taught how to use the strategies of predicting, questioning, making connections, and activating prior knowledge as they read to the elementary students. Family members became involved by helping the middle schoolers practice reading their books at home, participating in the training sessions for the middle schoolers, and attending the reading sessions at the elementary school.

• Combine efforts with teachers to promote reading activities beyond the regular school hours. One of the sixth-grade readers interviewed in the Worthy et al. (1999) study cited earlier indicated that she and some friends were starting a mother-daughter book club. In a recent issue of *Reading Today* ("Boys and Books," 2006), it was reported that "some communities have experimented with book clubs aimed at males" (p. 4). One such club, which was led by a man, met after school at a local bookstore. Additional book clubs for boys were organized due to the success of the initial club. Students might enjoy a Readers' Theatre club, a literary website club, a poetry club, a creative writing club, an online book review club, a drama club, or a club for writing lyrics to music. Clubs could share information and display projects in the school corridors and the media center.

• Once your students have a passion for reading you want it to stay alive. Work with teachers, the media specialist, and parents to keep students involved in reading during the summer. McGill-Franzen et al. (2005) summarized several activities for promoting reading during the summer. Among them were giving self-selected books to poor children in high-poverty schools, outfitting a recreational vehicle with books and making weekly neighborhood visits for students to exchange books, and allowing children not enrolled in summer school to use the school library.

Suggestions for Teachers

• Reflect on your beliefs about reading and expand your definition of reading to include the kind of reading that students, and especially boys, do outside of school. "Resist nostalgia" (Newkirk, 2006) and recognize that reading the sports page in newspapers, reviews of movies in magazines, and manuals for working on cars are all legitimate forms of reading.

• Let your passion for reading show. A ninth-grade student categorized as a "Reader" in the Strommen and Mates study (2004) said of one teacher, "it's like her one goal in life is to make everyone enjoy and love reading. She gets so into it. She loves it" (p. 187). Let your students see you reading and share quotes and passages from your reading with your students (Calkins, 1997).

91

CHAPTER 7

*All Children
and Adolescents
Have the Right
to Reading
Experiences That
Create a Passion
for Reading*

Hang posters and print on the walls that encourage reading. Create a colorful, attractive area in your room that contains lots of books and other reading material on students' interests and let students borrow them. Make a special bookshelf for boys and give it a catchy label such as Boys' Books or Guys Only. Have computers, DVD and video players, and materials to use with them. Create a work area for collaborative projects related to reading.

- Administer an interest inventory and use informal measures such as My Bag that was described earlier. Analyze the results and make a chart or table of topics your students are interested in reading about. Know your students' interests so well that you can make a personalized suggestion for reading (Brozo, 2006). The Scholastic (2006) study cited previously found that "medium frequency" and "low frequency" (p. 30) readers got most of their ideas about books to read from teachers.

- Read to your students dramatically and with expression every day. According to Trelease (1989), "reading aloud is the most effective advertisement for the pleasures of reading" (p. 201), and it "works directly on converting negative attitudes to positive ones" (p. 202). Read chapter books; articles from newspapers, magazines, and the Internet; poems; jokes and riddles; and facts from informational books and articles. Weave your reading aloud into your class periods at times that seem appropriate; you don't have to set aside a specific read-aloud time that seems artificial. One added benefit of reading aloud is that students often ask to borrow the reading material that you read because you have been successful in piquing their interest.

- Avoid overrelying on one format for reading such as round-robin oral reading or assigning a chapter or selection to be read for homework.

  - Consider a reading format called Everybody Read To (ERT) (Cunningham & Allington, 2007). Divide the reading assignment into reasonable segments and write a question to ask students before reading each segment to keep them focused. The question might be on the literal level with the answer stated in the book; it might be an inferential-level question where students have to use clues from the text, coupled with their background knowledge, to figure out a reasonable answer; it might be an evaluative question that requires students to use information in the text to make a judgment; or it might be a question that requires students to imagine and create. Only literal-level questions will have one right answer; the other types of questions may have several reasonable answers. When teaching, tell the students the pages to read, pose a question before reading, allow time for them to read in the format you have chosen, and follow the reading with a discussion of the answer to the question posed before reading.

  - Use teacher read-aloud as the format for reading difficult passages and passages that can be read with drama and expression. You might use teacher read-aloud at the beginning of a new chapter or at the beginning of a new story to spark interest.

  - Try choral reading as the format for some sections of the text that contain difficult words. Read a little louder than the students and control the rate. Poetry and texts with dialogue also work well for choral reading.

92

CHAPTER 7

*All Children
and Adolescents
Have the Right
to Reading
Experiences That
Create a Passion
for Reading*

Two boys enjoy reading with a partner.

- Select partner reading for some segments of the text. In this format, two students read the text together and answer questions, engage in discussion, or complete an activity. You could ask them to take turns reading pages orally in a whisper voice on some days. On other days, you might ask them to read silently and help each other with difficult words. Another possibility would be to let students decide how they will read the text together.
- Use a book club or literature circle format for groups of four or five students. The two formats are very similar; however, literature circles require each student to have a specific role to perform while in the group. If you are not required to teach from a single textbook, have several books for students to preview and then rate according to preference. Assign group members based on their preferred text. If you have a single required textbook, assign students to groups in order to have a mix of reading levels represented in each group, or let students decide how the groups will be formed. Alvermann (2003) reported that some students thought that students who liked to talk a lot should be together in groups while those who didn't talk much should be in other groups. In both book clubs and literature circles, students within each group decide how much they will read on a given day, the format for reading, and the way they will think about the text after reading. Encourage students to tell stories linking the

text to personal experiences and to role-play situations (Zigo, 2001). Other options for responding to the text are drama, dance, music, and the visual arts (Alvermann, Hagood, & Williams, 2001; Ballentine & Hill, 2000; Smith & Wilhelm, 2004). Smith and Wilhelm (2002) noted that "boys prefer active responses to reading in which they physically act out responses, do, or make something" (p. 11).

- Instead of making reading assignments to be completed outside of class, allow students to read in class. Cavazos-Kottke (2005) and his high school students created individual contracts indicating the books the students would read and the number of pages they would read during the semester. One boy who had lost interest in reading in middle school "wondered where his passion for reading had been for the past five years" (p. 183). Podl (1995) developed a program called Guided Independent Reading for her middle and high school English classes. In a given three-week period, the students read books of their choice in class, took tests on the books, and worked collaboratively to present their books to the class using a format of their choosing. One of the benefits of the activity, according to Podl, was an increase in students' enjoyment of reading.

- Tap into your students' interests in music and media (Alvermann, 2001a; O'Brien, 2001; Spires & Cuper, 2002; Vacca, 1998). Use song lyrics for teaching word families being taught in word study (Brozo, 2006) and movies and video games as springboards for writing (Newkirk, 2006). Introduce adolescents to Web-based book review sites where they can write and submit their own online reviews. Websites such as teenreads.com and teenlit.com might be of interest to your students.

- Select some teaching methods with boys in mind. Taylor (2004/2005) indicated that problem solving, inquiry, and interactive teaching are appropriate when teaching boys, as is the use of humor (Newkirk, 2002). Build on boys' existing competencies before reading by using prereading activities that require them to activate their prior knowledge and experiences and allow them to express their opinions. Also, plan challenging activities in which they can feel competent and successful (Smith & Wilhelm, 2002; Smith & Wilhelm, 2004; Williams, 2004/2005).

Putting Ideas into Action

Reflect on La Shondra's letter. If you were her teacher, what would you do? Would you try to persuade the administrator in your school to stop displaying points in the hallway? Would you propose incentives other than points? Would you emphasize intrinsic motivation rather than extrinsic motivation?

And what about La Shondra? She clearly knows the joys of reading, but she is feeling pressure with the tests and points. Would you tell La Shondra that she is a good reader who needs to read books with more point value and to try harder to get the number of points that she is capable of achieving? How do your ideas and insights about La Shondra connect to your own teaching practice?

*All Children
and Adolescents
Have the Right
to Reading
Experiences That
Create a Passion
for Reading*

1. We suggested that there should be equal emphasis on the cognitive and affective domains in today's schools. Do you agree or disagree with this position? Why? How much emphasis is put on the affective domain in your school? Should there be more or less attention to the affective domain in your school? Why?

2. We discussed the use of incentives to encourage students to read. What are some personal experiences you have had with incentives in your teaching? Based on your experiences and information in this chapter, do you think students read more because of them? Explain. Do you think students continue to read after the incentives are removed? Explain.

3. Think about the boys who attend your school. How do their test scores and grades compare to those of girls? What is your school doing to address the needs of boys? Does more attention need to be given to boys' reading needs in your school? Explain what could be done.

4. Refer to the questions in the Putting Ideas into Action section. Answer the questions as if you were La Shondra's teacher.

All Children and Adolescents Have the Right to Appropriate Reading Assessments

Dear Teacher,

Please don't make me repeat the fifth grade. My mother told me that if I don't do good on the test we are taking today, I will fail. This doesn't seem fair to me. I have studied my Social Studies and Science books real hard and have made good grades on all of my tests. I like to read and have even read Harry Potter all by myself. I like to write new adventures for the characters. Me and my friends act them out using action figures and a model of Hogwarts Hall I made. Honestly, I really am pretty smart. When I take a test, some of the stuff is boring, and I can't get into it so I kind of space out. I bet I could do good if they asked me about Harry Potter! I will just die of embarrassment if all my friends go on to middle school and I don't. Please save my life.

Sincerely,

Jonathan, grade 5

96

CHAPTER 8

*All Children
and Adolescents
Have the Right
to Appropriate
Reading
Assessments*

*I*n his letter, Jonathan conveys a concern that is a reality for many children and adolescents. This concern relates to the use of a single measure to determine students' academic achievement. For example, some children who did not pass the Florida Criterion Assessment Test in 2005 were retained in the third grade for the third time (Hirth, 2005). Florida, however, is not the only state that requires a passing score on mandated tests to pass to the next grade level (Neill, 2003). The use of single measures, such as norm-referenced standardized achievement tests used for state decision making, counters standards of best practices in literacy assessment (Winograd, Flores-Duenas, & Arrington, 2003). Professional organizations, such as the International Reading Association and the National Education Association, have called for the use of multiple assessments, including those that are sensitive to students' linguistic and cultural differences, to provide evidence of academic achievement and learning progress. And members of the American Educational Research Association (AERA) adopted assessment standards in 2000 that specifically call for *protection against high-stakes* decisions based on a single test score (AERA, 1999). When schools consider only standardized test scores to make high-stakes decisions such as whether to retain a student, children and adolescents can suffer. According to Shepard and Smith (1989), next to one's own death or the death of a parent, in-grade retention is a child's greatest fear. Children and adolescents who are retained have a higher likelihood of dropping out of school. Furthermore, retention is ineffective in raising achievement for most children (Allington & McGill-Franzen, 1995).

Students like Jonathan need advocates to ensure that important educational decisions are not made based on the results of a single test. In some cases, parents may take on the role of advocate, but many parents feel they cannot influence a school's decisions, and many children and adolescents do not believe they have the right to question the teacher or school policies (Risko, Matthews, Elish-Piper, Dasinger, & Bass, 2004). As a result, some children and adolescents suffer the consequences of inappropriate uses of assessments. If you were Jonathan's teacher, how would you respond to his letter? What other concerns might children and adolescents have related to testing? What are your personal experiences with high-stakes testing?

Jonathan's letter also raises issues related to classroom assessment. How are classroom assessments used for documenting student performance and learning? If classroom assessments are not used to inform decisions about instruction, the curriculum, and/or grade retention, then what is the value of classroom assessment? How do classroom assessments represent what the teacher values as knowledge and achievement? How can teachers use classroom assessments to identify what students know and can do as well as areas where they need further work and development? In this chapter we discuss these and other issues as they relate to *the right of all children and adolescents to be evaluated with appropriate reading assessments.*

Assessment and Evaluation

Currently, one of the most critical educational issues impacting teachers and their students is the appropriate use of assessments. The word *assessment* refers to the gathering of data to document what students know and can do and what they do not yet

97

CHAPTER 8

*All Children
and Adolescents
Have the Right
to Appropriate
Reading
Assessments*

know or cannot yet do. When the teacher reviews the assessments and makes a judgment, she is engaging in the evaluation process. For example, when the teacher reviews a student's daily work, performance on classroom activities, and observations from class discussions, she may evaluate the student's performance as being excellent, acceptable, or needs improvement. This process may lead to assigning grades, determining future instructional activities, or providing feedback to the student on goals and expectations. For the purpose of this chapter, we will use the term *assessment* to refer to both the gathering of data about student performance and the judgments made about performance.

As we suggest in this introduction, assessments are typically divided into two major categories: (1) norm-referenced standardized assessments meant to evaluate and compare school systems, document individual student achievement, and communicate that information to the public; and (2) classroom assessments meant to monitor student achievement and help teachers plan effective instruction (Farr, 1992). We will elaborate on these two types of assessments in the following sections.

Norm-Referenced Standardized Assessments

Norm-referenced standardized assessments measure student performance in specific areas of the curriculum and compare performance to a large representative sample of students (called the norming group). To ensure that these assessments are administered in a *standardized* or uniform way across settings, directions for administration are specific and teachers are required to follow the directions as written. When tests are scored at the local level or by a team selected by the state or by the publishers, specific scoring procedures provided by the test authors are to be followed carefully to ensure consistency of scoring across sites. While norm-referenced standardized tests can provide information about student performance for comparison purposes and about the effectiveness of instructional programs, they are not an effective instrument to support decisions concerning retention, classroom grouping, and/or placements in special and/or remedial classes. And these tests provide little to no useful information for teachers to use when making such decisions or when planning for effective instruction (Neill, 2003; Shepard & Smith, 1989).

Valencia and Riddle Buly (2004) claimed that knowing a child has failed a state test is "like knowing that you have a fever when you are feeling ill but having no idea of the cause or cure" (p. 134). When children and adolescents do not perform well on standardized tests, other measures should be administered to validate the test results or identify areas requiring further investigation. This is especially important when students' tests scores are not congruent with performance on classroom assignments. To substantiate their concerns about the use of scores on norm-referenced standardized tests for instructional purposes, Riddle Buly and Valencia (2002) administered additional assessments to fourth-grade students who failed their state achievement test. With the administration of these assessments they identified six different profiles of students and explained that students failed the state tests for different reasons, and thus required a different instructional response based on these reasons. For example, some students had strong comprehension skills but had difficulty identifying unknown words, some students had strong word-identification

CHAPTER 8

*All Children
and Adolescents
Have the Right
to Appropriate
Reading
Assessments*

skills but their focus on the words inhibited text comprehension, and some students had strong comprehension but weak vocabulary knowledge. These additional assessments provided the specific information required for differentiating instruction according to students' strengths and needs; the general score on the achievement test provided no such clues to aid instruction. It is incumbent upon the classroom teacher or reading specialist to use standardized tests as just one of several assessments when making educational decisions and to continue the assessment process until it reveals specific information that can guide instructional decisions.

Teachers must also be knowledgeable about the limitations of norm-referenced standardized tests, how to interpret them, and how to explain the scores to parents and children and adolescents in usable ways. For example, norm-referenced standardized tests are typically unable to measure much of the higher-level thinking required to be literate in today's world (Neill, 2003). In addition, many types of literacy skills are not best assessed through one format, such as written tests. Not all students are good test takers. Not all students learn in the same way or can demonstrate their learning in the same manner. Children and adolescents from diverse racial and ethnic groups may be at a disadvantage due to differences in language, learning styles, and cultures (see Chapter 3 on cultural responsiveness for a discussion of cultural bias in assessment). To be fair, children and adolescents should have the opportunity to represent their learning in many different formats and modalities, and teachers should use a wide variety of assessment tools to make instructional decisions about their students (Cambourne & Turnbull, 1990; Valencia, Hiebert, & Afflerbach, 1994). With the use of a broad range of assessment tools, teachers can develop a more complete picture of students' strengths and needs.

Teachers are expected to administer and interpret the results of norm-referenced standardized tests given in their classrooms and schools as well as construct and use alternative appropriate classroom assessments; therefore, they should understand issues related to the reliability, validity, and other characteristics of norm-referenced standardized and classroom assessments (Invernizzi, Landrum, Howell, & Warley, 2005). Validity is generally defined as "the degree to which evidence and theory support the interpretations of test scores entailed by proposed uses of tests" (AERA, 1999, p. 9). In other words, does the test measure what it says it measures? Reliability refers to the consistency of test scores (Lipson & Wixson, 2003). Would the test yield close to the same score if a student were administered the test again? Tests are only reliable and valid, regardless of published validity and reliability measures, if they are used for the purposes they were intended (Invernizzi et al., 2005).

A testing concept that is often not understood by teachers is the *standard error of measurement* (SEM) reported by test developers. Tests are not perfect, and test scores are not precise and fixed; their reliability fluctuates based on the SEM. The SEM allows a person to estimate the range within which an individual's *true score* probably lies. Thus, a reporting of an SEM score with the value of plus or minus 5 points indicates that a raw score of 25 actually falls somewhere within the range of 20 to 30. It is beyond the scope of this chapter to discuss other technical and statistical aspects of norm-referenced standardized tests. However, it is important for teachers to understand that test scores represent a range of scores rather than an absolute score. For a more in-depth discussion of validity, reliability, and SEM see *The Assessment and Instruction of Reading and Writing Difficulty: An Interactive Approach* (Lipson & Wixson, 2003).

99

CHAPTER 8

*All Children
and Adolescents
Have the Right
to Appropriate
Reading
Assessments*

Classroom assessments can be used to identify a student's strengths as well as areas where improvement is needed.

Two other testing concepts that can be confusing and difficult to interpret and explain are percentile ranks and grade equivalent scores. If a child scores at the 75th percentile, it does not mean that the child answered correctly 75 percent of the questions. Instead this score represents the percentage of students in the comparison group whose scores were equal to or lower than the target student's score. With a grade equivalent score, the reported score of 10.5 for an eighth-grade student indicates that the student's score is the same as the average score of students in the fifth month of the tenth grade if they had taken the eighth-grade test. It does not mean necessarily that the child can read and comprehend tenth-grade work. It does mean that if tenth graders took that particular test at the same time of the year, the typical score would be the same as this eighth grader's score. While there are additional difficulties related to grade equivalent scores, it is sufficient to note that these scores are so often misunderstood that the International Reading Association has encouraged test developers not to report the grade equivalent scores (Lipson & Wixson, 2003). The most important thing is for teachers to be knowledgeable about issues related to test validity and reliability so that reports of testing information to students, parents, and others are accurate.

Classroom Assessments

Classroom assessments can provide useful information for guiding teachers' instructional planning. Classroom assessments can help teachers identify student strengths

CHAPTER 8

*All Children
and Adolescents
Have the Right
to Appropriate
Reading
Assessments*

as well as areas where more instruction and support is needed. There are numerous literacy assessments that can be used at the classroom level for multiple examinations of students' learning and effectiveness of teaching practices (Winograd et al., 2003). These assessments vary in form and procedure and can include informal reading inventories, oral reading records and miscue analyses, vocabulary and comprehension tests that are content specific, conferences with individual students, student self-assessments, drawings and/or written responses to text content, multimedia development, and many others (Cooper, 2000). Uses of these assessments might follow state, district, and/or school policies, or the decision about their use may occur at the classroom level. Each assessment provides specific information that can be cross-referenced with information across measures and time to verify patterns of students' learning and progress. When used to represent learning and performance across different times and tasks and to represent learning and performance within the situated context of students' instruction, data collected on these assessments can guide adjustments in the curriculum or classroom instruction and help students understand their own progress and instructional needs.

And unlike norm-referenced standardized tests, the use of classroom-based assessments to inform curricular changes can provide specific directions for improving instruction. For example, teachers might work together to develop a rubric to evaluate students' writing samples. Teachers would then collect writing samples from all their students, score them using the rubric, and discuss the results with the other teachers and administrators in the school. This information might be used to make instructional adjustments to the writing curriculum or for particular students (Serafini, 1995). In some school systems teachers collect oral reading data during pre-specified time periods across the school year; often these assessments are referred to as benchmarks since they are used to mark progress and/or changes in student performance. Once these data are collected, they are aggregated (adding scores and determining school averages) to establish performance patterns and evaluate the effectiveness of the reading program.

Another use of classroom assessments is the sharing of assessment information with students so that teachers and students can work together to develop appropriate goals for learning. Collecting multiple forms of data across time with different assessment tools can help teachers, students, and parents feel more confident about instructional decisions.

Collecting multiple forms of information about a student's skills, strategies, interests, and background experiences invites teachers to construct knowledge about each student that is informed by the collected evidence. Imagine that a single piece of assessment data is a snapshot of a student's performance on a specific task at a particular point in time. By using multiple forms of assessment over time, the teacher is able to create a much more in-depth and accurate representation of a student's literacy strengths and needs, more like a photo album or even a video.

Appropriate Use of Assessments

In recognition of a need for multiple sources of assessment information, the International Reading Association in conjunction with the National Association of Teachers of English developed Standards for the Assessment of Reading and Writing (1994) (see Figure 8-1).

Using the International Reading Association Standards for the Assessment of Reading and Writing as an organizing framework, we suggest additional directions for enriching the classroom assessment process.

Assessments should be multidimensional, including a broad range of literacy tasks; be multimodal; and involve multiple literacies (Fehring, 2003). *Multimodal* refers to the multiple ways in which children and adolescents process information, that is, reading, writing, viewing, speaking, listening, drawing, and singing. There is strong evidence to support the use of art as a vehicle for learning and documenting learning. "Multiple choice answers and rote memorization do not adequately prepare students for the global marketplace. Art encourages children and adolescents to think critically, solve problems creatively, make evaluations, work within groups, and appreciate different points of view" (Cornett, 1999, p.1). All of the fine arts (e.g., writing lyrics, dance for text interpretations, dramatic performances) can be seen as ways of demonstrating comprehension and communicating what has been learned to others (Cornett, 2003).

Standards for the Assessment of Reading and Writing

1. The interests of the student are paramount in assessment.
2. The primary purpose of assessment is to improve teaching and learning.
3. Assessments must reflect and allow for critical inquiry into curriculum and instruction.
4. Assessments must recognize and reflect the intellectually and socially complex nature of reading and writing and the important roles of school, home, and society in literacy development.
5. Assessment must be fair and equitable.
6. The consequences of an assessment procedure are the first, and most important, consideration in establishing the validity of the assessment.
7. The teacher is the most important agent of assessment.
8. The assessment process should involve multiple perspectives and sources of data.
9. Assessment must be based in the school community.
10. All members of the education community—students, parents, teachers, administrators, policy makers, and the public—must have a voice in the development, interpretation, and reporting of assessment
11. Parents must be involved as active, essential participants in the assessment process.

Source: International Reading Association and National Council of Teachers of English Joint Task Force on Assessment, 1994.

Figure 8-1

Standards for Assessment

102

CHAPTER 8

*All Children
and Adolescents
Have the Right
to Appropriate
Reading
Assessments*

One of the authors and her colleague developed rubrics to guide evaluation of story information when assessing children's reading comprehension through illustration (Dasinger & Minor, 2004). Several children and adolescents who had difficulty retelling or writing about a story were able to document their understanding of the characters, setting, and the problem of the story with drawings. Teachers who used these rubrics told us that they provided important assessment information and acted as another window into the minds of their students. Children and adolescents can act out stories, create plays based on stories, write songs, create slide shows, and produce digital texts to document their learning (e.g., Damico with Riddle, 2006; Mahiri, 2006).

Multiliteracies, or New Literacies as they are sometimes called, extends the definition of literacy beyond traditional reading and written forms prevalent in the twentieth century (Street, 2003). Users of these expanded forms, such as new technologies, are required to adjust their skill and strategy use to accommodate these New Literacies. Today's students deal with gaming software, video technologies, Internet communities, search engines, and Web pages, to name a few (Leu, Kinzer, Coiro, & Cammack, 2004). (See Chapter 5 for a brief discussion of New Literacies.) If it is true that "What is tested is taught" it may be that teachers are not helping children and adolescents develop understandings and use of these New Literacies. Children and adolescents with teachers who teach them New Literacies and let them use these skills and strategies to document their learning will be at a distinct advantage as our society becomes more technologically advanced. Complex activities such as reading and writing are not easily assessed with multiple-choice or fill-in-the-blank assessments; instead, methods that require children and adolescents to apply their knowledge in multiple ways must be used. The arts and New Literacies can be incorporated into student projects that require application and higher-level thinking. The range of possibilities for such incorporation expand each day. One possibility includes the use of hypermedia. Hypermedia, using the definition in Meyers and Beach (2003), "is a combination of hypertext and multimedia that creates interactive experiences with media" (p. 245). Teachers who keep abreast of what's developing in hypertext and hypermedia possibilities expand their means to assess the multiple abilities of their students. A first place to look for information related to Storyspace, a tool useful for constructing text with other possibilities, is www.eastgate.com (Meyers & Beach, 2003).

Critical Inquiry into Curriculum and Instruction

In order to use assessments to improve instruction, many teachers across the country have become involved in professional learning communities (Darling-Hammond, 1998; Little, Gearhart, Curry, & Kafka, 2003; Seidel, 1998). These groups go by different names—Critical Friends (www.nsrfharmony.org/faq.html), Coalition of Essential Schools (www.essentialschools.org), or The Evidence Project (http://pzweb.harvard.edu/Research/Evidence.htm), but they have similar goals in that they examine student work and assessments to improve instruction. Participants discuss the work samples and assessments with their colleagues to receive productive feedback on their professional practice.

While looking at student work has always been a part of teaching, these professional learning communities emphasize the collective wisdom of groups of teachers and administrators that can inform the analysis of student performance and for adjusting instruction (Little et al., 2003). Members of these groups can check the alignment among learning outcomes, instruction, and assessments schoolwide (Seidel, 1998). There is also the potential for a consistent and all-school focus on issues of equity as participants work to increase the achievement of all students, especially those with diverse cultural and linguistic backgrounds. Participants learn specific protocols that help teachers focus on the important aspects of student work. For example, structured guidelines for discussion can help a teacher keep data on student participation to ensure that all students are engaged in classroom conversations.

Teaching has often been described as "solitary practice"; however, there is a growing understanding that a powerful collaboration and professional development can be achieved while looking at student work. The group must be a collaborative, integrated, ongoing project, and schools must organize for it. Also, teachers must be willing to put aside their personal comfort and be prepared to offer constructive feedback in order for the community to be effective. When teachers discuss student work and the instruments used to score them, there is potential for tremendous professional growth. For additional information on learning communities visit these websites: www.lasw.org, www.nsrfharmony.org, and www.pz.harvard.edu/research/evidence.htm.

Students and Parents as Important Stakeholders in Assessment

The consequences of assessment are too important to leave out two key stakeholders—students and their parents. Children and adolescents are the ones who have the most to gain or lose from assessment, but they are often excluded from the assessment process. However, it is important to provide many opportunities for children and adolescents to self-assess. Self-assessment by students can increase their self-esteem and motivation to read and write. Self-assessment leads to goal setting and self-direction. Self-assessment provides students with feedback that keeps them motivated and persistent in the pursuit of their goals. According to Gibbons (2004), "Self-direction is immobile without self-motivation and blind without self-assessment" (p. 464).

There are several ways children and adolescents can self-assess their literacy development and set personal goals. Students can keep book logs where they record how many books they have read as well as their favorite authors and illustrators (DeVries, 2004). Skill logs such as self-monitoring logs can help children and adolescents become conscious of the strategies they use or neglect when reading and decide which strategies they want to learn to improve their reading (Lenski, Wham, & Johns, 1999). A self-assessment for writing and spelling can be found in *Guided Readers and Writers (Grades 3–6): Teaching Comprehension, Genre, and Content Literacy* (Fountas & Pinnell, 2001); these criteria can be adjusted for students to assess their reading skills and strategies. Such assessments invite students to reflect on their growth as writers (and readers) and set goals for improvement.

103

CHAPTER 8
*All Children
and Adolescents
Have the Right
to Appropriate
Reading
Assessments*

CHAPTER 8

*All Children
and Adolescents
Have the Right
to Appropriate
Reading
Assessments*

It is important for parents to understand how and why their children and adolescents are being assessed and what can be learned from these assessments (Fredericks & Rasinski, 1990). There is a large body of research documenting the importance of parental involvement in supporting children's reading achievement (Rasinski & Padak, 2000; Sheldon & Epstein, 2002). While parents are often encouraged to become involved at school and to help with school work at home, there is limited discussion of the role parents should play in the assessment of their children and adolescents. We do know that when teachers communicate with parents concerning expectations for students and how their children and adolescents will be assessed, parents feel positive about working as partners with educators to improve learning (Guskey, 2003).

How can teachers communicate student performance standards and methods of assessment to parents? While newsletters and introductory letters are important, family nights and parental workshops related to assessment and evaluation can be more effective. During these sessions teachers can give examples of the standards, the assessments that will be used to assess those standards, and what the parents can do at home to help their children and adolescents meet the standards. This also gives the parents opportunities to ask questions. Scheduling a conference time for each family can be extremely useful for building common understandings and goals. For an excellent discussion of parental involvement and some guidelines for parent conferences see *Literacy Assessment and Intervention for the Elementary Classroom* (DeVries, 2004).

Why Is the Right to Appropriate Reading Assessments Important for Children and Adolescents?

There appears to be a "blame the victim" (the student) mentality in many public schools today (Hoover, 2005). Teachers are under tremendous pressure to raise test scores on norm-referenced standardized tests. Lack of student reading achievement is often blamed on children's socioeconomic status, differences in language patterns, or limited parental involvement. In addition, instead of receiving effective interventions, students are often retained in grade or placed in special education classrooms as a consequence of low test scores. Both practices have been shown to be ineffective for many children and adolescents (Allington & McGill-Franzen, 1995). Research indicates that teachers who monitor student achievement through ongoing classroom assessment can provide high-quality instruction based on students' strengths and needs, and guide students to high levels of achievement regardless of cultural and linguistic differences or socioeconomic status.

Some teachers think that the way to raise student reading achievement is to "teach to the test." This practice may show a short-term increase in test scores, but does not provide students with the higher-level literacy skills necessary for success in today's society. It has been said that what gets assessed is what gets taught, but we believe that teachers must continue to provide students with a rich curriculum that prepares them for our complex society, not just to pass tests. If children and adolescents are not succeeding on literacy tasks, teachers must critically evaluate the curriculum

105

CHAPTER 8

*All Children
and Adolescents
Have the Right
to Appropriate
Reading
Assessments*

Assessment results should inform instruction.

and methods of instruction (Allinder, Fuchs, & Fuchs, 1998) instead of spending excessive amounts of instructional time teaching to the test.

How Can the Right to Appropriate Reading Assessments Become a Reality in Today's Schools?

The appropriate use of literacy assessments is complex. As teachers, we must recognize that different assessments provide different kinds of information and are intended for different audiences. Norm-referenced standardized assessments are designed for the purposes of school accountability. They serve purposes such as description of achievement trends, school liability, school funding, and documentation of student achievement. The primary purpose of classroom assessment should be to determine students' strengths and needs and to help teachers improve their instruction. However, in all cases of assessment our primary focus should be on what is best for students. Are the assessments we use fair and equitable? Do they recognize and reflect the intellectually and socially complex nature of reading and writing? Do the assessments lead to improved teaching and learning? What are the consequences of the assessment for students and teachers? How valid and reliable are the assessments,

106

CHAPTER 8

*All Children
and Adolescents
Have the Right
to Appropriate
Reading
Assessments*

and are they being used appropriately? The following are some things you can do as a teacher to ensure the appropriate use of literacy assessments.

Putting Ideas into Action

At this point would you respond differently to Jonathan's letter than you did when you first read it? Now that you have read and discussed this chapter, use the following ideas to reflect on your own views about the right of all children and adolescents to have appropriate reading assessments:

- Become knowledgeable about the limitations of norm-referenced standardized tests and learn how to correctly interpret them and discuss the results with students, parents, and administrators. A good first place to start is the manuals that accompany the test. Read the manuals with colleagues. These provide useful information related to the appropriate and inappropriate uses of the test as well as information related to the validity, reliability, and the norming process and population.
- Take a standard instructional practice, perhaps writing a research report. How do you currently assess the report? How might you use multiple forms of assessment? For example, Carol Anderson Gibson and Debra J. Coffey designed a unit for high school students titled, "A Biography Study: Using Role-Play to Explore Authors' Lives," which uses multiple assessment methods. These include a timeline rubric, an author panel presentation rubric, checklists, peer editing, reading logs, and K-W-L- S charts. To review the unit and the assessments, go to www.readwritethink.org/lessons/lesson_view .asp?id=398 (retrieved October 19, 2006).
- Learn how to develop high-quality classroom assessments and scoring rubrics (Arter & McTighe, 2001). Teachers find the Internet a useful source for rubrics. Two helpful sites are http://edweb.sdsu.edu/webquest/rubrics/ weblessons.htm and http://rubistar.4teachers.org. Both sites provide templates teachers or students can use to create rubrics for a specific need. For example the second site provides templates for rubrics to assess: essays, research reports, lab reports, oral presentations, and online participation.
- Critically evaluate the assessments you use for cultural bias. Asa Hilliard, a psychologist and historian, has devoted much of his professional efforts arguing and critiquing the use of norm-referenced standardized assessments to evaluate the academic ability of African American students. His extensive writings on this topic began in the 1970s and continues to this day. One of his main arguments is that the tests we use have not been normed on African American populations as a group but rather includes them as a small proportion of the larger norming population. Join colleagues to study issues related to test bias.
- Allow students to self-assess on a consistent basis. One strategy middle and high school teachers find useful when assessing writing is Read-Around Groups (RAG) (Gossard, 1987). Gossard, a high school English teacher, uses RAG with her high school students throughout the writing of a paper. For ex-

ample, early in the writing process, students, organized into groups of four, read drafts of each other's paper, and examined how they introduced their writing. They continued to read and respond to each other's work throughout the writing process. At the conclusion of the written assignment, they read final drafts to review for editing, for example, issues, spelling, punctuation.

- Ask students to identify what makes good writing. Following a RAG activity, ask students to review a set of papers identified as examples of excellent papers. Students examine these papers and identify characteristics that distinguish these papers. As the teacher, you can identify categories; e.g., organization, voice, awareness of audience, to structure your students' review.
- Join a learning community. Work with colleagues to improve student learning. For example, you might form your own RAG with colleagues. Like Ms. Gossard's high school students, combine your expertise with others' to determine areas in which students in your school excel in writing and areas to strengthen. As they say, "Two heads are better than one."

*D*ISCUSSION QUESTIONS FOR STUDY GROUPS

1. What norm-referenced standardized tests are used in the school where you teach? What are the purposes of the tests? How are the results used? Are those uses appropriate—why or why not? What strengths do the tests offer; what limitations do they have? What insights can you draw about how you use scores from these tests in your school and classroom?

2. Most teacher candidates must take and pass one or more norm-referenced standardized test to be accepted for teacher certification. Reflect back on your own certification testing. What did the test measure effectively? What aspects of teaching was the test unable to measure? What do you think is the real purpose of these tests? How did you feel while preparing for and taking the test? By reflecting on your own experiences with standardized tests, what insights can you gain about standardized testing that you can apply to your own school and classroom?

3. Identify a unit of instruction you teach, and discuss the ways you use assessment in that unit. Do your methods of assessment allow you to learn about the most important aspects of student performance related to the unit? If not, what additional classroom assessments might you add to the unit to do a more thorough job of identifying students' strengths and needs in relation to the unit?

All Children and Adolescents Have the Right to Schools That Create a Climate for All to Learn

Dear Principal,

Thank you for helping us get down with high school. Before you came I used to think "What's up with this school?" Some of the teachers didn't care if we came to school or not and when we were here, they didn't seem to care if we learned anything. Kids would be loud and talking to each other and the teacher didn't say nothing. The walls of the classrooms were dirty and the halls were loaded with trash. Most of the computers in the rooms didn't work and the library computers were just as bad. It seemed that nobody cared about us so most of the kids didn't care either. Since you been here all that has changed. The teachers talk about important stuff—they say, "Keep stupid people out your ear. Who you hang with is what you're becoming. Start being what you want to be now by studying it." Most of the kids want to be here and they stay to graduate. You changed it all.

Sincerely,

Jamal, grade 9

CHAPTER 9

*All Children
and Adolescents
Have the Right
to Schools That
Create a Climate
for All to Learn*

*I*t is hard to believe that there are schools in America like the one Jamal described in his letter. But all across America there are high schools and middle schools that are physically run-down and neglected where students have no hope for the future because no one gives them the tools they need nor the encouragement to succeed (McNeely, Nonnemaker, & Blum, 2002). Jonathan Kozol (1995, 2005, 2006) describes many schools like these in poor sections of the South Bronx in New York as the "grimmest" schools he's ever seen. At Morris High, there is mold growing on the walls and the odors in the bathrooms are so terrible that the girls won't use them. They run home to use the bathroom as fast as they can after school, and if they can't wait until after school, they leave early. The students at Taft High School in the Bronx have such low self-esteem that they degradingly refer to Taft High as a place for "Training Animals for Tomorrow" (Kozol, 1995, p. 152). Many students each year are expelled from school for a variety of violations including poor attendance and violent behavior. Of the 1,436 children enrolled in the ninth grade in segregated New York schools during one academic year, six years later 80 percent had not graduated from high school. These schools lack a healthy school climate (Freiberg, 1998; Wagner & Masden-Copas, 2002). However, a positive school climate involves much more than just the physical environment. A positive school climate includes elements such as respectful relationships; safe, clean, and secure learning environments; and instructional priorities that support students and treats them as capable individuals (Freiberg & Stein, 1999).

While some schools have unhealthy or unsupportive climates such as the one described by Jamal in his letter at the beginning of this chapter, other schools across America are beating the odds by creating positive, supportive school environments (Biancarosa & Snow, 2004). These schools are sometimes referred to as 90-90-90 schools, in that they have more than 90 percent of students eligible for free and reduced lunch, a common indicator of low-income families; more than 90 percent of students from ethnic minorities; and more than 90 percent of students met or achieved high academic standards according to independently conducted tests of academic achievement (Reeves, 2000). These schools provide evidence to refute the commonly held belief that there is an unalterable correlation among poverty, ethnicity, and academic achievement factors. What is it about these schools and their climate that enables them to foster high levels of engagement and learning even when most of the students face challenges associated with poverty and discrimination? In this chapter, we describe factors contributing to a positive climate within effective schools, including those identified as 90-90-90 schools. As you read about the attributes of a positive school climate, compare those attributes to those of your own school climate. Think about how your school climate measures up to some of the best. How might you bring about changes that respond to the *right of all children and adolescents to a school climate that supports their learning?*

School climate has been defined in a variety of ways. Some researchers define school climate as: (1) the extent to which discipline problems affect a school (Esposito, 1999); (2) psychological factors in the school context affecting student learning and well-being, such as encouragement of the development of academic and social values among students (Kelley et al., 1986); (3) control of school management issues, positive staff attitudes, and school effectiveness (Wolf, Borko, Elliott, & McIver, 2000); or (4) a physical environment that is "welcoming and conducive to

110
....

CHAPTER 9

*All Children
and Adolescents
Have the Right
to Schools That
Create a Climate
for All to Learn*

learning" (Tableman, 2004). Alfie Kohn (1996) describes an ideal school climate as "one that promotes deep understanding, excitement about learning, and social as well as intellectual growth" (p. 54). Some of these factors are discussed further in Chapters 1 (caring, competent, highly qualified teacher), 3 (culturally relevant literacy instruction), and 7 (reading experiences that create a passion for reading and learning). Some educators include the infusion of technology as necessary for creating an effective school climate for learning (Peck, Cuban, & Kirkpatrick, 2002) because it provides opportunities to access rich sources of information and a different modality for learning. However it is defined, we know that many factors influence school climate and school effectiveness. And when these factors are part of the school fabric, they have a positive impact on teaching and student learning (Goddard, Sweetland, & Hoy, 2000; Smylie, Lazarus, & Brownlee-Conyers, 1996).

We believe that teacher factors and organizational factors make up school climate, with the school principal being primarily responsible for organizational issues. Teachers and literacy coaches also share the responsibility for creating a school climate in which all children and adolescents can learn. A review of research indicates that five general conditions contribute to supportive climates in effective schools: (1) strong leadership; (2) high teacher expectations for student achievement; (3) balance between emphasis on basic skills and higher-order thinking skills; (4) orderly environment, and (5) frequent, systematic evaluations of students (Astuto & Clark, 1985; Bossert, 1988). Stringfield and Herman (1996) identified similar characteristics when they observed in schools with positive climates and high academic achievement but also described what they called an "academic push" by administrators and teachers. An academic push or emphasis is the "extent to which a drive for academic excellence contributes to the behavioral and environmental press of the school" (Goddard, Sweetland, & Hoy, 2000, p. 684). In addition, teachers in these schools believe that students are capable of high levels of achievement. (We discuss the importance of teacher beliefs in Chapter 2.)

Positive student behaviors, such as engagement and expressing interest in reading, are associated with a positive school climate that includes this "academic push" (Goddard et al., 2000). In such schools, students work hard to succeed and respect others who do the same. They complete homework, make provisions to receive extra help from teachers, and seek assignments to receive extra credit. In schools with positive climates, both teachers and students plan more, are persistent, accept responsibility for achievement, and overcome temporary setbacks. And an academic emphasis within classes and across the school conveys that schools are organized to support students and their learning (Teddlie & Reynolds, 2000).

Another important consideration for a positive school climate is school connectedness (McNeely et al., 2002). Students with school connectedness feel cared for by the adults at school. They are encouraged to make decisions and to be self-managing. In smaller schools and schools with discipline policies that involve students in setting goals, students have higher levels of school connectedness. A high level of participation in extracurricular activities is also highly correlated with a feeling of school connectedness. Administrators in a school program that increased school connectedness and promoted self-discipline found that after one year there was a 30 percent to 100 percent decrease in discipline referrals, depending on the level of implementation (Freiberg, 1989).

An example of how to foster school connectedness is provided by Dennis Loftus, a principal in the Syracuse City School District in New York (Curtis, 2005). Curtis uses an activity called "2 by 10." He chooses a student who he knows is having behavioral or academic problems to talk with informally for two minutes on ten consecutive days. He asks about their families, how they are doing, and the sources of their concerns. He believes that these students are often seeking attention and that this positive attention helps them establish a relationship with someone that they can go to when they have difficulties. He believes that children and adolescents will work hard for someone they think likes and cares about them. He has seen positive results from this approach to making connections with each student. Many other activities for developing connections that affect a positive school climate can be found at the website for Discipline with Dignity: www.disciplineassociates.com/dwd.htm.

In the recent *Reading Next* report, Biancarosa and Snow (2004) cited fifteen elements of effective adolescent literacy programs. These elements were divided into organizational and instructional factors. Several of the organizational factors they cited were related to school climate. For example, they noted the importance of school leaders who have a solid understanding of how to teach reading and writing in ways that make connections to the diverse population of students in today's schools. To enhance instruction, they recognized the importance of a comprehensive and coordinated literacy program that is interdisciplinary and interdepartmental and coordinates with the local community. They concluded that teacher teams should meet regularly to discuss student progress and to coordinate the curriculum so that students are receiving explicit and individualized instruction in comprehension strategies using content-area material. Additional key elements are the use of technology,

Relationships are an important part of a positive school climate.

CHAPTER 9

*All Children
and Adolescents
Have the Right
to Schools That
Create a Climate
for All to Learn*

ongoing formative assessment of students, and extended time for literacy—all elements that can foster high engagement and appropriate instruction within a healthy, productive school climate.

A positive school climate can also be supported or undermined by district level administration (Teddlie & Stringfield, 1993). Although efforts to create and maintain a positive climate at the school level have the most direct impact on student learning, boards of education and district staff must be actively engaged in supporting such efforts (Chrispeels, 2002). In describing the California Center for Effective Schools and its partnership with the Oxnard School district, Chrispeels cites the establishment of a district leadership team as an essential element of a school improvement process that has a positive impact on school climate. This leadership team should have the capacity to collect and analyze achievement data, involve teachers and administrators in developing action plans that lead to a redesign of instruction where needed and to implementing instruction that is both standards based and appropriate for the particular student population.

While these studies serve as a review of the characteristics of effective schools with a positive school climate, there are additional characteristics that have been identified within 90-90-90 schools where, because of large populations of poor and minority students, some might expect low levels of achievement (Education Trust, 2006). A series of studies was conducted in Milwaukee public schools using test data collected from over 130,000 students in 228 elementary, middle, and high school buildings from 1995 to 1998 (Reeves, 2000, 2005). An analysis of these data yielded some characteristics of 90-90-90 schools that were consistent across locations. These common characteristics were:

- a focus on academic achievement,
- clear curriculum choices,
- frequent assessment of student progress and multiple opportunities for improvement,
- an emphasis on nonfiction writing, and
- collaborative scoring of student work. (Reeves, 2005, p. 365)

These 90-90-90 schools had what was described as a "laser-like" focus on student achievement (Reeves, 2000, p. 187). The walls of the school were lined with charts, graphs, and tables displaying improvement in student test scores. The schools identified five areas in which to focus on improvement, rather than a lengthy list of unfocused efforts. The message to students seemed to be "It's not how you start here that matters, but how you finish" (p. 187). Some students who struggled with reading and writing received up to three hours a day in literacy interventions. One of the most interesting facts was no specific intervention program was used across schools, nor was there any consistent use of expensive programs. *Student success appeared to be the result of replicable professional practices implemented by caring, highly qualified teachers.* The emphasis that 90-90-90 schools place on student achievement is coupled with the supports needed for helping students succeed. This combination of high expectations and various forms of support interact to create a climate where students are engaged and successful because they and their teachers believe success is possible and they work hard to make it happen. More information about additional 90-90-90 schools can be accessed at www2.edtrust.org and www.just4kids.org. At this latter website, authors provide a self-assessment measure for viewers to examine how their schools compare with these high-performing schools.

Although cited as an important component of school climate by some (Biancarosa & Snow, 2004; Peck, Cuban, & Kirkpatrick, 2002), the impact of technology is not prominent in most descriptions of school climate. (Refer to Chapter 5 for an in-depth discussion of the role of technology in middle and high schools.) It appears from a review of the literature that there are mixed results about the impact of technology on student achievement, attitudes, and climate (Schlacter, 1999). James Kulik (1994) conducted a meta-analysis of over five hundred research studies of computer-based instruction, including tutorial, drill and practice, and Integrated Learning Systems. Kulik found that, on average, students who used computer-based instruction scored at the 64th percentile on standardized reading achievement tests compared to students in the control conditions without computers who scored at the 50th percentile. Student data indicated more positive attitudes, however, toward classes that used technology.

Baker, Gearhart, and Herman (1994) assessed the impact of interactive technologies on learning in five schools in four different states. They found no significant difference on the standardized tests scores for vocabulary, comprehension, mathematical concepts, or study skills between those students who did not have access to computers or to teaching and learning reforms implemented in Apple Classrooms of Tomorrow schools and those students who did. Student attitudes were not assessed. Overall, it could be that opportunities to use technology are viewed positively by students, but more information is needed to differentiate how students rate particular technology applications according to interest (e.g., access to online discussion groups versus producing digital texts) and how specific applications may have a differential impact on student engagement and learning within different content areas.

Let's now look at several examples of schools that foster positive climates even in the face of challenging situations. Norview High School in Norfolk, Virginia, is a high-poverty urban school working to improve student reading achievement and to narrow the achievement gap between Caucasian and minority students (Norview High School Report Card, 2004/2005). Seventy-two percent of its students come from minority groups, and 54 percent are eligible for subsidized lunch. In this school, the teachers formed teams to review the state standards, adopt shared curriculum guides, and review student work. They developed common assessments to compare and analyze school assessment data. Norview teachers used challenging, relevant texts to motivate students to read and taught specific comprehension strategies when needed. In 2004, 93 percent of students passed the state reading and writing exams. High engagement in school projects and learning activities was observed. The achievement gap was cut in half in almost every subject. Additional information is available at the school website at http://cf.nps.k12.va.us/.

Another school that has turned challenges into opportunities to create a positive, productive school climate is Horizonte High School in Utah (Andersen, Floisand, Martinez, & Robinson, 1997). The school population of 1,800 is 45 percent Latino, with the other 55 percent comprising Pacific Islanders, African Americans, Asians, Eastern Europeans, and Native Americans. Most of the students had been unsuccessful at other schools. In this school, kindness and respect for cultural differences are the hallmarks. The school offers the students many choices including the ability to select their own schedules and teachers. Students meet in student-parent-advisor teams to set goals. There is an emphasis on service learning and integrating the

114

....

CHAPTER 9

*All Children
and Adolescents
Have the Right
to Schools That
Create a Climate
for All to Learn*

curriculum. For example, archaeological digs have been used to teach math, social studies, science, English, and humanities. Horizonte High School has posted impressive performance gains (Andersen et al., 1997). Ninety percent of the school's students passed the Salt Lake City School District writing competency test. Students with ethnic-minority and low socioeconomic backgrounds who had been at Horizonte for one or more years achieved the greatest Scholastic Assessment Test (SAT) performance gains among secondary schools in the district.

Recovering the Gifted Child Academy on Chicago's West Side (Pool & Hawk, 1997) has created a positive school climate that emphasizes achievement, success, and responsibility. The school, founded in 1990, has 45 African American students in grades 4 through 7. These children live in poverty and have not been successful in other schools because of reported behavior problems, truancy, disrupted family life, homelessness, drugs, child abuse, and other problems. However, in spite of these challenges, the school boasts of increased reading scores, higher overall test scores, and higher graduation rates when compared to other public schools. The academy is run like a business. Students go to school from 8:15 A.M. to 5:00 P.M., business dress is required, students complete time cards, and students receive paychecks with "school money." The money comes from student-run businesses and partnerships. According to the school's founder, Corla Hawkins, a caring environment and parent involvement are the keys to the success of the academy. She stated that an unwillingness to let any child fail is the mission of the school, and this belief forms the foundation of the academy's positive school climate.

Another model, the Consistency Management and Cooperative Discipline, strives to promote caring, supportive classrooms and schools that create a climate for learning through the emphasis of democratic principles. The more than ten thousand K through 12 classrooms in Texas where this program is implemented are described as "people centered." Teachers strive to prevent discipline problems by developing a sense of community, where students share ownership of classroom duties, self-regulation is encouraged, and the emphasis is on intrinsic rewards. Longitudinal studies of the project show that students of teachers in low-performing, inner-city schools who use the program earned scores significantly higher on national standardized tests and state-criterion reference tests than comparison students. Furthermore, four years after implementing the program, there were significant differences in how students viewed their learning environments based on survey data. Discipline referrals were down in all schools using the program and the rate of suspensions five years after the implementation of the program was half that of nonprogram schools.

What should one expect to see in a classroom where the climate promotes learning? The elements of caring, kindness, and respect are highly visible in the classrooms of the schools we describe. These elements foster trust and knowledge that teachers are supportive; they are in direct contrast to the emphasis on control and obedience found in too many classrooms today, especially at the middle and high school levels (Freiberg, 1996). Additionally, Alfie Kohn (1996) specifies attention to the setup of the physical environment (so that work areas facilitate interaction and collaboration), positive displays of student work, a clean and orderly environment, teachers working directly with small groups and individual students, and students asking questions and frequently initiating discussions.

How can educators assess their school climate to determine strengths and areas for improvement? Freiberg (1998) suggests using entrance and exit interviews, stu-

*All Children
and Adolescents
Have the Right
to Schools That
Create a Climate
for All to Learn*

A positive classroom enviornment is caring and collaborative.

dent concern surveys, and ambient noise checklists to determine if a school has a healthy climate. His School Climate Survey assesses students' perceptions of: (1) achievement motivation, (2) fairness, (3) order and discipline, (4) parent involvement, (5) sharing of resources, (6) student interpersonal relationships, and (7) student-teacher relationships. He asserts that these elements, or the lack thereof, influences student behavior. For example, he argues that students can become aggressive when noise levels are high. Freiberg states that if adults want to assess the school climate, they should also ask themselves whether they enjoy being in the climate of their school.

If we look at the common characteristics of schools with positive climates, we can see that they embody the correlates of the Effective Schools movement. The original correlates were discussed by Ronald Edmonds in an article published in 1979. Since that time, there have been many research studies to support the correlates of effective schools (Hoffman, 1991; Shavelson & Berliner, 1988). The most current version of specific attributes of schools with positive climates include:

- a clearly stated and focused school mission,
- a safe and orderly climate/physical environment for learning,
- high expectations for students, teachers, and administrators,
- opportunities to learn and student time-on-task,
- instructional leadership by all administrators and staff members,
- frequent monitoring of student progress,
- ongoing curriculum improvement based on assessment results, and
- positive home/school relations.

116

·······························

CHAPTER 9

*All Children
and Adolescents
Have the Right
to Schools That
Create a Climate
for All to Learn*

Why Is the Right to Schools That Create a Climate for All to Learn Important for Children and Adolescents?

The quality of the school climate can have serious positive or negative consequences for children and adolescents. When students attend schools with negative or even toxic climates, such as those described by Kozol (2005), the outcomes can be devastating, as students question their very value as human beings when attending filthy, poorly equipped, overcrowded, and unsafe schools. On the other hand, schools with healthy, positive climates impact students in favorable ways, such as increased engagement and achievement, as illustrated by the 90-90-90 schools described earlier in this chapter. School climate influences whether students are engaged and able to learn to their full potentials. Climate also influences whether students will stay in school, graduate from high school, and go on to college. All children and adolescents deserve to attend schools with positive climates that allow them to learn, prosper, and dream of the futures they wish to pursue.

What Can You Do to Promote a Positive School Climate Where All Students Can Learn?

As supported by our previous discussion, teacher and organizational factors influence school climate. Think about Jamal's letter and how an enhancement in school climate improved the students' belief that they could be successful and encouraged them to come to school. If you believe that a positive school climate ensures all children will be given an opportunity to learn, think of ways to improve the climate in your school. Listed are some ideas for you to consider:

- Use Alfie Kohn's (1996) checklist for assessing a positive classroom climate to evaluate your own classroom and school and then set goals for improvement.
- Use Freiberg's (1998) School Climate Survey to assess students' perceptions of school climate. Use the findings to identify strengths and areas where additional work is needed. Create a team to develop an action plan for addressing aspects of the climate that need improvement. The team should include administrators, teachers, students, parents, and community members to ensure that the voices of all important stakeholders are included in the process.
- Create a warm, inviting classroom environment where students feel respected, valued, and significant. Providing time for students to share their ideas, offering student choice, seeking student input on classroom decisions, and demonstrating respect in your words and actions will provide a foundation for such an environment.
- Read additional information about the Consistency Management and Cooperative Discipline model from the Discipline with Dignity program. Make changes to bring about a more democratic atmosphere in your classroom where the students have a sense of ownership and self-regulation is empha-

sized. Consult the following website for more information www.ed.gov/pubs/ToolsforSchools/cmcd.html.

117

CHAPTER 9

*All Children
and Adolescents
Have the Right
to Schools That
Create a Climate
for All to Learn*

- Build school connectedness (McNeely et al., 2002) by reaching out to students in your classes through informal discussions in the hallways, honest and open classroom discussions, extracurricular activities, and techniques such as "2 by 10" (Curtis, 2005) described in this chapter.
- At the beginning of the school year, get to know all students' names quickly, call them by name, and greet them each time you see them in and out of school. Use interest inventories, questionnaires, or open-ended writing activities to learn about your students' interests, goals, and lives. Use this information to build relationships with your students.
- Check to see if you are doing all you can to encourage parental involvement. Call parents or send notes home when students are doing well. Seek ways to develop partnerships with parents and deepen their involvement in their children's education. (See Chapter 10 for additional ideas to encourage parent involvement.)
- Look at the physical condition of your school. Enlist the help of parent groups and student clubs and organizations to clean or paint the school or improve the school grounds. Ask the principal to add "homey touches" to the school such as plants and flowers, artwork, bird feeders and birdhouses, and comfortable lobby furniture.
- Check your attitude toward students of color and students from poor socioeconomic backgrounds. Do you truly hold the same high expectations for all the children in your classroom? Do you provide the support needed to help all students make progress toward those high expectations?
- Analyze your classroom curriculum. Do you have a balance between basic skills and higher-order thinking skills? Do you incorporate art, music, and movement into your lessons to create interest and reach students with varying learning strengths?
- Establish leadership teams or learning communities, if you are a literacy coach, where the teachers and administrators meet together to make instructional decisions. If you are not a literacy coach, encourage your literacy coach or administrator to develop such a learning community. Work to improve the communication in your building so the entire staff is "on the same page" regarding priorities and key goals.
- Help develop a cohesive reading program and encourage your administrators to continue the program long enough to evaluate its effectiveness. Ask yourself and others if the components of your reading program build on and support each other or are they just fragmented programs with no cohesion.
- Evaluate critically the use of technology in your school. Are there sufficient computers in the classrooms and are they in good condition? Is there a variety of software used for drill and practice, simulation, and higher-order thinking skills? Are learners matched appropriately to technology based on their learning needs? Are the teachers trained to match learners to technology?
- Assess learners so that appropriate instruction can be provided for all students. Are learners assessed in a frequent, systematic manner? Does your school district have a data collection system that enables your school to make data-driven decisions?

118

CHAPTER 9

*All Children
and Adolescents
Have the Right
to Schools That
Create a Climate
for All to Learn*

• Examine how you and your fellow educators feel about the climate at your school. Ask yourselves, is this a place we enjoy spending time? Would we want our own children to attend this school? Why or why not? Students can sense when their teachers are unhappy in their schools. If we want children and adolescents to feel safe, secure, and valued in their schools, educators must also feel this way themselves. Explore ways to build positive feelings among the school staff about your school (e.g., open forums for discussions, team-building activities, and shared leadership).

Putting Ideas into Action

Although the role of school climate in the effectiveness of schools is complex, it is worth evaluating. How do your classroom and school rate in the area of school climate? Does your school feel like there is an atmosphere of kindness and caring? Is there an atmosphere of academic emphasis or push? Is your school successful with those students who have difficulty in traditional school settings? Positive school climate may be the important element that helps students improve literacy achievement, graduate from high school, go on to college, and become productive members of our democratic society.

*D*ISCUSSION QUESTIONS FOR STUDY GROUPS

1. Are there any schools in your district or state that are considered 90-90-90 schools? What specific practices have they implemented? What ideas from these 90-90-90 schools can you apply to your own building?

2. What is your feeling about the practice of posting charts that show improvements in test scores in the halls? What would be the benefit of this practice?

What might be the danger of this practice?

3. Policy makers and educators rate school performance according to different criteria. Access at least three different websites identified in this chapter to determine how your school is rated. Analyze the results and set goals to address any areas that require improvement.

All Children and Adolescents Have the Right to an Education That Involves Their Families and Communities in Meaningful Ways

Dear Teacher,

I don't want to hurt your feelings, but everything we read and do in class is pointless to me. I know you have to teach us certain books and how to write term papers. But I wonder why we can't read books with characters we can identify with. Why can't we talk about current books, movies, TV shows, and world events that are real to us? When my mom asks, "What are you studying in English class?" she's surprised that I'm reading the exact same books she did when she was in high school. She even admitted that she didn't understand Chaucer's Canterbury Tales too much so she can't help me figure out what I'm supposed to know for the test. Can't we just read or study something that matters in my life or that relates to the world I live in?

Your Student,

Amber, grade 11

CHAPTER 10

*All Children
and Adolescents
Have the Right to
an Education That
Involves Their
Families and
Communities in
Meaningful Ways*

*A*mber works hard in school, and she is an average student. Her mother, Judy, is a single parent who works long hours as a nurse's assistant. Amber dreams of going to college to study business, but she has many challenges facing her. In addition to the typical issues of limited finances and admission tests, Amber will be the first person in her entire family to ever go to college. She also knows very few people who have attended college, let alone graduated. Judy works hard to save money to help pay for Amber's college tuition, but she is concerned that she can't help Amber with studying for classes or her preparation for college admissions tests. Judy is worried that Amber seems less interested and motivated to do her homework and to complete her assigned readings than in previous years, but she doesn't know what she can do to help. When Amber shows her mother her books, class notes, and assignments, Judy finds them dull and unrelated to Amber's life, or to the life of any typical teenager, but she doesn't say this to Amber. Judy wonders, however, what she can do to help Amber become more connected to her schoolwork and be successful so she can pursue her dream of going to college.

We believe that in order to make schooling relevant and effective, *all children and adolescents have the right to an education that involves their families and communities in meaningful ways.* This right is important, but it becomes challenging to put into action as students move beyond the primary grades because the curriculum shifts to content that may be far removed from the lived experiences of students and their families. In addition, as students mature, the roles that parents play in their lives and their education change (Catsambis, 1998). What, then, can we do to reach out and involve families in the learning of their sons and daughters? How can teachers incorporate the strengths, experiences, and talents of families and community members into the curriculum? What are the outcomes on student achievement for making such connections? In this chapter we will draw on ideas from our previous research, including extensive interviews with students and their parents, the professional literature, and our experiences as teachers and parents to address these questions.

Family Involvement and Education

All children and adolescents live in the nested contexts of their families, communities, and cultures (Enomoto, 1997; Heath, 1983). Their learning, literacy, socialization patterns, language, and worldviews are shaped and influenced by the lives they lead (González, Moll, & Amanti, 2005; Schultz & Hull, 2002). In other words, Amber, who lives in a small apartment with her mother in a low-income part of a large city, is influenced by her interactions with her mother and other family members, by her culture, and by her community. Amber's classmate Roberto lives in another part of the city that is mainly populated by immigrants, and the unique aspects of his family, neighborhood, culture, and language shape his life. Another classmate, Shanette, lives with her mother and stepfather in a condominium in a trendy neighborhood on the north side of the city. Shanette is also affected by her culture, family, and community as they interact to shape who she is, what she believes, and the choices she makes. While Amber, Roberto, and Shanette are enrolled in the same eleventh-grade English class and are expected to complete the same readings and assignments, the perspectives, lived experiences, and family expectations and support they bring to their school tasks differ widely. One common thread, however, is that Amber, Roberto, and Shanette all question how what they study in school relates to their lives. And another thread connects their families as they worry about how to support, encourage, motivate, and help their children succeed in school (Rudney, 2005).

The National Educational Goals Panel (1994) stated in Goal 8 that "By the year 2000, every school will promote partnerships that will increase parent involvement and participation in promoting the social, emotional, and academic growth of children." We are well beyond the year 2000, and this goal has not been met in the lives of Amber, Roberto, Shanette, or countless other children and adolescents. A national survey of teachers conducted by Metropolitan Life Insurance Company (1998) concluded that students perceive parent involvement in education as helpful, productive, and supportive. In addition, this survey indicated that teachers felt parents viewed their involvement as important to the success of their children and adolescents. Furthermore, the survey found that teachers typically felt that family involvement in education was important and contributed to students' success in school. While it is clear that students, parents, and teachers value the contributions that families make to students' learning and success in school, the issue of family involvement in education is complex and fraught with challenges.

The cultural expectations that families have for schools and teachers differ from one family to the next. For example, in some Latino families, like Roberto's, the teacher is perceived as the authority on schooling and families tend to see their job as taking care of issues at home rather than interfering with what happens at school (Carger, 1996; Valdés, 1996). This might be the clearest explanation for why Roberto's mother and father have not attended his school's open house or requested a conference with his science teacher even though he had difficulty all semester in his advanced chemistry class. They do, however, talk to him about school each evening, provide a quiet nook in their apartment for him to complete his homework, and encourage him to do his best in school. In some families the schooling experiences of family members may influence how they approach schooling and whether they choose to be directly involved with their children's schools or not (Smith & Elish-Piper, 2002). For example, Amber's mother, Judy, dropped out of high school when she was a senior because she was pregnant. She eventually earned her GED through a night school program, but Judy feels unprepared and inadequate to help Amber with her school work. Judy does, however, do many things to support Amber's learning. For example, she purchased a computer and has an Internet connection for Amber to use for her homework and school projects. She also arranged for a tutor from the community center to help Amber earlier this year when she had difficulty with her math class.

In other families, like Shanette's, the expectations of schools and families are closely aligned, resulting in more direct connections between home and school (Wang, Haertl, & Walberg, 1997). Shanette's family assumes that she will graduate from college because that is the norm in their family. Her mother and stepfather have enrolled her in test prep classes to prepare her to take the Scholastic Aptitude Test (SAT) for admission to college. They also help her study for tests and proofread her essays for school. Her mother is very involved in the after-school activities Shanette

121

CHAPTER 10

All Children and Adolescents Have the Right to an Education That Involves Their Families and Communities in Meaningful Ways

CHAPTER 10

*All Children
and Adolescents
Have the Right to
an Education That
Involves Their
Families and
Communities in
Meaningful Ways*

participates in—volleyball, the drama club, and student council. While each of these families supports their sons and daughters in different ways, all their contributions are important and supportive of learning (Epstein, 1995; Mueller, 2001). Family involvement at the middle and high school levels is correlated with high school completion (Anguiano, 2004), higher grade point averages, higher test scores (both standardized and classroom-based), enrollment in more challenging academic programs, and better attendance rates (Henderson & Mapp, 2002).

Community Involvement and Education

The communities where children and adolescents live shape their viewpoints, experiences, and realities. The people students interact with both in and out of school influence their perceptions of self, views of school, and goals for the future. Knowing the community where our students live is critical (González et al., 2005). Recently, one of us was talking to a student teacher in an urban middle school about the importance of knowing the community in order to make instruction relevant. The student teacher replied, "I'm not going to walk around that neighborhood—it's too dangerous for me," yet she reported having no concerns that her sixth-grade students lived in the very housing projects and apartment buildings that she refused to visit. When probed about why she felt this way, she replied, "It's where they live so it feels normal to them, but it scares me to think about going there." How sad it is when teachers don't find ways to get to know their students' communities. We know many teachers who take part in community activities, such as those situated in community centers or sponsored by houses of worship, as a way to understand their students' communities better. And once involved they can begin to know, understand, and value the communities where they teach and their students live. When teachers are disconnected from their students and their lives, it is difficult to build effective teaching and learning relationships (Stipek, 2006). We believe that it is only when teachers know, understand, and embrace the communities where their students live that they will be able to provide instruction, support, encouragement, and guidance that is congruent with the lives and realities of their students (Diller, 1999).

A variety of community members influence children and adolescents. For example, in some communities religious leaders play significant roles—the local minister who offers an after-school tutoring program; the rabbi who talks each Friday at temple to parents and their children about the importance of schooling; the priest who urges parents to attend all school functions and share family dinner conversations; and the imam who speaks to families at the local mosque about the importance of studying in their spiritual and worldly lives (Sanders & Herting, 2000). In addition, others in the community may have a strong influence on children and adolescents. These important adults may include coaches, leaders of groups or clubs, business leaders, politicians, those in the helping professions such as teachers and medical personnel, business owners, community agency employees, caring neighbors, family friends, and others. When teachers understand who the influential adults are in their students' lives, they can forge connections with individuals to build bridges between students' out-of-school lives and the classroom (Moll, Amanti, Neff, & González, 1992).

Why Is the Right to Have an Education That Involves Families and Communities in Meaningful Ways Important for Children and Adolescents?

123

CHAPTER 10

All Children and Adolescents Have the Right to an Education That Involves Their Families and Communities in Meaningful Ways

Children and adolescents whose parents are involved in their education and schooling tend to be more successful in school (McCarthey, 2000). A longitudinal study of home and school settings for students in elementary and middle school concluded that the most supportive learning contexts are created when students have both strong teachers and good family support (Snow, Barnes, Chandler, Goodman, & Hemphill, 1991). More specifically, when adolescent students have strong support at home and at school, they are less disruptive in school, earn higher grades, and are more likely to go to college (Gutman & Midgley, 2000; Sanders & Herting, 2000). While all students benefit when their families are involved in their education, those students who are having the most difficulty in school make the greatest gains when their families become involved in their education (Jordan, Orozco, & Averett, 2000). Beyond academic gains, middle school students also tend to have more positive attitudes toward school when their families are involved in their homework, discuss assignments, and understand teacher expectations for homework (Shumow & Miller, 2001; Sui-Chu & Willms, 1996).

The effective inclusion of families and communities in education is about (1) supporting and teaching; (2) enjoying children and adolescents; (3) working together to promote positive outcomes for children and adolescents, including school

Community members are an important influence on adolescents.

124

CHAPTER 10

*All Children
and Adolescents
Have the Right to
an Education That
Involves Their
Families and
Communities in
Meaningful Ways*

completion, achievement, opportunity to learn, and socialization; and (4) creating conditions that support all children and adolescents as learners (Christenson, 1995). We agree that we can improve schools, education, and student learning through partnerships among parents, schools, and communities (Epstein et al., 2002). Family and community involvement in education can be described as a safety net to promote students' learning and school success. Research by Christenson and Sheridan (2001) concludes that this safety net is most important for low-income students and those who struggle with learning; however, all students benefit when their families and communities are involved in their education. It is important to note that family and community involvement do not take only one form; rather, such involvement runs along a continuum from fundamental to supplemental, as summarized in Figure 10-1.

An important consideration for building partnerships with all families is an awareness and appreciation for multiculturalism. In such a perspective, teachers view *all* families as valuable contributors to their students' learning (González et al., 2005; Hidalgo, Sui, & Epstein, 2004). A "funds-of-knowledge approach" (Hidalgo et al., 2004, p. 711) is a useful framework for adopting a multicultural stance. This approach helps teachers create lessons that draw on knowledge sources in families, incorporate multicultural literature, and engage parents and others from the community as intellectual resources for lessons. In addition, by using the funds of knowl-

Figure 10-1

*The Framework
for Comprehensive
Partnerships*

Type One: Parenting—Workshops and other activities that help families understand child and adolescent development and how to support student learning at home. In addition, this type of partnership includes ways that family cultural traditions can be used to support students' learning.

Type Two: Communicating—Provision of information about school programs and student progress through letters, memos, notices, phone calls, email messages, conferences, and other methods. Translation and interpreter services are necessary to make this information available to all families.

Type Three: Volunteering—Opportunities for families to volunteer to assist teachers, administrators, and students. Being an audience for student performances is a common way for families to volunteer in middle and high schools.

Type Four: Learning at Home—Involvement of families with learning activities at home, including homework. The Teachers Involve Parents in Schoolwork (TIPS) approach is one example of this type of involvement (Epstein, Simon, & Salinas, 1997).

Type Five: Decision Making—Decisions are made about the school, governance, and advocacy through PTA/PTO, school councils, committees, and other groups that involve families.

Type Six: Collaborating with the Community—Coordination of resources and services for families, students, and the school with businesses, agencies, and other groups. This type of involvement also includes families, students, and the school providing services to the community such as recycling projects, art displays, and cultural performances.

Source: Epstein, 1990

edge, teachers and students are able to work together to develop positive views of cultural diversity. Within the funds of knowledge approach, the teacher serves as an ethnographer (cultural anthropologist) to learn about the types of knowledge and resources available in the homes and community of her students (González et al., 2005). She then taps into this knowledge and these skills to make connections to the curriculum and to demonstrate respect for the resources and strengths that exist in the families and communities served by the school. (See Chapter 3 for more information on funds of knowledge.)

125

CHAPTER 10

*All Children
and Adolescents
Have the Right to
an Education That
Involves Their
Families and
Communities in
Meaningful Ways*

How Can the Right to an Education That Involves Families and Communities in Meaningful Ways Become a Reality in Today's Schools?

Family and community involvement have been directly correlated with student achievement (Henderson & Mapp, 2002), and students, parents, and teachers perceive such involvement as important to student success (Metropolitan Life Insurance Company, 1998). What can teachers do, then, to make this right a reality in the

Talking about homework is one way parents can support their adolescents in school.

126

CHAPTER 10

*All Children
and Adolescents
Have the Right to
an Education That
Involves Their
Families and
Communities in
Meaningful Ways*

classrooms, schools, and communities where they teach? First, we believe that teachers must get to know the families and communities where their students live. Second, we assert that teachers must strive to find real, meaningful connections between the curriculum of the school and the "curriculum of the home and the community" (Heath, 1983). Third, we contend that teachers and schools must reach out to families and the community to help them work collaboratively with the school to support student learning. Fourth, we believe that good communication with families is essential. And finally, we contend that teachers have a responsibility to help families advocate for high-quality instruction and meaningful educational opportunities for their children.

Involving Families and Communities in Education: One School's Story

Miller Middle School is an example of how a school can make family and community involvement an integral part of its mission. Miller is a large middle school with 62 percent of its students classified as low income, 27 percent are English language learners, and over 60 percent of the students are students of color. The moment you arrive at Miller, you feel welcome because of the large sign that includes greetings in all of the languages represented by students in the school. Student-made flags of all of the countries of origin for students in the school hang from the rafters in the three main hallways of the building.

At the beginning of each quarter, each team of teachers at Miller develops a plan for contacting parents, inviting families and community members to the school for learning activities, and examining connections between the curriculum and students' lives. During their weekly team meetings, the teachers share information about contacts they have made with families and discuss upcoming units of study and possible ways to make the curriculum relevant by making connections to current events, popular culture, community events, and common experiences and concerns of middle school students.

While preparing for a unit on mysteries in her eighth-grade language arts class, Monique wondered how to make the genre of mystery relevant for her students, who were often reluctant readers. Javier, the social studies teacher, mentioned that the television show *Cold Case* provided historically accurate cases of unsolved crimes and murders and guided the viewer through the process of solving each mystery. When Monique polled her class, she found that many of her students had watched the show previously, along with other popular shows such as *CSI*, *Without a Trace*, and *Unsolved Mysteries*. Monique then used excerpts from some of these shows (carefully selected for content appropriate for middle school students) to tie together her mystery unit. At Javier's suggestion, she also brought in newspapers with articles about several high-profile mysteries that remained unsolved. At the end of the unit, Monique reported that her students responded very favorably and were extremely motivated to complete the readings.

On a recent visit to this school, one of us met with a seventh-grade team of teachers to discuss their upcoming World Expo celebration. This event was to be the culmination of units of study in the social studies, language arts, art, music, and family and consumer classes. Students conducted research, created oral histories, and collected artifacts for countries represented by students on the seventh-grade team. The event provided an opportunity for students, family members, and community members to celebrate the students' knowledge and also the various countries and cultures represented at Miller Middle School. Another example of this type of family and community learning event was the Storytelling Festival that a sixth-grade team implemented recently. Students read folktales from around the world and then had the option to write their own, develop a storytelling performance, or create another representation of a folktale (e.g., artistic interpretation, drama, music, dance or movement, computer presentation). Students then invited their families and community members to listen to the students' stories and also to share their own stories. Miller Middle School provides such celebrations of learning once each quarter.

At Miller Middle School, connections to students' families are an integral part of teachers' daily work. Teachers commit to making parent contacts each day during their planning times so each family is contacted by each teacher at least one time per quarter. Using a survey as part of the school registration process, families indicate their preferred method of communication (e.g., phone, email, written correspondence, face-to-face meetings). Teachers strive to contact families for positive reasons (e.g., good attendance, academic achievement, effort, improvement), as well as when problems arise. Each team of teachers at Miller also shares the responsibility for writing a biweekly newsletter that is sent home every other Friday to inform families of important information and upcoming events. The newsletter is translated into Spanish, Gujarati, and Polish because of the large numbers of families that speak these languages at Miller Middle School. The translation duties are shared by several paraprofessionals hired by the school district to serve as translators and community liaisons.

While Miller Middle School is an example of how an entire school can prioritize family and community involvement and connections, some teachers work in schools and districts where this type of commitment does not yet exist. There are still many things that you can do to forge meaningful and productive relationships and connections with your students' families and communities, whether you are working alone or with a team of other teachers in your school or district.

- What, then, can you do as a teacher to get to know your students' families and communities?
  - Contact parents to find out the hopes, goals, dreams, and concerns they have for their sons and daughters. This can be done through a questionnaire sent home, at open house, through phone or email conversations, during conferences, or through family stories gathered during face-to-face meetings (Edwards, Pleasants, & Franklin, 1999).
  - Survey your students to find out how their families and communities support their learning.
  - At the beginning of the school year, send a letter to parents introducing yourself and describing key information about your class (i.e., topics you will study, homework policy, major projects, testing schedule, and ideas for how families can support, encourage, and help students succeed in your class).
  - Walk through the neighborhoods where your students live to observe daily activities and gain an understanding about what life is like there. Be

127

CHAPTER 10

All Children and Adolescents Have the Right to an Education That Involves Their Families and Communities in Meaningful Ways

128

CHAPTER 10

*All Children
and Adolescents
Have the Right to
an Education That
Involves Their
Families and
Communities in
Meaningful Ways*

sure to visit places like supermarkets, libraries, community centers, restaurants, and other locations to gain insight into daily life in the community. By looking at the types of literacy, print, and interactions in the community, you will learn a great deal about the context where your students live (Orellana & Hernandez, 1999).

• Attend community events such as neighborhood festivals, plays at the local community center, religious services, and cultural events to learn more about the community where students and their families live.

• What can you do as a teacher to make meaningful connections from school curricula to home and community?

• Have students interview family members about specific times or events in history (e.g., Vietnam, the Civil Rights Movement, Desert Storm) or complete other family-focused assignments such as reading and responding to a current events article as a family, completing an oral history of a family member, or interviewing or surveying family members about an issue related to the curriculum (Kyle, McIntyre, Miller, & Moore, 2006).

• Provide an opportunity for students to research the history of the cultures represented in the school by doing oral history projects; conducting Internet searches; completing library research, and visiting museums, historical societies, and community locations.

• Ensure that your students will be able to make real-life connections to what you are teaching (Schultz & Hull, 2002). For example, if you are studying history, find parallels in current events. If you are reading a novel, make connections to current movies, TV programs, public figures, or students' lived experiences. If you are conducting research projects, allow students to choose topics that have personal significance for them. If you are studying scientific concepts, ask students to examine the ramifications on daily life (e.g., the impact of space travel on our lives, how computer technology is a part of daily life, how a specific invention or discovery has affected modern society, or the ethical considerations of cloning, DNA analysis, or stem cell research). Make these connections explicit to students so they understand how school learning is related to their lives.

• Work with a local cable access station to develop and offer educational television programming as has been done in Dallas (Cooter et al., 1999). Or create original programming that highlights student projects, performances, and classroom vignettes as has been presented on the local television station in Williamson County, Tennessee (V. J. Risko, personal communication, May 19, 2005). Students can take ownership of the process by serving as script writers, producers, and on-camera reporters for these productions. Families and community members can learn more about what is happening in your school by viewing these programs.

• What can you do as a teacher to invite families and community members to participate in students' education?

• Provide concrete suggestions to parents—via newsletter, Web page, email, or at open houses or conferences—about how they can create opportunities for their sons and daughters to succeed in their studies and in school. These suggestions may include setting general ground rules such as no TV or phone calls during homework time, having a set time for school work, and developing an organizational system for assignments, notes, and other school materials.

- Build on the expertise and funds of knowledge (Moll et al., 1992) present in students' families and communities. This can be accomplished by inviting guest speakers to your classroom to share their life experiences, travels, hobbies, or cultures. Another way to structure this process is to hold a community learning celebration that highlights the many talents and experiences of community members and families (McIntyre, Kyle, Moore, Sweazy, & Greer, 2001). Possible topics for presentations, demonstrations, and displays include careers, music, horticulture, art, drama, and crafts (Kyle et al., 2006).

- Form a committee at your school to develop evening enrichment classes for parents, students, and community members. These classes may be taught by high school students, teachers, parents, or community members who have special skills or talents such as Web page design, digital photography, oil painting, dancing, yoga, scrapbooking, or cooking.

- Hold special events highlighting student learning and projects and invite families and community members. For example, in conjunction with a study of astronomy, high school students collaborated with university researchers to analyze complex data and then participate in community "star parties" that were held to invite astronomy enthusiasts and families to share their learning and to pursue questions of mutual interest (Alvarez, 1996).

- Provide homework that promotes involvement at home. One model called Teachers Involve Parents in Schoolwork (TIPS) has been correlated with improved student achievement in the middle school grades (Epstein, Simon, & Salinas, 1997). In this approach teachers assign homework that requires students to demonstrate or discuss some aspect of their learning with a family member. This involvement may include interviewing family members, discussing real-world applications of content, or eliciting family input into texts students have written. During the TIPS process, parents monitor and support their children, but they are not expected to teach content, read assignments, or direct projects because those tasks are the responsibility of the students. Each TIPS assignment also includes a section for home to school communication where family members are asked to share observations, comments, or questions regarding the assignment. Teachers typically assign TIPS activities no more than once per week, and they provide two or more days to complete the assignment to accommodate families' busy schedules. For more information on this approach to homework and sample TIPS lessons, consult the TIPS website sponsored by the National Network of Partnership Schools by using the following URL: www.csos.jhu.edu/p2000/tips/TIPSmain .htm.

- What can you do as a teacher to communicate effectively with families?
  - Establish two-way communication with families to gain insights into parents' understandings of their sons' and daughters' learning and to identify ways to incorporate these ideas into the classroom (Mueller, 2001).

129

CHAPTER 10

All Children and Adolescents Have the Right to an Education That Involves Their Families and Communities in Meaningful Ways

130

CHAPTER 10

*All Children
and Adolescents
Have the Right to
an Education That
Involves Their
Families and
Communities in
Meaningful Ways*

- Send home a newsletter periodically throughout the year to keep families informed of what is happening in your class. The frequency of newsletters may be as often as weekly if you teach in an elementary setting, monthly if you teach in a team setting in a middle school, or once each semester if you teach in a high school. The main purposes of the newsletter are (1) to inform families of what students are studying and expected to do in your class, (2) to offer suggestions for how families can support students in school (e.g., study tips, the importance of talking about school with their sons and daughters, the importance of letting their children and adolescents know that school and learning are valued by the family, and the importance of talking about current events, community happenings, and other issues), (3) to make connections to community resources that can support students and families (e.g., a display of art at the local library, an author presentation at a local bookstore, a cultural festival, a performance of a play, a guest speaker at the local community college, or a television program or talk show featuring information of interest), and (4) to invite parents and community members into the classroom as resources (e.g., to teach an art lesson, to share songwriting experiences, or to participate in class activities or projects). Professionally written newsletters with general tips and ideas for parents and families are also available for schoolwide use at the middle school and high school levels. Samples and ordering information for can be found on the Parent Institute website located at www.parent-institute.com.

- Contact parents when students are not succeeding in your classes. This can be done through regular progress reports, phone calls, or email messages. Informing parents that their child or adolescent is earning a low grade in your class will provide time and opportunities for improvement rather than waiting until report cards are issued.

- When you need to contact families to resolve concerns regarding student performance, motivation, behavior, or engagement in the classroom, apply the "my son or daughter test." In other words, try to think about the situation as if the student were your son or daughter. Doing so tends to result in greater empathy with families and an increased likelihood of effective communication (Canter & Associates, 1999).

- Work with the school counselor, social worker, or other support professionals in your school when you are concerned about a student and want to discuss issues with parents. Sometimes these support personnel already have a relationship with the student and the student's family that you can use as a resource to improve communication.

- Use multiple methods of communication to reach more families. For example, some teachers have a website that lists homework assignments and other important information; you may choose to record a daily voice mail message listing homework and announcements; or you may use email messages, phone calls, newsletters, and progress reports to communicate with families.

- Consider language issues when contacting parents who may speak a language other than English or who may have low levels of literacy (Smith & Elish-Piper, 2002). Locate bilingual individuals in your school or community who can translate written materials, and arrange for interpreters for parent-teacher conferences when language is an issue. Prepare all written materials to be shared with families so they are clear, concise, and easy to read.

131

CHAPTER 10

All Children and Adolescents Have the Right to an Education That Involves Their Families and Communities in Meaningful Ways

* What can you do as a teacher to promote advocacy with families?
  * Encourage parents to advocate for the needs of their sons and daughters. Help them understand the structure of the school hierarchy so they can solve problems and access resources for their children and adolescents (Rudney, 2005).
  * Look at the policies in your school and identify any that work against families. Work with your colleagues and administrators to change these policies so your school is more supportive of students and their families. For example, one of us works with a school district that requires any Mexican American students who leave school during the school year to visit Mexico for more than two weeks to re-enroll in the district upon their return. Once they complete the paperwork and procedures for enrollment, they are automatically assigned to a different classroom than they attended prior to the trip. The stated purpose of this policy is to discourage families from taking students out of school for long periods of time; however, in reality, this policy places a burden on families and slows down academic progress as students must become acclimated to the new classroom, teacher, and instructional methods. This is a policy that clearly works against students and families, and it is one that could be modified if teachers and families advocated for a change.
  * Work with parent groups in your school to recruit membership from groups that are underrepresented. Encourage diverse parents to serve on parent committees and take on leadership roles so that the voices of all families are heard as decisions are made in the school. If interpreters are needed to allow linguistically diverse families access to meetings and the decision-making process, work with your administrators to make this resource available.

Putting Ideas into Action

Think about Amber's letter at the beginning of this chapter. If you were Amber's teacher, how would you respond to her? How would you address the concerns of her mother, Judy, about supporting Amber at home so she can be more engaged and successful in school? What would you do to try and make the curriculum you teach more relevant to Amber's life? Some ideas we considered include making connections between Chaucer's *Canterbury Tales* and current movies so Amber and her classmates can see the timeless conflicts people encounter in literature and in life. In addition, we might ask Amber and her peers to put themselves into the story line of one of Chaucer's *Canterbury Tales* and consider what they would do, how they would feel, and how they would react if they were in that situation. Providing such opportunities to see themselves in the literature they read helps students become directly engaged in their learning (Wilhelm, 1996).

132

CHAPTER 10

*All Children
and Adolescents
Have the Right to
an Education That
Involves Their
Families and
Communities in
Meaningful Ways*

As you ponder the issues Amber and her mother raised, think about your own students, their families, and their communities. How connected are you to your students' families and communities? What have you been successful with in terms of family and community involvement? What obstacles or challenges have you faced when trying to make family and community connections? What options, resources, and creative ideas can you think of to address these obstacles or challenges? Think of an aspect of family or community involvement that would enhance your teaching and your students' learning. What steps can you take to implement your idea? Share your ideas with a teaching colleague and develop a plan for making your idea happen. Your efforts will be well worth the hard work because family and community connections do make a difference for student learning. This point is clearly illustrated in Amber's words, "I seem to learn best and be the most fired-up to study when what I'm learning makes sense to me—in my life—in my world. I wish more teachers would think about this." And as Amber's mother, Judy, noted, communication and connections with teachers can enhance family support as demonstrated in her statement, "I want Amber to graduate and go on to college. I try to encourage her as much as I can, but I just want the teachers to tell me what else I can do to help my child succeed."

DISCUSSION QUESTIONS FOR STUDY GROUPS

1. Family involvement is typically stressed at preschool and early elementary levels. Critics of family involvement at the middle and high school levels often cite the need for students to take responsibility for their own learning as the reason that family involvement should be limited with older students. Using information and insights from the chapter and from your own professional and personal experiences, how would you respond to these critics? What reasons, experiences, and assumptions underlie your response?

2. Students develop a positive view of learning, education, and themselves when they find their schooling experiences are relevant to their lives. Amber did not find relevance in her high school studies, including the assigned reading of Chaucer. If you were Amber's teacher, what could you do to make the curriculum come alive and connect to Amber's life as a modern teen? What obstacles might you encounter as you tried to make the curriculum become more relevant to Amber and her classmates? What could you do to overcome or address these obstacles?

3. Imagine you taught in the school that had the policy that required Mexican American students who left school for more than two weeks to re-enroll and be placed into different classrooms upon their return. Your principal explained to the teachers that the reason for the policy was to discourage parents from removing their students from school and disrupting their learning. How would you respond to the policy in terms of the disruption of student learning?

4. How can you use the funds of knowledge approach in your classroom or school? What process would you go through to learn about the funds of knowledge in your students' families and communities? What are some possible ways you could make connections from the funds of knowledge to your curriculum?

Epilogue

Recently, one of us had a conversation with a high school teacher who, three years earlier, began her teaching career in a ninth-grade English class. The poor, rural area in North Carolina where the school was located differed considerably from the suburban, upscale area she called home. When she arrived in January to teach her first class, the students boasted they had already "run off" several teachers in the previous four months. The students let her know by their words and behavior they expected that she, like the others, would leave. It took a few weeks before they realized she was different; she was there to stay. When they said, "Hey you'll leave just like the rest," she responded, "I'm not leaving. I promise. I will be here with you on the last day of school." Slowly, the students began to trust her.

When asked what advice she could offer to others, she responded, "It's simple. Be yourself, show you care, and listen." Listen she did. When they spoke of "rims," she asked, "What are rims?" When one of the tires was flat on her car, and two of her students came to her aid, she marveled at how easily they could perform a task that neither she nor her husband could manage. When she recounted this incident in class the next day, it stimulated an impromptu conversation about how time and place have a lot to do with how we develop reading, writing, and speaking strategies and skills. It was through everyday conversations like these that these students and this teacher forged a relationship—a relationship between two parties genuinely interested in the thoughts and experiences of the other.

We are not hopeless idealists; we know that teaching middle and high school students presents unique challenges. By their developmental nature, learners of this age strive for independence and autonomy, which at times are demonstrated by resistance to rules and authority. Although this movement toward independence and autonomy is typical and healthy, occasionally its consequences can test teachers.

Adding to this challenge is the unevenness in students' development of school-based reading strategies and skills. For example, some lack a firm understanding of the basics of reading (e.g., oral reading fluency, an adequate sight vocabulary), while others lack facility with the strategies needed to comprehend the content of the texts and literature used in their classes. When students are assessed as having a comprehension problem in school, yet they can comprehend the layout of a friend's website or navigate with ease the complexity of a video game, is that a comprehension problem? Or is it that they have not been taught specific strategies for accessing content in textbooks or that teachers have missed opportunities to help students make connections between their prior knowledge and text concepts? Sometimes teachers' attention to their students' specific reading needs is distracted by external pressures to increase test scores or to teach with curricula that don't match the needs of the students in their classrooms.

Often students find that the reading experiences in school are so far removed from their lives, that they can't see their relevance. This lack of relevance is significant and was a primary stimulus for writing this book. In several chapters we argue that the school experiences and assignments do not build on what students know and are able to do. They do not build on the expertise *all* bring with them to school—an expertise described in Chapter 3 when we discuss *funds of knowledge* and in Chapter 4 when we discuss *provisions*.

We consciously designed this book to be a resource of ideas for teachers so they could create this relevance. In Chapters 3 and 10, we suggest using culturally relevant readings and experiences and inviting family and community members to the classroom to share their expertise. Suggestions are described in Chapter 6 for providing at least some choice in what students read in schools and in how students represent their learning. In Chapter 5, we present strategies for creating environments rich in the variety of materials available and in how students use these materials during instruction. In Chapter 7, we discuss the stimulating power of readings and experiences that engage and motivate children and adolescents. And in Chapter 9, we describe characteristics of schools perceived by children and adolescents as places where they want to be and as places where they believe they are able to learn. Intuitively, we all know the teacher is central to how students perceive their schools. Thus, we chose to begin our book by talking about ways teachers demonstrate care for their students' learning and the significance for teachers to invest in their own learning so they can match this care with competence, Chapter 1. A critical tool for designing effective instruction is the ethical and appropriate use of assessments. In Chapter 8, we address how such use can be accomplished. In the end, all students must feel respected and in Chapter 2 but really within each chapter, we examine elements useful for creating an environment of respect.

Although the capabilities and needs of preadolescent and adolescent readers vary, all deserve reading experiences that recognize these variations and honor their rich cultural and language backgrounds. The title of this book establishes how we believe this can be achieved. *A Declaration of Readers' Rights* reflects our belief that access to quality reading instruction and experiences is the inalienable right of every student. The subtitle, *Renewing Our Commitment to Students*, expresses the need to bring the student to the forefront of the debates on literacy reform. Currently, so much attention is directed toward curriculum standards, accountability, and demands for increasing test scores that the student has slowly faded from consideration. Many teachers share our concerns, as evidenced by this statement from a high school teacher, "We have focused so long on how to teach and what to teach that we've forgotten who we teach."

Along similar lines, Carol Santa (2006), the former president of the International Reading Association and a longtime advocate of adolescent literacy, says that decades of research have produced a lot of information about what constitutes effective literacy instruction for this age learner. Her current role as coowner of the Montana Academy, a boarding school for adolescents with emotional and academic struggles, has only served to reinforce her belief that, "Successful learning in the classroom has far more to do with human relationships and classroom community than with the content of our lessons" (p. 467). We concur wholeheartedly.

In the introduction, we stated our desire for this book to be a vehicle for us to converse with many teachers. To that end, we now turn the conversation over to you. What are your next steps? Are there colleagues you might invite into the conversation? Perhaps the following actions will stimulate such conversation.

1. *Choose one right on which to focus.* Teachers in our graduate courses often feel overwhelmed when, during their studies, they are introduced to many new ideas and resources and desire to make a wholesale change in their literacy program. As we suggest to these teachers, we urge you to identify one aspect on which to focus. So, choose one right; refer to the chapter related to that right, and select one or two suggestions to try.

2. *Take five.* Your schedules are tight. Your students are numerous. The demands placed on you are great. With that said, commit five minutes during each class to developing a relationship with your students. One simple strategy you might try is to begin each class with a statement such as, "Hey, you know what?" The class responds, "What?" Quickly share something that's going on in your life. Then invite others to repeat, "Hey, you know what?" and to share. It won't be long before you will have students eager to share something that's going on in their lives.

3. *Consider: Why do I teach the way I do?* This question provides the framework for a master's program at Georgia State University. During the fifteen-month program, the teachers are involved in many course experiences, such as discussing reading cases and viewing video clips of teaching examples to stimulate discussions about the beliefs which guide their literacy teaching. Questions are used to guide these discussions. *Who's doing the thinking? Who's doing the talking? What evidence is there that the students' background is being used to teach the concept? What role is the teacher assuming? The students?* And then, based on the answers to these questions, *How does this teacher define literacy teaching and learning?* Invite a group of colleagues to participate with you in similar activities to gain insights into why you teach the way you do. Such insights can lead to more intentional rather than incidental instructional decision making.

4. *Read and become informed.* During the past few years, preadolescent and adolescent literacy has garnered a lot of attention. In response, several reports have been written regarding the state and the promise of this age learner. Many are free and can be accessed on the Web. ("Adolescent Literacy and the Achievement Gap: What Do We Know and Where Do We Go from Here?")

www.carnegie.org; *Effective Literacy Instruction for Adolescents* (Alvermann, 2001a), http://nrconline.org; *Reading Next: A Vision for Action and Research in Middle and High School Literacy* (Biancarosa & Snow, 2004), www.carnegie.org). Also, keep up with what's going on in the field. Subscribe to a journal such as the *Journal of Adolescent and Adult Literacy*, which focuses on the older learner.

5. *Read stories that recount the success of other teachers who teach literacy to older children and adolescents.* All too often, the negative events and issues in education get the attention, but there are many success stories too. Read to gain a clearer perspective of the possibilities. (A few of our favorites are *Lifer: Learning from At-Risk Adolescent Readers*, by Pamela N. Mueller [2001]; *Going with the Flow: How to Engage Boys (and Girls) in their Literacy Learning*, by Michael Smith and Jeffery D. Wilhelm; *To Be a Boy, To Be a Reader: Engaging Teen and Preteen Boys in Active Literacy*, by William Brozo [2002]; *On the Brink: Negotiating Literature and Life with Adolescents*, by Susan Hynds [1997]; *The Freedom Writer's Diary: How a Teacher and 150 Teens Used Writing to Change Themselves and the World around Them*, by Erin Gruwell [1999]).

In the introduction, we shared portions of a letter written by Al. Yes, there is an Al, and the sentence which opens his letter, "The teacher has all the power in the classroom," is his. Although Al is only one adolescent, his words mirrored the comments expressed by other young people with whom we interacted. We found his words penetrating, and so we return to Al to close this book and to offer his ideas on how teachers might create what he termed "An Enjoyable, Respectful Classroom":

The teacher has to capture the students' attention with open discussions and a positive attitude. The discussions should not just be for the teachers' favorites but open to all who want to chime in. There should be debates on current events like global warming or the headlines in the daily news. And, the teacher must be trustworthy. The students should be able to discuss personal matters without fear of being talked about behind their backs. Finally, the class should prepare the students for the later stages of their lives and the teacher should treat all as though he believes all could be future leaders, not lifelong failures.

We hope this book provides you with the encouragement to pursue reading experiences with your students as though reading is their inalienable right. We hope this book creates or reinforces your will to renew your commitment to the students in your classroom. In the end, teaching is a relationship—a relationship initiated by the teacher. A relationship founded on a deep respect of what learners bring to that relationship and a relationship motivated by a sincere desire to guide young people to fulfill their great promise.

Reader's Bill of Rights Parent Survey*

Directions for Use

The Reader's Bill of Rights Parent Survey is a quick survey of parents' perceptions of the rights their children have as readers. It consists of twenty items and takes approximately five to ten minutes to complete.

The first ten items are related to recreational reading, which is reading that is done during students' free time outside of school. The second ten items are related to reading during school lessons or assignments. Think carefully about each item and answer the item as honestly as possible.

If you have any comments, please make those on the last page. Please indicate if your child is a boy or a girl and his/her grade in school.

*Risko et al., 2004

Reader's Bill of Rights Parent Survey

Please complete the following information about your child and make comments if you choose to do so.

My child is   Female   Male

My child is in the _____ grade.

Comments:

PART I DIRECTIONS

Sometimes students read during their free time just because they want to read. Mark each item according to your children's rights as readers.

	Strongly Agree	Agree	Not Sure	Disagree	Strongly Disagree
1. When my children read during their free time, they should be allowed to choose not to read.	A	B	C	D	E
2. When my children read during their free time, they should be allowed to skip pages.	A	B	C	D	E
3. When my children read during their free time, they should be allowed to not finish what they read.	A	B	C	D	E
4. When my children read during their free time, they should be allowed to reread.	A	B	C	D	E
5. When my children read during their free time, they should be allowed to read anything.	A	B	C	D	E
6. When my children read during their free time, they should be allowed to escape from the real world.	A	B	C	D	E
7. When my children read during their free time, they should be allowed to read anywhere.	A	B	C	D	E
8. When my children read during their free time, they should be allowed to glance through what they're reading.	A	B	C	D	E
9. When my children read during their free time, they should be allowed to read out loud.	A	B	C	D	E
10. When my children read during their free time, they should be allowed not to explain their choice of reading material.	A	B	C	D	E

PART II DIRECTIONS

139

APPENDIX A

*Reader's Bill
of Rights
Parent Survey*

Sometimes students read during their free time because they have lessons or assignments given to them by a teacher. Mark each item according to your children's rights as readers.

	Strongly Agree	Agree	Not Sure	Disagree	Strongly Disagree
1. When my children read for lessons or assignments, they should be allowed to choose not to read.	A	B	C	D	E
2. When my children read for lessons or assignments, they should be allowed to skip pages.	A	B	C	D	E
3. When my children read for lessons or assignments, they should be allowed to not finish what they read.	A	B	C	D	E
4. When my children read for lessons or assignments, they should be allowed to reread.	A	B	C	D	E
5. When my children read for lessons or assignments, they should be allowed to read anything.	A	B	C	D	E
6. When my children read for lessons or assignments, they should be allowed to escape from the real world.	A	B	C	D	E
7. When my children read for lessons or assignments, they should be allowed to read anywhere.	A	B	C	D	E
8. When my children read for lessons or assignments, they should be allowed to glance through what they're reading.	A	B	C	D	E
9. When my children read for lessons or assignments, they should be allowed to read out loud.	A	B	C	D	E
10. When my children read for lessons or assignments, they should be allowed not to explain their choice of reading material.	A	B	C	D	E

Reader's Bill of Rights Survey for Teachers*

1. Your gender: **A.** female   **B.** male

2. Professional position   **A.** elementary teacher   **B.** middle school teacher
   or goal: **C.** secondary teacher   **D.** special education teacher
                    E. other (specify) _____

3. Degree being sought: **A.** B.A. or B.S.   **B.** M.A. or M.S.   **C.** Ed.D. or Ph.D.   **D.** None

4. If a teacher, what grade   **A.** Pre-K   **B.** K   **C.** 1
   do you currently teach?   **D.** 2 or 3   **E.** 6–8   **F.** 9–12
                    G. other (specify) _____

5. Teaching Experience: **A.** 1–3 years   **B.** 4–10 years   **C.** over 10 years   **D.** over 15 years

Daniel Pennac, in his book *Better Than Life,* proposed the Reader's Bill of Rights. The researchers would like to know your thoughts and feelings about these proposed rights.

For the first ten statements, how much is each of the ten phrases like you (e.g., does it describe you as a reader?)?

For the next ten statements, to what degree do you as a teacher agree or disagree that students should have the rights listed?

*Elish-Piper et al., 1999, 2000

As a reader, I believe I have:

	Strongly Agree	Agree	Uncertain	Disagree	Strongly Disagree
1. The right to choose not to read.	A	B	C	D	E
2. The right to skip pages.	A	B	C	D	E
3. The right to not finish what I read.	A	B	C	D	E
4. The right to reread.	A	B	C	D	E
5. The right to read anything.	A	B	C	D	E
6. The right to escapism.	A	B	C	D	E
7. The right to read anywhere.	A	B	C	D	E
8. The right to browse.	A	B	C	D	E
9. The right to read out loud.	A	B	C	D	E
10. The right to not have to defend my taste.	A	B	C	D	E

**As a teacher or prospective teacher, I believe
my students should have:**

	Strongly Agree	Agree	Uncertain	Disagree	Strongly Disagree
11. The right to choose not to read.	A	B	C	D	E
12. The right to skip pages.	A	B	C	D	E
13. The right to not finish what they read.	A	B	C	D	E
14. The right to reread.	A	B	C	D	E
15. The right to read anything.	A	B	C	D	E
16. The right to escapism.	A	B	C	D	E
17. The right to read anywhere.	A	B	C	D	E
18. The right to browse.	A	B	C	D	E
19. The right to read out loud.	A	B	C	D	E
20. The right to not have to defend their taste.	A	B	C	D	E

Student Interview Guide: Reader's Rights*

My job is to work with teachers to help them teach reading, and it helps me in my work with teachers to know how students feel about reading. I want to ask you a few questions about reading. There are no right or wrong answers to the questions. Your answers will not have any effect on your grades, and your teachers will not know what your answers are. I just want you to think about the questions and give your honest opinion.

I don't want to forget what you say, so I'm going to tape-record our conversation. Later, once the interview is over, I will play the tape back for myself and take some notes on what you said. Your teacher will not hear the tape.

The interview will take about twenty minutes. First, I'll ask you what you think about reading. Next, I will ask you questions about when you read assignments for school work, and then I'll ask you the same questions about when you read things you choose on your own time. If you don't understand a question or don't understand what some of the words mean, please tell me and I will try to explain them for you.

Student's Perceptions of Reading

1. What do you think a good reader is?

2. Do you think you are a good reader? Explain.

3. Do your teachers think you are a good reader? Explain.

4. What makes reading easy for you?

5. What makes reading hard for you?

---

*Matthews et al., 2001; Bass et al., 2002

6. What do teachers do that makes reading easy?

7. What do teachers do that makes reading hard?

Students' Perceptions of Their Rights as Readers

We will now begin the next part of our interview. I will ask you several questions. The first ten questions are about when you have to read for your school assignments. This includes any books or chapters in books that your teacher asks you to read.

(Suggested prompts for all questions: Anything else? Or repeat the student's answer and then say: Anything else?)

ACADEMIC READING

1. When reading for an assignment, do you think it is OK to choose not to read something? Explain.

2. When reading for an assignment, do you think it is OK to skip pages? Explain.

3. When reading for an assignment, do you think it is OK not to finish something you are reading? Explain.

4. When reading for an assignment, do you think it is OK to reread? Explain.

5. When reading for an assignment, do you think it is OK to read anything you want to read for that assignment? Explain.

6. When reading for an assignment, do you think it is OK to use your imagination and escape to another place? Explain.

7. When reading for an assignment, do you think it is OK to read anywhere? Explain.

8. When reading for an assignment, do you think it is OK to browse or just look through the pages? Explain.

9. When reading for an assignment, do you think it is OK to read out loud? Explain. (If yes, say: Can you give me an example of when you might read out loud?)

10. When reading for an assignment, do you think it is OK not to defend or not to explain why you like the things you read? Explain.

I asked you a lot of questions. Do you want to add anything to what you said? Were there any questions that were hard to answer? Were there any that were confusing?

Now, I will ask you the same questions, but this time I want you to think about when you read for recreation or fun. This might be a book, a magazine, a newspaper, or any reading you choose to do on your own time.

1. When reading something you choose to read on your own time, do you think it is OK to choose not to read something? Explain.

2. When you are reading something you choose to read on your own time, do you think it is OK to skip pages? Explain.

3. When you are reading something you choose to read on your own time, do you think it is OK not to finish what you are reading? Explain.

4. When you are reading something you choose to read on your own time, do you think it is OK to reread? Explain.

5. When you are reading something you choose to read on your own time, do you think it is OK to read anything you want to read? Explain.

6. When you are reading something you choose to read on your own time, do you think it is OK to use your imagination and escape to another place? Explain.

7. When you are reading something you choose to read on your own time, do you think it is OK to read anywhere? Explain.

8. When you are reading something you choose to read on your own time, do you think it is OK to browse or just look through the pages? Explain.

9. When you are reading something you choose to read on your own time, do you think it is OK to read out loud? Explain. (If yes); Can you give me an example of when you might read out loud?

10. When you are reading something you choose to read on your own time, do you think it is OK not to defend or not to explain why you like the things you read? Explain.

I asked you a lot of questions. Do you want to add anything to what you said? Were there any questions that were hard to answer? Were there any that were confusing?

We're finished. You have been great. Your ideas will help me in my work with teachers. Do you have anything else you want me to know?

References

Adler, M., Rougle, K., Kaiser, E., & Caughlan, S. (2004). Closing the gap between concept and practice: Toward more dialogic discussion in the language arts classroom. *Journal of Adolescent & Adult Literacy, 47,* 312–322.

Alderman, M. K. (1990). Motivation for at-risk students. *Educational Leadership, 48*(1), 27–30.

Alexander, P. A. (2003). Profiling the developing reader: The interplay of knowledge, interest, and strategic processing. In C. M. Fairbanks, J. Worthy, B. Maloch, J. V. Hoffman, & D. L. Schallert (Eds.), *Fifty-second yearbook of the National Reading Conference* (pp. 47–65). Chicago, IL: National Reading Conference.

Alexander, P. A. (2005). The path to competence: A lifespan developmental perspective on reading. *The Journal of Literacy Research, 37,* 413–436.

Alliance for Excellent Education. (2006, March). *Straight A's: Public education policy and progress, 6*(5). Retrieved October 31, 2006, from http://www.all4ed.org/publications/StraightAs/Volume6No5.html.

Allinder, R. M., Fuchs, L. S., & Fuchs, D. (1998). Curriculum based assessment. In H. B. Vance (Ed.), *Psychological assessment of children: Best practices for school and clinical settings* (2nd ed., pp. 106–129). San Francisco: Jossey-Bass.

Allington, R. L. (2005, June/July). The other five "pillars" of effective reading instruction. *Reading Today.* Newark, DE: International Reading Association.

Allington, R. L. (2006). *What really matters for struggling readers: Designing research-based programs* (2nd ed.). Boston: Pearson Education.

Allington, R. L., & McGill-Franzen, A. (1995). Flunking: Throwing good money after the bad. In R. L. Allington & S. A. Walmsley (Eds.), *No quick fix: Rethinking literacy programs in America's elementary schools* (pp. 45–60). New York: Teachers College Press.

Almasi, J. F. (1995). The nature of fourth graders' sociocognitive conflicts in peer-led and teacher-led discussions of literature. *Reading Research Quarterly, 30,* 314–351.

Alvarez, M. C. (1996). Explorers of the universe: Students using the World Wide Web to improve their reading and writing. In B. Neate (Ed.), *Literacy saves lives* (pp. 140–145). Winchester, England: United Kingdom Reading Association.

Alvermann, D. E. (2001a). *Effective literacy instruction for adolescents.* Executive summary and paper commissioned by the National Reading Conference. Chicago, IL: National Reading Conference.

Alvermann, D. E. (2001b). Reading adolescents' reading identities: Looking back to see ahead. *Journal of Adolescent & Adult Literacy, 44,* 676–690.

Alvermann, D. E. (2003). *Seeing themselves as capable and engaged readers: Adolescents and re/mediated instruction.* Naperville, IL: Learning Point Associates. Retrieved February 22, 2006, from www.ncrel.org/litweb/readers.pdf.

Alvermann, D. E., & Hagood, M. C. (2000). Random and critical media literacy. *Journal of Adolescent & Adult Literacy, 43,* 436–446.

Alvermann, D. E., Hagood, M. C., & Williams, K. B. (2001, June). Image, language, and sound: Making meaning with popular culture texts. *Reading Online, 4*(11). Retrieved February 17, 2006, from www .readingonline.org/newliteracies/lit_ index.asp?

Alvermann D. E., & Heron, A. H. (2001). Literacy identity work: Playing to learn with popular media. *Journal of Adolescent & Adult Literacy, 45,* 118–122.

American Educational Research Association, American Psychological Association, & National Council on Measurement in Education. (1999). *Standards for educational and psychological testing.* Washington, DC: American Educational Research Association. Retrieved 2000 from www.aera .net/about/policy/stakes.htm.

Andersen, J. P., Floisand, B., Martinez, D., & Robinson, D. (1997). Horizonte—where students come first. *Phi Delta Kappan, 54,* 50–52.

Anderson, L. W., & Pellicer, L. O. (1990). Synthesis of research on compensatory and remedial education. *Educational Leadership, 48*(1), 10–16.

Anderson, R., Wilson, P., & Fielding, L. (1988). Growth in reading and how children spend their time outside of school. *Reading Research Quarterly, 23,* 286–303.

Anguiano, R. P. V. (2004). Families and schools: The effect of parental involvement on high school completion. *Journal of Family Issues, 25,* 61–85.

Arter, J., & McTighe, J. (2001). *Scoring rubrics in the classroom: Using performance criteria for assessing and improving student performance.* Thousand Oaks, CA: Corwin Press.

Artiles, A. J., Klingner, J. K., & Tate, W. F. (2006). Representation of minority students in special education: Complicating traditional explanations. Editor's introduction. *Educational Researcher, 35,* 3–5.

Astuto, T. A., & Clark, D. L. (1985). Strength of organizational coupling in the instructionally effective school. *Urban Education, 19,* 331–356.

Au, K. (2000). A multicultural perspective on policies for improving literacy achievement: Equity and excellence. In M. L. Kamil, P. B. Mosenthal, P. D. Pearson, & R. Barr (Eds.), *Handbook of reading research: Vol. 3* (pp. 835–851). Mahwah, NJ: Erlbaum.

August, D., & Hakuta, K. (Eds.). (1997). *Improving schooling for language minority children: A research agenda.* Washington, DC: National Academy Press.

Ayers, W., Hunt, J. A., & Quinn, T. (Eds.). (1998). *Teaching for social justice: A democracy and education reader.* New York: Teachers College Press.

Baker, E. L., Gearhart, M., & Herman, J. L. (1994). Evaluating the Apple Classrooms of tomorrow (SM). In E. L. Baker & H. F. O'Neil, Jr. (Eds.), *Technology assessment in education and training* (pp. 173–198). Hillsdale, NJ: Erlbaum.

Baker, M. I. (2002). Reading resistance in middle school: What can be done? *Journal of Adolescent & Adult Literacy, 45,* 364–366.

Balfanz, R., & Legters, N. (2005). *Locating the dropout crises.* Retrieved October 31, 2006, from www.csos.jhu.edu/tdhs/rsch/ Locating_Dropouts.pdf.

Ball, A. F. (2000). Teachers' developing philosophies on literacy and their use in urban schools: A Vygotskian perspective on internal activity and teacher change. In C. D. Lee & P. Smagorinsky (Eds.), *Vygotskian perspectives on literacy research: Constructing meaning through collaborative inquiry* (pp. 226–255). Cambridge, England: Cambridge University Press.

Ball, A. F., & Farr, M. (2003). Language varieties, culture and teaching the English language arts. In J. Flood, D. Lapp, J. Squire, & J. Jensen (Eds.), *Handbook of research on teaching the English language arts* (2nd ed., pp. 435–445). Mahwah, NJ: Erlbaum.

Ballentine, D., & Hill, L. (2000). Teaching beyond once upon a time. *Language Arts, 78,* 11–20.

Banks, J. A. (2004). Multicultural education: Historical development, dimensions, and practice. In J. A. Banks & C. M. Banks (Eds.), *Handbook of research on multicultural education* (2nd ed., pp. 3–29). San Francisco: Jossey-Bass.

Bartolome, L. (1994). Beyond the methods fetish: Toward a humanizing pedagogy. *Harvard Educational Review, 64*(2), 173–194.

Barton, D., & Hamilton, M. (2000). Literacy practices. In D. Barton, M. Hamilton, & R.

Ivanic (Eds.), *Situated literacies: Reading and writing in context* (pp. 7–15). London: Routledge.

Bass, J. A. (2005). READ IT: A multifaceted strategy for decoding words. *Tennessee Reading Teacher, 33*(2), 14–19.

Bass, J. A., Dasinger, S., Risko, V. J., Matthews, M. W., Elish-Piper, L., & Johns, J. L. (2002). Students' perceptions of their rights as readers: Including students' voices in the dialogue. *Yearbook of the American Reading Forum, 22*. Retrieved January 27, 2003, from www.americanreadingforum.org.

Bean, T. W. (2002). Making reading relevant for adolescents. *Educational Leadership, 60*(3), 34–37.

Bear, D. R., Invernizzi, M., Templeton, S., & Johnston, F. (2004). *Words their way: Word study for phonics, vocabulary, and spelling instruction* (3rd ed.). Upper Saddle River, NJ: Pearson.

Bialystok, E. (1997). Effects of bilingualism and biliteracy on children's emerging concepts of print. *Developmental Psychology, 33*(3), 429–440.

Biancarosa, G., & Snow, C. E. (2004). *Reading next—A vision for action and research in middle and high school literacy: A report to Carnegie Corporation of New York.* Washington, DC: Alliance for Excellent Education.

Biggers, D. (2001). The argument against Accelerated Reader. *Journal of Adolescent & Adult Literacy, 45,* 72–75.

Bintz, W. P. (1993). Resistant readers in secondary education: Some insights and implications. *Journal of Reading, 36,* 605–615.

Bloom, D. (2000). What will be the social implications of schooling in the next millennium? *Reading Research Quarterly, 35,* 423–424.

Bossert, S. T. (1988). School effects. In N. J. Boyan (Ed.), *Handbook of research on educational administration* (pp. 341–352). New York: Longman.

Bourdieu, P. (1991). *Language and symbolic power.* Cambridge, England: Policy Press.

Boys and books. (2006, August/September). *Reading Today, 24,* 1, 4.

Brandt, R. (1995). Punished by rewards? A conversation with Alfie Kohn. *Educational Leadership, 53*(1), 13–16.

Brozo, W. G. (2002). *To be a boy, to be a reader: Engaging teen and preteen boys in active literacy.* Newark, DE: International Reading Association.

Brozo, W. G. (2006). Bridges to literacy for boys. *Educational Leadership, 64*(1), 71–74.

Brozo, W. G., & Simpson, M. L. (1991). *Readers, teachers, learners: Expanding literacy in secondary schools.* New York: Merrill.

Bruck, M., & Genesee, F. (1995). Phonological awareness in young second language learners. *Child Language, 22,* 307–334.

Buehl, D. (2001). *Classroom strategies for interactive learning* (2nd ed.). Newark, DE: International Reading Association.

Calkins, L. (1997, January/February). Five ways to nurture a lasting love of reading. *Instructor—Primary, 106*(5), pp. 32–33.

Cambourne, B., & Turnbull, A. (1990). Assessment in whole language classrooms: Theory into practice. *The Elementary School Journal, 90,* 337–349.

Canfield, J. (1990). Improving students' self-esteem. *Educational Leadership, 48*(1), 48–50.

Canter & Associates (1999). *First-class teacher: Success strategies for new teachers.* Santa Monica, CA: Canter & Associates.

Carger, C. L. (1996). *Of borders and dreams: A Mexican-American experience of urban education.* New York: Teachers College Press.

Cassidy, J., Garrett, S. D., & Barrera, E. S., IV (2006). What's hot in adolescent literacy 1997–2006. *Journal of Adolescent & Adult Literacy, 50,* 30–37.

Castle, M. (1994). Helping children choose books. In E. H. Cramer, & M. Castle (Eds.), *Fostering the love of reading: The affective domain in reading education* (pp. 145–168). Newark, DE: International Reading Association.

Catsambis, S. (1998). *Expanding knowledge of parental involvement in secondary education: Effects on high school academic success.* CRESPAR (Center for Research on the Education of Students Placed at Risk), Report No. 27. Retrieved April 1, 2006, from the Johns Hopkins University website: http://www.csos.jhu.edu/crespar .Reports/report27entire.htm.

Cavazos-Kottke, S. (2005). Tuned out but turned on: Boys' (dis)engaged reading in and out of school. *Journal of Adolescent & Adult Literacy, 49,* 180–184.

Chard, D. J., Pikulski, J. J., & McDonagh, S. H. (2006). Fluency: The link between decoding and comprehension for struggling readers. In T. Rasinski, C. Blachowicz, & K. Lems (Eds.), *Fluency instruction: Research-based best practices* (pp. 39–61). New York: Guilford Press.

Chrispeels, J. (2002). The California Center for effective schools: The Oxnard School District partnership. *Phi Delta Kappan, 83,* 382–387.

Christenson, S. L. (1995). Supporting home-school collaboration. In A. Thomas & J. Grimes (Eds.), *Best practices in school psychology III* (pp. 253–267). Washington, DC: National Association of School Psychologists.

Christenson, S. L., & Sheridan, S. M. (2001). *Schools and families: Creating essential connections for learning.* New York: Guilford Press.

Civic Enterprises. (2006). The Silent Epidemic: New report offers solutions to graduation rate crisis based on interviews with dropouts. *Alliance for Excellent Education, 6*(5), 3–5. Available at http://www.civicenterprises.net/pdfs/thesilentepidemic3-06.pdf.

Civil Rights Project at Harvard University. (2005). Available at http://www.all4ed.org/publications/StraightAs/Volume5No7.html#Harvard.

Clifford, M. M. (1990). Students need challenge, not easy success. *Educational Leadership, 48*(1), 22–26.

Cochran-Smith, M. (2004). *Walking the road: Race, diversity, and social justice in teacher education.* New York: Teachers College Press.

Cole, J. E. (2002/2003). What motivates students to read? Four literacy personalities. *The Reading Teacher, 56,* 326–336.

Conniff, C. (1993). How young readers perceive reading and themselves as readers. *English in Education, 27*(2), 19–25.

Cooper, J. D. (2000). *Literacy: Helping children construct meaning* (4th ed.). New York: Houghton Mifflin.

Cooter, R. B., Mills-House, E., Marrin, P., Mathews, B. A., Campbell, S., & Baker, T. (1999). Family and community involvement: The bedrock of reading success. *The Reading Teacher, 52,* 891–896.

Cornett, C. E. (2003). *Creating meaning through literature and the arts.* Upper Saddle River, NJ: Merrill Prentice-Hall.

Cornett, C. E. (1999). *The arts as meaning makers: Integrating literature and the arts throughout the curriculum.* Upper Saddle River, NJ: Prentice-Hall.

Cramer, E. H., & Castle, M. (Eds.). (1994). *Fostering the love of reading: The affective domain in reading education.* Newark, DE: International Reading Association.

Csikszentmihalyi, M. (1991). Literacy and intrinsic motivation. In S. R. Graubard (Ed.), *Literacy: An overview of 14 experts* (pp. 115–140). New York: Hill & Wang.

Cummins, J., Brown, K., & Sayers, D. (2007). *Literacy, technology, and diversity: Teaching for success in changing times.* Boston: Pearson/Allyn & Bacon.

Cunningham, P. M., & Allington, R. L. (2007). *Classrooms that work: They can all read and write* (4th ed.). Boston: Pearson.

Curtis, D. (2005). *10 tips for creating a caring school.* Retrieved March 15, 2006, from www.glef.org.

Damico, J. (with Riddle, R.). (2006). Exploring freedom and leaving a legacy: Enacting new literacies with digital texts in the elementary classroom. *Language Arts, 84,* 34–44.

Darling-Hammond, L. (1997). *The right to learn.* San Francisco, CA: Jossey-Bass.

Darling-Hammond, L. (1998). Teacher learning that supports student learning. *Educational Leadership, 55*(5), 6–11.

Darling-Hammond, L. (1999). *Teacher quality and student achievement: A review of state policy evidence.* Seattle, WA: Center for the Study of Teaching and Policy, University of Washington.

Darling-Hammond, L., & Falk, B. (1997). Using standards and assessments to support student learning. *Phi Delta Kappan, 79*(3), 190–199.

Darling-Hammond, L., Wise, A., & Klein, S. (1999). *A license to teach: Raising standards for teaching.* San Francisco: Jossey-Bass.

Dasinger, S., & Minor, L. (2004, February). *Creating meaning: Using the arts as assessment tools.* Paper presented at the Georgia

Reading Association Conference, Atlanta, GA.

Davidson, A. (1999). Negotiating social differences: Youths' assessment of educators' strategies. *Urban Education, 34*, 338–369.

Deci, E. L. (1992). The relation of interest to the motivation of behavior: A self-determination theory perspective. In K. A. Renninger, S. Hidi, & A. Crapp (Eds.), *The role of interest in learning and development* (pp. 43–70). Hillsdale, NJ: Erlbaum.

Deeds, B. (1981). Motivating children to read through improved self-concept. In A. J. Ciani (Ed.), *Motivating reluctant readers* (pp. 78–89). Newark, DE: International Reading Association.

Delpit, L. (1992). Education in a multicultural society: Our future's great challenge. *Journal of Negro Education, 61*, 237–249.

Delpit, L. (1995). *Other people's children: Cultural conflict in the classroom.* New York: New Press.

Delpit, L, & Dowdy, J. K. (Eds.). (2002). *The skin that we speak: Thoughts on language and culture in the classroom.* New York: The New Press.

Devine, J. (1994). Literacy and social power. In B. M. Feldman, R. M. Weber, & A. G. Ramirez (Eds.), *Literacy across languages and cultures* (pp. 221–237). Albany: SUNY Press.

De Vries, B. A. (2004). *Literacy assessment and intervention for the elementary classroom.* Scottsdale, AZ: Holcomb Hathaway.

Diller, D. (1999). Opening the dialogue: Using culture as a tool in teaching young African American children. *The Reading Teacher, 52*, 820–828.

Dillon, D. R. (1989). Showing them that I want them to learn and that I care about who they are: A micro ethnography of the social organization of a secondary low-track English-reading classroom. *American Educational Research Journal, 26*, 227–259.

Dillon, D. R., & Moje, E. B. (1998). Listening to the talk of adolescent girls: Lessons about literacy, school, and life. In D. E. Alvermann, K. A. Hinchman, D. W. Moore, S. F. Phelps, & D. R. Waff (Eds.), *Reconceptualizing the literacies in adolescents' lives* (pp. 193–223). Mahwah, NJ: Erlbaum.

Dillworth, M. E. (1994). *Being responsive to cultural differences: How teachers learn.* Thousand Oaks, CA: Corwin Press.

Dispelling the myth program. (n.d.) Retrieved October 4, 2006, from http://www.edtrust.org.

Dixey, B. P., & Dasinger, S. B. (2006). Unraveling assessments: A guide for classroom teachers. Unpublished manuscript.

Doherty, R. W., Hilberg, R. S., Pinal, A., & Tharp, R. G. (2003). Five standards and student achievement. *NABE Journal of Research and Practice, 1*(1), 1–24.

Draper, S. M. (2000). *Teaching from the heart: Reflections, encouragement, and inspiration.* Portsmouth, NH: Heinemann.

Duffy, G. (1997). Powerful models or powerful teachers: An argument for teachers as entrepreneurs. In S. A. Stahl & D. A. Hayes (Eds.), *Instructional models in reading* (pp. 351–365). Mahwah, NJ: Erlbaum.

Edelsky, C. (2002). We need education rights movements. *Talking Points, 13*(2), 11–15.

Edmonds, R. (1979). Effective schools for the urban poor. *Educational Leadership*, 22–27.

Edmunds, K. M., & Bauserman, K. L. (2006). What teachers can learn about reading motivation through conversations with children. *The Reading Teacher, 59*, 414–424.

Education Trust. (2006). *Yes we can: Testing truths and dispelling myths about race and education in America.* Retrieved October 22, 2006, from http://www2.edtrust.org/edtrust.

Edwards, P. A., Pleasants, H. M., & Franklin, S. H. (1999). *A path to follow: Learning to listen to parents.* Portsmouth, NH: Heinemann.

Eisner, E. W. (2003). The arts and the creation of mind. *Language Arts, 80*, 340–344.

Elish-Piper, L., Matthews, M. W., Bass, J. A., Dasinger, S., Johns, J., & Lewis, J. (2002, December). *Examining students' perceptions of reading and readers' rights in varied contexts.* Paper presented at the meeting of the American Reading Forum, Sanibel Island, FL.

Elish-Piper, L., Matthews, M. W., Johns, J. L., & Risko, V. (1999). An exploration of the Reader's Bill of Rights. In R. J. Telfer (Ed.), *Literacy conversations: Family, school, community* (pp. 95–106). Whitewater, WI: American Reading Forum.

Elish-Piper, L., Matthews, M. W., Risko, V. J., Johns, J. L., Bass, J. A., Dasinger, S., & Illig-Aviles, B. (2000). The Reader's Bill of Rights: Analysis, issues, and insights. In R. J. Telfer (Ed.), *Literacy transitions into the next millennium: Where have we been? Where are we going?* (pp. 1–15). Whitewater, WI: American Reading Forum.

Enomoto, E. K. (1997). Schools as nested communities: Sergiovanni's metaphor extended. *Urban Education, 32,* 512–531.

Epstein, J. L. (1995). School/family/community partnerships: Caring for the children we share. *Phi Delta Kappan, 76,* 701–712.

Epstein, J. L. (2001). *School, family, and community partnerships: Preparing educators and improving schools.* Boulder, CO: Westview Press.

Epstein, J. L., Sanders, M. G., Simon, B. S., Salinas, K. C., Jansorn, N. R., & Van Voorhis, F. L. (2002). *School, family, and community partnerships: Your handbook for action* (2nd ed.). Thousand Oaks, CA: Corwin Press.

Epstein, J. L., Simon, B. S., & Salinas, K. C. (1997). Involving parents in homework in the middle grades. *Research Bulletin,* No. 18. Retrieved May 24, 2005, from http://www.pdkintl.org/edres/resbul18.htm.

Esposito, C. (1999). Learning in urban blight: School climate and its effect on the school performance of urban, minority, and low-income children. *School Psychology Review, 28,* 365–378.

Exeter Academy. (n.d.). The history of Harkness. Retrieved October 12, 2006, from www.exeter.edu/admissions/147_harkness.aspx

Fall, R., Webb, N. M., & Chudowsky, N. (2000). Group discussion and large-scale language arts assessment: Effects on students' comprehension. *American Educational Research Journal, 37,* 911–941.

Farnan, N. (1996). Connecting adolescents and reading: Goals at the middle level. *Journal of Adolescent & Adult Literacy, 39,* 436–445.

Farr, R. (1992). Putting it all together: Solving the reading assessment puzzle. *The Reading Teacher, 46,* 26–37.

Fehring, H. (2003). Understanding the influences on teachers' judgments in the process of assessing and reporting students' literacy in the classroom. In H. Fehring (Ed.), *Literacy assessment: A collection of articles from the Australian Literacy Educators' Association* (pp. 10–38). Newark, DE: International Reading Association.

Feldman, R. S. (2006). *Development across the life span* (4th ed.). Upper Saddle River, NJ: Pearson/Prentice-Hall.

Finders, M. J. (1997). *Just girls: Hidden literacies and life in junior high.* Urbana, IL: Teachers College Press.

Fisher, D. (2004). Setting the "opportunity to read" standard: Resuscitating the SSR program in an urban high school. *Journal of Adult & Adolescent Literacy, 48,* 138–156.

Fountas, I., & Pinnell, G. S. (2001). *Guided readers and writers: Teaching comprehension, genre, and content literacy.* Portsmouth, NH: Heinemann.

Fredericks, A. D., & Rasinski, T. V. (1990). Involving parents in the assessment process. *The Reading Teacher, 44,* 346–349.

Freiberg, H. J. (1989). Turning around at-risk schools through consistency management. *Journal of Negro Education, 58,* 372–382.

Freiberg, H. J. (1996). From tourists to citizens in the classroom. *Educational Leadership, 54*(1), 32–36.

Freiberg, H. J. (1998). Measuring school climate: Let me count the ways. *Educational Leadership, 56*(1), 22–26.

Freiberg, H. J., & Stein, T. A. (1999). Measuring, improving, and sustaining healthy learning environments. In H. J. Freiberg (Ed.), *School climate* (pp. 11–29). Philadelphia: Falmer.

Freire, P. (2000). *Pedagogy of the oppressed* (30th anniversary edition). New York: Continuum.

Galda, L. (1982). Assuming the spectator stance: An examination of the responses of young readers. *Research in the Teaching of English, 16,* 1–20.

Gambrell, L. B. (1996). What research reveals about discussion. In L. Gambrell, & J. Almasi (Eds.), *Lively discussions! Fostering engaged reading* (pp. 25–38). Newark, DE: International Reading Association.

Gambrell, L. B., & Marinak, B. A. (1997). Incentives and intrinsic motivation to read. In J. T. Guthrie & A. Wigfield (Eds.),

Reading engagement: Motivating readers through integrated instruction (pp. 205–217). Newark, DE: International Reading Association.

Gambrell, L. B., Palmer, B. M., Codling, R. M., & Mazzoni, S. A. (1996). Assessing motivation to read. *The Reading Teacher, 49,* 518–533.

Gaskin, I. W., Gensemer, E. W., & Six, L. M. (2003). Tailoring a middle school language arts class to meet the needs of struggling readers. In R. L. McCormack & J. R. Paratore (Eds.), *After intervention, then what? Teaching struggling readers in grades 3 and beyond* (pp. 137–157). Newark: DE: International Reading Association.

Gee, J. P. (2003). *What video games have to teach us about learning and literacy.* New York: Palgrave.

Gee, J. P., & Green, J. L. (1998). Discourse analysis, learning, and social practice: A methodological study. *Review of Research in Education, 23,* 119–169.

Geva, E., & Wade-Woolley, L. (1998). Component processes in becoming English-Hebrew biliterate. In A. Y. Durgunoglu & L. T. Verhoeven (Eds.), *Literacy development in a multilingual context: Cross-cultural perspectives* (pp. 85–110). Mahwah, NJ: Erlbaum.

Gibbons, M. (2004). Pardon me, didn't I just hear a paradigm shift? *Phi Delta Kappan, 85,* 461–467.

Gilligan, C. (1982). *In a different voice: Psychological theory and women's development.* Cambridge, MA: Harvard University Press.

Gipe, J. P. (2002). *Multiple paths to literacy: Classroom techniques for struggling readers* (5th ed.). Upper Saddle River, NJ: Merrill.

Gipps, C. (1999). Sociocultural aspects of assessment. In A. Iran-Nejad & P. D. Pearson (Eds.), *Review of Research in Education* (pp. 355–392). Washington, DC: American Educational Research Association.

Goddard, R. D., Sweetland, S. R., & Hoy, W. K. (2000). Academic emphasis of urban elementary schools and student achievement in reading and mathematics: A multilevel analysis. *Educational Administration Quarterly, 36,* 683–702.

González, N., Moll, L. C., & Amanti, C. (2005). Introduction: Theorizing practices.

In N. González, L. C. Moll, & C. Amanti (Eds.), *Funds of knowledge: Theorizing practices in households and classrooms* (pp. 1–28). Mahwah, NJ: Erlbaum.

Gossard, J. (1987). Using Read-Around Groups to establish criteria for good writing. In C. B. Olson (Ed.), *Practical ideas for teaching writing as a process* (pp. 148–153). Irvine, CA: California State Department of Education.

Graves, D. H. (2001). *The energy to teach.* Portsmouth, NH: Heinemann.

Gregory, E., & Williams, A. (2000). *City literacies: Learning to read across generations and cultures.* London: Routledge.

Gruwell, E. (1999). *The freedom writer's diary: How a teacher and 150 teens used writing to change themselves and the world around them.* New York: Broadway Books.

Gunning, T. G. (1995). Word building: A strategic approach to the teaching of phonics. *The Reading Teacher, 48,* 484–488.

Gurian, M., & Stevens, K. (2005). *The minds of boys: Saving our sons from falling behind in school and life.* San Francisco: Jossey-Bass.

Guskey, T. (2003). How classroom assessments improve learning. *Educational Leadership, 60*(5), 6–11.

Guthrie, J., & Humerick, N. (2004). Motivating students to read: Evidence for classroom practices that influence reading motivation and achievement. In P. McCardle & V. Chhabra (Eds.), *The voice of evidence in reading research* (pp. 329–354). Baltimore: Brookes.

Guthrie, J. T., & McCann, A. D. (1997). Characteristics of classrooms that promote motivations and strategies for learning. In J. T. Guthrie & A. Wigfield (Eds.), *Reading engagement: Motivating readers through integrated instruction* (pp. 128–140). Newark, DE: International Reading Association.

Guthrie, J. T., Schafer, W., Wang, Y. Y., & Afflerbach, P. (1995). Relationships of instruction to amount of reading: An exploration of social, cognitive, and instructional connections. *Reading Research Quarterly, 30,* 8–25.

Guthrie, J. T., & Wigfield, A. (1997). Reading engagement: A rationale for theory and teaching. In J. T. Guthrie & A. Wigfield

(Eds.), *Reading engagement: Motivating readers through integrated instruction* (pp. 1–12). Newark, DE: International Reading Association.

Gutierrez, K. D. (2005). The persistence of inequality: English-language learners and educational reform. In J. Flood & P. L. Anders (Eds.), *Literacy development of students in urban school: Research and policy* (pp. 288–313). Newark, DE: International Reading Association.

Gutierrez, K. D., Baquedano-Lopez, P., & Alvarez, H. H. (2001). Literacy as hybridity: Moving beyond bilingualism in urban classrooms. In M. L. Reyes & J. Halcon (Eds.), *The best for our children: Critical perspectives on literacy for Latino students* (pp. 122–141). New York: Teachers College Press.

Gutman, L. M., & Midgley, C. (2000). The role of protective factors in supporting the academic achievement of poor African American students during the middle school transition. *Journal of Youth and Adolescence, 29*, 223–248.

Haberman, M. (1995). Selecting "star" teachers for children and youth in urban poverty. *Phi Delta Kappan, 76*, 777–781.

Handel, R. D. (1995). Family reading at the middle school. *Journal of Reading, 38*, 528–540.

Harmon, J. M. (2000). Assessing and supporting independent word learning strategies of middle school students. *Journal of Adolescent & Adult Literacy, 43*, 518–527.

Harvey, S., & Goudvis, A. (2000). *Strategies that work: Teaching comprehension to enhance understanding.* Portland, ME: Stenhouse.

Haselkorn, D., & Harris, L. (1998). *The essential profession: A 1998 national survey of public attitudes towards teaching, educational opportunity and school reform.* Belmont, MA: Recruiting New Teachers.

Heath, S. B. (1983). *Ways with words.* Cambridge, England: Cambridge University Press.

Heckelman, R. G. (1969). A neurological impress method. *Academic Therapy Quarterly, 4*, 277–282.

Henderson, A. T., & Mapp, K. L. (2002). *A new wave of evidence: The impact of school, family, and community connections on student achievement.* Austin, TX: National Center for Family and Community Connections with Schools.

Henk, W. A., & Melnick, S. A. (1995). The Reader Self-Perception Scale (RSPS): A new tool for measuring how children feel about themselves as readers. *The Reading Teacher, 48*, 470–482.

Henning-Stout, M. (1994). *Responsive assessment: A new way of thinking about learning.* San Francisco: Jossey-Bass.

Hibbert, C. (1990). *Redcoats and rebels: The American revolution through British eyes.* Boston: Avon.

Hicks, D. (2004). Coming of age in working-poor America: Lessons from ethnography and teaching. In D. S. Strickland & D. E. Alvermann (Eds.), *Bridging the literacy achievement gap, grades 4–12* (pp. 30–55). New York: Teachers College Press.

Hidalgo, N., Sui, S. F., & Epstein, J. (2004). Research on families, schools, and communities: A multicultural perspective. In J. A. Banks & C. A. M. Banks (Eds.), *Handbook for research on multicultural education* (pp. 631–655). San Francisco: Jossey-Bass.

High school survey of student engagement. (2005). *National survey of student engagement.* Bloomington, IN: Center for Postsecondary Education. Available at http://nsse.iub.edu/pdf/NSSE2005_annual_report.pdf.

Hilliard, A. G. (2002). Language, culture, and the assessment of African American children. In L. Delpit, & J. K. Dowdy (Eds.), *The skin that we speak: Thoughts on language and culture in the classroom* (pp. 87–105). New York: The New Press.

Hinchman, K. A., Alvermann, D. E., Boyd, F. B., Brozo, W. G., & Vacca, R. T. (2004). Supporting older readers' in- and out-of-school literacies. *Journal of Adolescent & Adult Literacy, 47*, 304–310.

Hirth, D. (2005, June 6). Understanding FCAT reports. *The Tallahassee Democrat.*

Hoffman, J. V. (1991). Teacher and school effects in learning to read. In R. Barr, M. Kamil, P. B. Mosenthal, & P. D. Pearson (Eds.), *Handbook of reading research, Vol. II* (pp. 911–950). New York: Longman.

Hoover, J. (2005). Differentiating curriculum and instruction for English-language learners with special needs. *Intervention in School & Clinic, 40,* 231–236.

Howard, G. R. (1999). *We can't teach what we don't know. White teachers, multi-racial school.* New York: Teachers College Press.

Hibbert, C. (1990). *Redcoats and rebels: The American Revolution through British eyes.* Boston: Avon.

Hynds, S. (1997). *On the brink: Negotiating literature and life for adolescents.* New York: Teachers College Press.

Ingersoll, R. (2001). *Teacher quality and educational inequality.* Seattle, WA: Center for the Study of Teaching and Policy, University of Washington.

International Reading Association. (2000). *Making a difference means making it different: Honoring children's rights to excellent reading instruction.* Position Statement of the International Reading Association. Newark, DE: International Reading Association.

International Reading Association. (2003a). *Standards for reading professionals.* Newark, DE: International Reading Association. Retrieved October 10, 2006 from www.reading.org/downloads/resources/545standards2003/index.html.

International Reading Association. (2003b). *Prepared to make a difference: Research evidence on how some of America's best college programs prepare teachers of reading.* Newark, DE: International Reading Association.

International Reading Association. (2003c). *The role of reading instruction in addressing the overrepresentation of minority children in special education in the United States: A position statement of the International Reading Association.* Newark, DE: International Reading Association.

International Reading Association. (2006). *Standards for middle and high school literacy coaches.* Newark, DE: International Reading Association.

International Reading Association and National Council of Teachers of English (1994). *Standards for the assessment of reading and writing.* Newark, DE: International Reading Association.

International Reading Association and National Middle School Association. (2001). *Supporting young adolescents' literacy learning: A joint position statement of the International Reading Association and the National Middle School Association.* Newark, DE: International Reading Association.

Invernizzi, M., Landrum, T., Howell, J., & Warley, H. (2005). Toward the peaceful coexistence of test developers, policymakers, and teachers in an era of accountability. *The Reading Teacher, 58,* 610–618.

Ivanic, R., & Moss, W. (1991). Bringing community writing practices into education. In D. Barton & R. Ivanic (Eds.), *Writing in the community* (pp. 193–223). Newbury Park, CA: Sage.

Ivey, G. (1999a). A multicase study in the middle school: Complexities among young adolescent readers. *Reading Research Quarterly, 34,* 172–192.

Ivey, G. (1999b). Reflections on teaching struggling middle school readers. *Journal of Adolescent & Adult Literacy, 42,* 372–381.

Ivey, G., & Broaddus, K. (2001). "Just plain reading": A survey of what makes students want to read in middle school classrooms. *Reading Research Quarterly, 36,* 350–377.

Jimenez, R. T. (2003). Literacy and Latino students in the United States: Some considerations, questions, and new directions. *Reading Research Quarterly, 38,* 122–128.

Johns, J. L., & Berglund, R. L. (2002). *Fluency: Questions, answers, and evidence-based strategies.* Dubuque, IA: Kendall/Hunt.

Johnston, P. H. (2004). *Choice words: How our language affects children's learning.* Portland, ME: Stenhouse.

Jordan, C., Orozco, E., & Averett, A. (2001). *Emerging issues in school, family, and community connections.* Austin, TX: National Center for Family and Community Connections with Schools.

Kasten, W. C., & Wilfong, L. G. (2005). Encouraging independent reading with ambience: The Book Bistro in middle and secondary school classes. *Journal of Adolescent & Adult Literacy, 48,* 656–663.

Kelley, E. Glover, J., Keefe, J., Halderson, C., Sorenson, C., & Seth, C. (1986). *School climate survey.* Reston, VA: National Association of Secondary School Principals.

King, K., & Gurian, M. (2006). With boys in mind/ Teaching to the minds of boys. *Educational Leadership, 64*(1), 56–61.

Knapp, M. S. (1995). *Teaching for meaning in high-poverty classrooms.* New York: Teachers College Press.

Kohn, A. (1996). What to look for in a classroom. *Educational Leadership, 54*(1), 54–55.

Kozol, J. (1995). *Amazing Grace: The lives of children and the conscience of a nation.* New York: Crown.

Kozol, J. (2005). *The shame of the nation: The restoration of apartheid schooling in America.* New York: Crown.

Kozol, J. (2006). *Equal opportunity for all students.* Presentation at the 51st annual meeting of the International Reading Association, Chicago, Illinois.

Kulik, J. A. (1994). Meta-analysis studies of findings on computer-based instruction. In E. I. Baker & H. F. O'Neil, Jr. (Eds.), *Technology assessment in education and training.* Hillsdale, NJ: Lawrence Erlbaum.

Kyle, D. W., McIntyre, E., Miller, K. B., & Moore, G. H. (2006). *Bridging home and school through family nights.* Thousand Oaks, CA: Corwin.

Kymes, A. (2005). Teaching online comprehension strategies using think-alouds. *Journal of Adolescent & Adult Literacy, 48,* 492–501.

Ladson-Billings, G. (1994). *The dreamkeepers: Successful teachers of African American children.* San Francisco: Jossey-Bass.

Ladson-Billings, G. (1995). Toward a theory of culturally relevant pedagogy. *American Educational Research Journal, 32,* 465–491.

Ladson-Billings, G., & Tate IV, W. F. (1995). Toward a critical race theory of education. *Teachers College Record, 97,* 47–68.

Landis, D., Kalieva, R., Abitova, S., Izmukhanbetova, S., & Musaeva, Z. (2006). Learning through ethnographic dialogues. *Language Arts, 83,* 192–202.

Langer, J. A. (2000). *Beating the odds: Teaching middle and highschool students to read and write well.* Retrieved October 4, 2006, from the National Research Center on English Learning & Achievement website: http://cela.Albany.edu/eie2/index.html.

Langer, J. A. (2001). Beating the odds: Teaching middle and high school students to read and write well. *American Educational Research Journal, 38,* 837–880.

Lankshear, C., & Knobel, M. (2003). *New literacies: Changing knowledge and classroom learning.* Buckingham, England: Open University Press.

Learning Point Associates. (2005). *Using student engagement to improve adolescent literacy: Implementing the No Child Left Behind Act.* Naperville, IL: Author. Retrieved March 16, 2006, from http://www.rcrel.org/litweb/adolescent/qkey10/.

Lee, C. D. (2004). African American students and literacy. In. D. S. Strickland & D. E. Alvermann (Eds.), *Bridging the literacy achievement gap, grades 4–12* (pp. 70–85). New York: Teachers College Press.

Lee, V. E., Smith, J., & Croninger, R. (1995). Another look at high school restructuring. In *Issues in Restructuring Schools,* No. 9. Madison: University of Wisconsin, Center on Organization and Restructuring of Schools.

Lenhart, A., Madden, M., & Hitlin, P. (2005). *Teens and technology.* Retrieved October 5, 2006, from http://www.pewinternet.org.

Lenski, S. D., & Johns, J. L. (2000). *Improving writing: Resources, strategies, assessments.* Dubuque, IA: Kendall/Hunt.

Lenski, S. D., Wham, M. A., & Johns, J. L. (1999). *Reading and learning strategies for middle and high school students.* Dubuque, IA: Kendall/Hunt.

Leu, D. J., Kinzer, C. K., Coiro, J. L., & Cammack, D. W. (2004). *Toward a theory of new literacies emerging from the processes of reading* (5th ed., pp. 1570–1613). Newark, DE: International Reading Association. Available at http://www.readingonline.org/new literacies/lit_index.asp?HREF=leu/.

Lewis, C. (2001). *Literacy practices as social acts: Power, status, and cultural norms in the classroom.* Mahwah, NJ: Erlbaum.

Lipson, M. Y., & Wixson, K. K. (2003). *Assessment & instruction of reading and writing difficulty: An interactive approach* (3rd ed.). Boston: Allyn & Bacon.

Little, J. W., Gearhart, M., Curry, M., & Kafka, J. (2003). Looking at student work for teacher learning, teacher community, and school reform. *Phi Delta Kappan, 84,* 185–192.

Lloyd, S. L. (2004). Using comprehension strategies as a springboard for student talk. *Journal of Adolescent & Adult Literacy, 48,* 114–124.

Lopez, M. E. (1999). *When discourses collide: An ethnography of migrant children at home and at school.* New York: Peter Lang.

Luchner, K. (n.d.). The pros and cons of discussion. Retrieved October 10, 2006, from www.readwritethink.org/lessons/ lesson-view.asp?id=819.

Mahiri, J. (2006). Digital DJ-ing: Rhythms of learning in an urban school. *Language Arts, 84,* 55–62.

Malikow, M. (2006). Teaching the affective domain: Turning a crier into a crier. *Kappa Delta Pi Record, 43,* 36–38.

Mann, N. R. (1987). *The keys to excellence: The Deming philosophy.* Los Angeles: Prestwick.

Matthews, M. W., & Cobb, M. B. (2005). Broadening the interpretive lens: Considering individual development along with sociocultural views of learning to understand young children's interactions during socially mediated literacy events. *Journal of Literacy Research, 37,* 325–364.

Matthews, M. W., Elish-Piper, L., Johns, J. L., Bass, J. A., Dasinger, S., Risko, V. J., & Illig-Aviles, B. (2001). An exploration of students' perceptions of their rights as readers. In G. B. Moorman, & W. R. Trathen (Eds.), *Multiple perspectives in the millennium, 21* (pp. 99–115). Boone, NC: American Reading Forum.

McCarthey, S. J. (2000). Home-school connections: A review of the literature. *The Journal of Educational Research, 93,* 145–153.

McCarthey, S. J. (2002). *Students' identities and literacy learning.* Newark, DE: International Reading Association and Chicago: National Reading Conference.

McDermott, R., Goldman, S., & Varenne, H. (2006). The cultural work of learning disabilities. *Educational Researcher, 35,* 12–17.

McFann, J. (2004, August/September). Boys and books. *Reading Today,* pp. 20–21.

McGill-Franzen, A., Allington, R., Solic, K., Williams, L., Zmach, C., Graff, J., et al. (2005). The rich/poor achievement gap: Contributions of summer reading loss. *Tennessee Reading Teacher, 34*(1), 8–30.

McIntyre, E., Kyle, D., Moore, G., Sweazy, R. A., & Greer, S. (2001). Linking home and school through family visits. *Language Arts, 78,* 264–272.

McKenna, M. C. (1994). Toward a model of reading attitude acquisition. In E. H. Cramer & M. Castle (Eds.), *Fostering the love of reading: The affective domain in reading education* (pp. 18–40). Newark, DE: International Reading Association.

McKenna, M. C., & Kear, D. J. (1990). Measuring attitude toward reading: A new tool for teachers. *The Reading Teacher, 43,* 626–639.

McMahon, S., & Raphael, T. (Eds.). (1997). *The book club connection: Literacy learning and classroom talk.* New York: Teachers College Press & Newark, DE: International Reading Association.

McNeely, C. A., Nonnemaker, J. M., & Blum, R. W. (2002). Promoting school connectedness: Evidence from the National Longitudinal Study of Adolescent Health. *Journal of School Health, 72*(4), 138–146.

Melton, C., Smothers, B., Anderson, E., Fulton, R., Replogle, W., & Thomas, L. (2003). A study of the effects of the accelerated reader program on fifth grade students' reading achievement growth. *Reading Improvement, 4*(1), 18–23.

Metropolitan Life Insurance Company. (1998). *The Metropolitan Life survey of the American teacher: Building family-school partnerships.* Retrieved May 24, 2005, from http://www.metlife.com/WPSAssets/ 17708507701018400929V1Flifesurv-98 .pdf.

Meyers, J., & Beach, R. (2003). Hypermedia authoring as critical literacy. In B. C. Bruce (Ed.), *Literacy in the information age: Inquiries into meaning making with new technologies* (pp. 233–246). Newark, DE: International Reading Association.

Michaels, S. (1984). Listening and responding: Hearing the logic in children's classroom narratives. *Theory into Practice, 23,* 218–224.

Moje, E. B., Collazo, T., Carrillo, R., & Marx, R. W. (2001). Maestro, what is quality?: Language, literacy, and discourse in project-based science. *Journal of Research in Science Teaching, 38,* 469–498.

Moje, E. B., Peek-Brown, D., Sutherland, L. M., Marx, R. W., Blumenfeld, P., & Krajcik, J. (2004). Explaining explanations: Developing scientific literacy in middle school project-based science reforms. In D. S. Strickland & D. E. Alvermann (Eds.), *Bridging the literacy achievement gap, grades 4–12* (pp. 227–251). New York: Teachers College Press.

Moll, L. C. (1992). Bilingual classroom studies and community analysis. *Educational Researcher, 21,* 20–24.

Moll, L. C. (2000). Inspired by Vygotsky: Ethnographic experiments. In C. D. Lee & P. Smagorinsky (Eds.), *Vygotskian perspectives on literacy research: Constructing meaning through collaborative inquiry* (pp. 256–279). New York: Cambridge University Press.

Moll, L. C. (2003, February). *Biliteracy development in "marked" children: Sociocultural considerations.* Presentation given at Vanderbilt University, Nashville, Tennessee.

Moll, L. C., Amanti, C., Neff, D., & González, N. (1992). Funds of knowledge for teaching: Using a qualitative approach to connect homes and classrooms. *Theory into Practice, 31,* 132–141.

Moll, L. C., & Greenberg, J. B. (1990). Creating zones of possibilities: Combining social contexts for instruction. In L. C. Moll (Ed.), *Vygotsky and education: Instructional implications and applications of sociohistorical psychology* (pp. 319–348). Cambridge, England: Cambridge University Press.

Moll, L. C., Saez, R., & Dworin, J. E. (2001). Exploring biliteracy: Two student case examples of writing as a social practice. *The Elementary School Journal, 101,* 435–449.

Moll, L. C., Tapia, J., & Whitmore, K. (1993). Living knowledge: The social distribution of cultural resources for thinking. In G. Saloman (Ed.), *Distributed cognitions: Psychological and educational considerations* (pp. 139–163). Cambridge, England: Cambridge University Press.

Monson, D. L., & Sebesta, S. L. (1991). Reading preferences. In J. Flood, J. M. Jensen, D. Lapp, & J. R. Squire (Eds.), *Handbook of Research on Teaching the English Language Arts* (pp. 664–673). New York: Macmillan.

Montecel, M. R., & Cortez, J. D. (2002). Successful bilingual education programs: Development and dissemination of criteria to identify promising and exemplary practices in bilingual education at the national level. *Bilingual Research Journal, 26,* 1–22.

Moore, D. W., Bean, T. W., Birdyshaw, D., & Rycik, J. A. (1999). *Adolescent literacy: A position statement for the Commission on Adolescent Literacy of the International Reading Association.* Newark, DE: International Reading Association.

Morrow, L. M. (2004, April/May). Motivation: The forgotten factor. *Reading Today,* 6.

Mueller, P. N. (2001). *Lifers: Learning from at-risk adolescent readers.* Portsmouth, NH: Heinemann.

National Assessment of Educational Progress. (2005). *National Association of Educational Progress: The Nation's Report Card: Reading 2005, U. S. Department of Education Institute of Education Services NCES 2006-451.* Retrieved October 21, 2006, from http://nces.ed.gov/nationsreport card/.

National Center for Education Information. (2005). *Alternative routes to teacher certification.* Retrieved June 28, 2005, from http://www.ncei.com/Alt-Teacher-Cert.htm.

National Commission on Teaching and America's Future. (1996). *What matters most: Teaching for America's future.* Washington DC: National Commission on Teaching and America's Future.

National Commission on Teaching and America's Future. (2003). *No dream denied: A pledge to America's children.* Washington, DC: National Commission on Teaching and America's Future.

National Educational Goals Panel. (1994). *Goals 2000: Educate America Act.* Washington, DC: U.S. Government Printing Office. Retrieved May 10, 2005, from http://www.ed.gov/legislation/GOALS2000/TheAct/index.html.

National Reading Panel. (2000). *Teaching children to read: An evidence-based assessment of the scientific research literature on reading and its implications for reading instruction.* NIH Publication No. 00-4769. Washington, DC: U. S. Government Printing Office.

Neill, M. (2003). The dangers of testing. *Educational Leadership, 60*(5), 43–46.

Neuman, S. B., Celano, D. C., Greco, A. N., & Shue, P. (2001). *Access for all: Closing the book gap for children in early education.* Newark, DE: International Reading Association.

Newkirk, T. (2002). *Misreading masculinity: Boys, literacy, and popular culture.* Portsmouth, NH: Heinemann.

Newkirk, T. (2006). Media and literacy: What's good? *Educational Leadership, 64*(1), 62–66.

Newman, F. M., Marks, H. M., & Gamoran, A. (1995). Authentic pedagogy: Standards that boost study performance. In *Issues in Restructuring Schools,* No. 8. Madison, WI: Center on Organization and Restructuring Schools.

Nieto, S. (2000). *Affirming diversity: The sociopolitical context of multicultural education.* New York: Longman.

Noddings, N. (1984). *Caring: A feminine approach to ethics and moral education.* Los Angeles: University of California Press.

Noddings, N. (2004). *Happiness and education.* Cambridge, England: Cambridge University Press.

Norview High School Report Card. (2004/2005). Retrieved October 10, 2006, from http://cf.nps.k12.va.us/.

Obiddah, J. E. (1998). Black-mystery: Literate currency in everyday schooling. In D. E. Alvermann, K. A. Hinchman, D. W. Moore, S. F. Phelps, & D. R. Waff (Eds.), *Reconceptualizing the literacies in adolescents' lives* (pp. 51–71). Mahwah, NJ: Erlbaum.

O'Brien, D. (2001). "At-risk" adolescents: Redefining competence through the multi-literacies of intermediality, visual arts, and representation. *Reading Online, 4*(11). Retrieved March 16, 2006, from http://readingonline.org/newliteracies/lit_index.asp?HREF=/newliteracies/obrien/index.html.

O'Brien, D. G., & Bauer, E. B. (2004). New literacies and the institution of old learning. *Reading Research Quarterly, 40,* 120–131.

O'Brien, D. G., Stewart, R., & Moje, E. B. (1995). Why content literacy is difficult to infuse into the secondary school: Complexities of curriculum, pedagogy, and school culture. *Reading Research Quarterly, 30,* 442–463.

Ogbu, J. (1988). Cultural diversity and human devilment. In D. T. Slaughter (Ed.), *Black children and poverty: A developmental perspective* (pp. 11–28). San Francisco: Jossey-Bass.

Orellana, M. F., & Hernandez, A. (1999). Talking the walk: Children reading urban environmental print. *The Reading Teacher, 52,* 612–619.

Osterman, K. (2000). Students' need for belonging in the school community. *Review of Educational Research, 70,* 323–367.

Palmer, P. (1998). *The courage to teach: Exploring the inner landscape of a teacher's life.* San Francisco: Jossey-Bass.

Pappas, C. (2002). Becoming literate in the borderlands. *The Review of Education, Pedagogy, and Cultural Studies, 24,* 228–260.

Peck, C., Cuban, L., & Kirkpatrick, H. (2002). Techno-promoter dreams, student realities. *Phi Delta Kappan, 83,* 472–480.

Pennac, D. (1999). *Better than life.* (D. Homel, Trans.). York, ME: Stenhouse. (Original work published 1992).

Perez, B. (Ed.). (2004). *Sociocultural contexts of language and literacy* (2nd ed.). Mahwah, NJ: Erlbaum.

Perkins-Gough, D. (2006). Special report/Do we really have a "boy crisis"? *Educational Leadership, 64*(1), 93–94.

Pflaum, S. W., & Bishop, P. A. (2004). Student perceptions of reading engagement: Learning from the learners. *Journal of Adolescent & Adult Literacy, 48,* 202–214.

Podl, J. B. (1995). Introducing teens to the pleasures of reading. *Educational Leadership, 53*(1), 56–57.

Pollard, R., & Pollard, C. (2004). Research priorities in educational technology: A Delphi study. *Journal of Research on Technology in Education, 37,* 142–147.

Pool, C. R., & Hawk, M. (1997). Hope in Chicago. *Phi Delta Kappan, 54,* 33–36.

Prensky, M. (2005/2006). Listen to the natives. *Educational Leadership, 63*(4), 8–13.

Pressley, M. (2000). What should comprehension instruction be the instruction of? In M. L. Kamil, P. B. Mosenthal, P. D. Pearson, & R. Barr (Eds.), *Handbook of reading research: Vol. 3* (pp. 545–561). Mahwah, NJ: Erlbaum.

Pressley, M. (2004). Comprehension strategies instruction: A turn-of-the-century status report. In R. D. Robinson, M. C. McKenna, & J. M. Wedman (Eds.), *Issues and trends in literacy education* (3rd ed.) (pp. 133–150). Boston: Pearson.

Pressley, M., & Harris, K. R. (1990). What we really know about strategy instruction. *Educational Leadership, 48*(1), 31–34.

Purcell-Gates, V. (1995). *Other people's words: The cycle of low literacy.* Cambridge, MA: Harvard University Press.

Purcell-Gates, V. (2002). "... As soon as she opened her mouth!": Issues of language, literacy, and power. In L. Delpit & J. K. Dowdy (Eds.), *The skin that we speak: Thoughts on language and culture in the classroom* (pp. 121–141). New York: The New Press.

Rasinski, T., & Padak, N. (2000). *Effective reading strategies: Teaching children who find reading difficult* (2nd ed.). Columbus, OH: Merrill Prentice-Hall.

Readence, J. E., Bean, T. W., & Baldwin, R. S. (2001). *Content area literacy: An integrated approach* (7th ed.). Dubuque, IA: Kendall/Hunt.

Reeves, A. R. (2004). *Adolescents talk about reading: Exploring resistance to and engagement with text.* Newark, DE: International Reading Association.

Reeves, D. B. (2000). The 90/90/90 schools: A case study. In *Accountability in action: A blueprint for learning organizations,* (2nd ed.). Englewood, CO: Advanced Learning Press. Available at http://www.making standardswork.com.

Reeves, D. B. (2005). High performance in high poverty schools: 90/90/90 and beyond. In J. Flood & P. L. Anders (Eds.), *Literacy development of students in urban schools: Research and policy* (pp. 362–388). Newark, DE: International Reading Association.

Reutzel, D. R., & Cooter, R. B., Jr. (2004). *Teaching children to read: Putting the pieces together* (4th ed.). Upper Saddle River, NJ: Pearson.

Riches, C., & Genesee, F. (2006). Cross-linguistic and crossmodal issues. In F. Genesee, K. Lindholm-Leary, W. Saunders & D. Christian (Eds.), *Educating English Language Learners: A synthesis of research evidence* (pp. 64–87). New York: Cambridge University Press.

Riddle Buly, M., & Valencia, S. (2002). Below the bar: Profiles of students who fail state reading assessments. *Educational Evaluation and Policy Analysis, 24,* 219–232.

Risko, V. J. (2005). A loss of equity, excellence, and expectations through overrepresentation of culturally and linguistically diverse students in special education: A response to Cheryl Utley, Festus Obiakor, and Elizabeth Kozleski In J. Flood & P. Anders (Eds.), *Literacy development of students in urban schools: Research and policy* (pp. 345–359). Newark, DE: International Reading Association.

Risko, V., Matthews, M., Elish-Piper, L., Dasinger, S., & Bass, J. (2004). Parents' voices in the discussion of the rights of readers. In W. Trathen & B. Schlagal (Eds.), *It is reading research: Has it made a difference in student learning?* Boone, NC: American Reading Forum.

Roller, C. (1996). *Variability not disability: Struggling readers in a workshop classroom.* Newark, DE: International Reading Association.

Rosenblatt, L. M. (1994). The transactional theory of reading and writing. In R. B. Ruddell, M. R. Ruddell, & H. Singer (Eds.), *Theoretical models and processes of reading* (pp. 1057–1092). Newark, DE: International Reading Association.

Rosenthal, R., & Jacobson, L. (1968). *Pygmalion in the classroom: Teacher expectation and pupils' intellectual development.* New York: Holt, Rinehart & Winston.

Rubenstein-Avila, E. (2003/2004). Conversing with Miguel: An adolescent English language learner struggling with later literacy development. *Journal of Adolescent & Adult Literacy, 47,* 290–301.

Ruddell, R. B. (1995). Those influential literacy teachers: Meaning negotiators and motivation builders. *The Reading Teacher,* 48, 454–463.

Rudney, G. L. (2005). *Every teacher's guide to working with parents.* Thousand Oaks, CA: Corwin.

Rueda, R. (2005). Culture, context, and diversity: A perspective on urban school reform: A response to Kris Gutierrez. In J. Flood & P. Anders (Eds.), *Literacy development of students in urban schools: Research and policy* (pp. 305–313). Newark, DE: International Reading Association.

Sachar, L. (1998). *Holes.* New York: Random House.

Sanacore, J. (2002). Questions often asked about promoting lifetime literacy efforts. *Intervention in School & Clinic, 37,* 163–168.

Sanders, M. G., & Herting, J. R. (2000). Gender and the effects of school, family, and church support on the academic achievement of African-American urban adolescents. In M. G. Sanders (Ed.), *Schooling students placed at risk: Research, policy, and practice in the education of poor and minority adolescents* (pp. 141–161). Mahwah, NJ: Erlbaum.

Santa, C. (2006). A vision for adolescent literacy: Ours or theirs? *Journal of Adolescent & Adult Literacy, 49,* 466–476.

Saunders, W., & Goldenberg, C. (1999). The effects of instructional conversations and literature logs on the story comprehension and thematic understanding of English proficient and limited English proficient students. *Elementary School Journal, 99,* 277–301.

Schiefele, U. (1991). Interest, learning, and motivation. *Educational Psychologist, 26,* 299–323.

Schlacter, J. (1999). *The impact of technology on student achievement: What the most current research has to say.* Retrieved January 23, 2007, from www.emporia.edu/idt/graduateprojects/fall04/BaldwinMeagan/baldwin.pdf.

Scholastic, Inc. (2006, June). *Kids and family reading report.* Retrieved September 15, 2006, from http://www.scholastic.com/readingreport.

Schultz, K., & Hull, G. (2002). Locating literacy theory in out-of-school contexts. In G. Hull & K. Schultz (Eds.), *School's out!:* *Bridging out-of-school literacies with classroom practice* (pp. 11–31). New York: Teachers College Press.

Schunk, D. H., & Zimmerman, B. J. (1997). Developing self-efficacious readers and writers: The role of social and self-regulatory processes. In J. T. Guthrie & A. Wigfield (Eds.), *Reading engagement: Motivating readers through integrated instruction* (pp. 34–50). Newark, DE: International Reading Association.

Schwartz, A., & Rubinstein-Avila, E. (2006). Understanding the manga hype: Uncovering the multimodality of comic-book literacies. *Journal of Adolescent & Adult Literacy, 50,* 40–49.

Schwartz, W. (2003). *Helping underachieving boys read well and often.* ERIC Digest (Contract No. R189002001). Washington, DC: U.S. Department of Education. (ERIC Document Reproduction Service No. ED467687)

Seidel, S. (1998). Collaborative assessment conferences for the consideration of project work [Data File]. Harvard Graduate School of Education: Project Zero. Retrieved March 23, 2005, from www.pz.harvard.edu/.

Serafini, F. (1995). Reflective assessment. *Talking Points: Conversations in the whole language community, 6*(4), 10–12.

Shannon, P. (1995). *Texts, lies, and videotape: Stories about life, literacy, and learning.* Portsmouth, NH: Heinemann.

Shannon, P. (1996). Critical issues: Literacy and educational policy. Part two (Poverty, literacy, and politics: Living in the USA). *Journal of Literacy Research, 28,* 429–449.

Shavelson, R. J., & Berliner, D. (1988). Evasion of the education research infrastructure: A reply to Finn. *Educational Researcher, 17,* 9–11.

Sheldon, S. B., & Epstein, J. L. (2002). Present and accounted for: Improving student attendance through family and community involvement. *The Journal of Educational Research, 95,* 308–314.

Shepard, L., & Smith, H. (1989). Synthesis of research on grade retention. *Educational Leadership, 47*(8), 84–88.

Shepard, L. A., Taylor, G. A., & Kagan, S. L. (1996). *Trends in early childhood assessment: policies and practices.* Los Angeles: Center for Research on Evaluation, Standards, and Testing.

Short, K. (1996). Caring teachers. *Teacher Talk* (1). Retrieved March 6, 2006, from http://www.education.indiana.edu/cas/tt/v1i1/caring.html.

Shulman, L. S. (1987). Knowledge and teaching: Foundations of the new reform. *Harvard Educational Review, 57*(1), 1–22.

Shumow, L., & Miller, J. D. (2001). Parents' at-home and at-school academic involvement with young adolescents. *Journal of Early Adolescence, 21,* 68–91.

Sivin-Kachala, J. (1998). *Report on the effectiveness of technology in schools, 1990–1997.* Software Publisher's Association.

Smith, H. L. (2004). Literacy and instruction in African American communities: Shall we overcome? In B. Perez, (Ed.), *Sociocultural contexts of language and literacy* (2nd ed., pp. 207–245). Mahwah: NJ: Lawrence Erlbaum.

Smith, M. C., & Elish-Piper, L. (2002). Primary-grade educators and adult literacy: Some strategies for assisting low-literate parents. *The Reading Teacher, 56,* 156–165.

Smith, M. W., & Wilhelm, J. D. (2002). *"Reading don't fix no Chevys": Literacy in the lives of young men.* Portsmouth, NH: Heinemann.

Smith, M. W., & Wilhelm, J. D. (2004). "I just like being good at it": The importance of competence in the literate lives of young men. *Journal of Adolescent & Adult Literacy, 47,* 454–461.

Smith, M. W., & Wilhelm, J. D. (2006). *Going with the flow: How to engage boys (and girls) in their literacy learning.* Portsmouth, NH: Heinemann.

Smylie, M. A., Lazarus, V., & Brownlee-Conyers, J. (1996). Instructional outcomes of school-based participative decision making. *Educational Evaluation and Policy Analysis, 18,* 181–198.

Snipp, C. M. (2004). American Indian studies. In J. A. Banks & C. M. Banks (Eds.), *Handbook of research on multicultural education* (2nd ed., pp. 315–331). San Francisco: Jossey-Bass.

Snow, C. E., Barnes, M. S., Chandler, J., Goodman, I. F., & Hemphill, L. (1991). *Unfulfilled expectations: Home and school influences on literacy.* Cambridge, MA: Harvard University Press.

Snow, C. E., Burns, M. S., & Griffin P. (Eds.). (1998). *Preventing reading difficulties in young children.* Washington, DC: National Academy Press.

Solano-Flores, G., & Trumbull, E. (2003). Examining language in context: The need for new research and practice paradigm in the testing of English-language learners. *Educational Researcher, 32,* 3–13.

Sparks, D. (2003). We care, therefore they learn: Interview/ Ronald F. Ferguson. *National Staff Development Council, 24*(4), 42–47.

Spires, H., & Cuper, P. (2002, September). Literacy junction: Cultivating adolescents' engagement in literature through Web optionality. *Reading Online, 6*(2). Retrieved March 16, 2006, from http://www.readingonline.org/articles/art_index.asp?HREF=spires/index.html.

Stephenson F. J. (Ed.). (2001). *Extraordinary teachers: The essence of excellent teaching.* Kansas City, MO: Andrews McMeel.

Stipek, D. J. (1988). *Motivation to learn: From theory to practice.* Englewood Cliffs, NJ: Prentice-Hall.

Stipek, D. J. (2006). Relationships matter. *Educational Leadership, 64*(1), 46–49.

Street, B. (2003). What's "new" in New Literacy studies? Critical approaches to literacy in theory and practice. *Current Issues in Comparative Education, 5*(2), 1–14.

Stringfield, S., & Herman, R. (1996). Assessment of the state of school effectiveness research in the United States of America. *School Effectiveness and School Improvement, 7,* 159–180.

Strommen, L. T., & Mates, B. F. (2004). Learning to love reading: Interviews with older children and teens. *Journal of Adolescent & Adult Literacy, 48,* 188–201.

Sturtevant, E. G. (2003). *The literacy coach: A key to improving teaching and learning in secondary schools.* Retrieved March 15, 2006 from http://www.all4ed.org/publications/LiteracyCoach.pdf.

Sui-Chu, E. H., & Willms, J. D. (1996). Effects of parental involvement on eighth-grade achievement. *Sociology of Education, 69,* 126–141.

Sweet, A. P. (1997). Teacher perceptions of student motivation and their relation to literacy learning. In J. T. Guthrie & A. Wigfield (Eds.), *Reading engagement: Motivating readers through integrated instruction* (pp. 86–101). Newark, DE: International Reading Association.

Tableman, B. (2004). School climate and learning. *Best Practice Briefs, 31*, 1–10.

Tatum, A. W. (2000). Breaking down barriers that disenfranchise African American adolescent readers in low-level tracks. *Journal of Adolescent & Adult Literacy, 44*, 52–64.

Tatum, A. W. (2006, March 15). *Motivating African American teenage boys to read text.* Ohio Resource Center for Mathematics, Science, and Reading. http://ohiorc.org.

Taylor, D. L. (2004/2005). "Not just boring stories": Reconsidering the gender gap for boys. *Journal of Adolescent & Adult Literacy, 48*, 290–298.

Teddlie, C., & Reynolds, D. (2000). *The international handbook of school effectiveness research.* New York: Falmer.

Teddlie, C., & Stringfield, S. (1993). *Schools make a difference: Lessons learned from a 10-year study of school effects.* New York: Teachers College Press.

Tolkien, J. R. R. (1979, December). *Sir Gawain and the Green Knight: Pearl and Sir Orfeo* (reissue ed.). New York: Random House.

Tomlinson, C. A. (2001). *How to differentiate instruction in mixed-ability classrooms* (2nd ed.). Alexandria, VA: Association for Supervision and Curriculum Development.

Tompkins, G. E. (2007). *Literacy for the 21st century: Teaching reading and writing in prekindergarten through grade 4.* Upper Saddle River, NJ: Pearson.

Topping, K. J. (2006). Paired reading: Impact of a tutoring method on reading accuracy, comprehension, and fluency. In T. Rasinski, C. Blachowicz, & K. Lems (Eds.), *Fluency instruction: Research-based best practices* (pp. 173–191). New York: Guilford Press.

Torres-Guzman, M. E. (1992). Stories of hope in the midst of despair: Culturally responsive education for Latino students in an alternative high school in New York City. In M. Saravia-Shore & S. F. Arvizu (Eds.), *Cross-cultural literacy: Ethnographies of communication in multi-ethnic classrooms* (pp. 477–490). New York: Garland.

Trelease, J. (1989). Jim Trelease speaks on reading aloud to children. *The Reading Teacher, 42*, 200–206.

Tyre, P., Murr, A., Juarez, V., Underwood, A., Springen, K., & Wingert, P. (2006, January 30). The trouble with boys. *Newsweek, 147*, 44–52.

United States Department of Education. (2001). *No Child Left Behind Act.* Retrieved February 2, 2004, from http://www.ed.gov/policy/elsec/leg/esea02/107-110.pdf.

Utley, C., Obiakor, F., & Kozleski, E. (2005). Over representation of culturally and linguistically diverse students in special education in urban schools: A research synthesis. In J. Flood & P. Anders (Eds.), *Literacy development of students in urban schools: Research and Policy* (pp. 314–344). Newark, DE: International Reading Association.

Vacca, R. T. (1998). Let's not marginalize adolescent literacy. *Journal of Adolescent & Adult Literacy, 41*, 604–610.

Vacca, R. T., & Vacca, J. L. (1989). *Content area reading* (3rd ed.). Glenview, IL: Scott Foresman.

Valdés, G. (1996). *Con respeto: Bridging the distances between culturally diverse families and schools.* New York: Teachers College Press.

Valencia, S., & Riddle Buly, M. (2005). Behind test scores: What struggling readers really need. *The Reading Teacher, 57*, 520–531.

Valencia, S., Hiebert, E., & Afflerbach, P. (1994). *Authentic assessment: Practices and possibilities.* Newark, DE: International Reading Association.

Viadero, D. (2006, March 15). Concern over gender gap shifting to boys. *Education Week, 1*, 16, 17.

Vogt, M. (2000). Active learning: Dramatic play in the content areas. In M. McLauglin & M. Vogt (Eds.), *Creativity and innovation in content area teaching* (pp. 73–90). Norwood, MA: Christopher-Gordon.

Vygotsky, L. S. (1978). *Mind in society.* Cambridge, MA: Harvard University Press.

Wagner, C., & Masden-Copas, P. (2002). An audit of the culture starts with two handy tools. *Journal of Staff Development, 23*(3), 1–4.

Walker, A. (1982). *The color purple.* Orlando, FL: Harcourt.

Walker, B. J., Mokhtari, K., & Sargent, S. (2006). Reading fluency: More than fast and accurate reading. In T. Rasinski, C. Blachowicz, & K. Lems (Eds.), *Fluency instruction: Research-based best practices* (pp. 86–105). New York: Guilford Press.

Wang, M. C., Haertl, G. D., & Walberg, H. J. (1997). *What do we know: Widely implemented school improvement programs.* Philadelphia: Temple University Center for Research in Human Development and Education, Laboratory for Student Success.

Wasserstein, P. (1995). What middle schoolers say about their schoolwork. *Educational Leadership, 53*(1), 41–43.

Wayne, A. J., & Youngs, P. (2003). Teacher characteristics and student achievement gains: A review. *Review of Educational Research, 73,* 89–122.

Weiner, H., & Cohen, A. R. (2003, November). *Dispositions in teacher education programs: An opportunity for reform.* Paper presented at the Second Annual National Conference on Teacher Dispositions, Richmond, Kentucky.

Wigfield, A. (1997). Children's motivations for reading and reading engagement. In J. T. Guthrie & A. Wigfield (Eds.), *Reading engagement: Motivating readers through integrated instruction* (pp. 14–33). Newark, DE: International Reading Association.

Wigfield, A. (2004). Motivation for reading during the early adolescent and adolescent years. In D. S. Strickland & D. E. Alvermann (Eds.), *Bridging the literacy achievement gap, grades 4–12* (pp. 56–69). New York: Teachers College Press.

Wilhelm, J. D. (1996). *"You gotta be the book": Teaching engaged and reflective reading with adolescents.* New York: Teachers College Press.

Williams, B. T. (2004/2005). Are we having fun yet? Students, social class, and the pleasures of literacy. *Journal of Adolescent & Adult Literacy, 48,* 338–342.

Williams, R., & Rivers, W. (1972). *Mismatches in testing from Black English.* Paper presented at the meeting of the American Psychological Association, Honolulu, Hawaii.

Willis, S. (1991, September). The complex art of motivating students. *ASCD Update, 33,* 1, 4–5.

Winograd, P., Flores-Duenas, L. A., & Arrington, H. (2003). Best practices in literacy assessment. In L. M. Morrow, L. B. Gambrell, & M. Pressley (Eds.), *Best practices in literacy instruction* (2nd ed., pp. 201–238). New York: Guilford Press.

Wolf, S., Borko, H. Elliott, R., & McIver, M. (2000). That dog won't hunt: Exemplary school change efforts within the Kentucky reform. *American Educational Research Journal, 37,* 349–393.

Wood, C. (1997). *Yardsticks: Children in the classroom ages 4–14: A resource for parents and teachers.* Greenfield, MA: Northeast Foundation for Children.

Worthy, J., & McKool, S. S. (1996). Students who say they hate to read: The importance of opportunity, choice, and access. In D. J. Leu, C. K. Kinzer, & K. A. Hinchman (Eds.), *Literacies for the 21st century: Research and practice. 45th yearbook of the National Reading Conference* (pp. 245–256). Chicago: National Reading Conference.

Worthy, J., Moorman, M. G., & Turner, M. (1999). What Johnny likes to read is hard to find in school. *Reading Research Quarterly, 34,* 12–27.

Yatvin, J. (2004). *A room with a differential view: How to serve all children as individual learners.* Boston: Pearson Education.

Zentella, A. C. (1997). *Growing up bilingual: Puerto Rican children in New York.* Oxford, England: Basil Blackwell.

Zhou, M., & Bankston, C., III. (1998). *Growing up American: How Vietnamese children adapt to life in the United States.* New York: Russell Sage Foundation.

Zigo, D. (2001). From familiar worlds to possible worlds: Using narrative theory to support struggling readers' engagements with texts. *Journal of Adolescent & Adult Literacy, 45,* 62–70.

Zutell, J., Donelson, R., Bevans, J., & Todt, P. (2006). Building a focus on oral reading fluency into individual instruction for struggling readers. In T. Rasinski, C. Blachowicz, & K. Lems (Eds.), *Fluency instruction: Research-based best practices* (pp. 265–278). New York: Guilford Press.

Index